Dining in the Raw
Cooking with "the Buff"

RITA ROMANO

Illustrations by Nancy Jolly

Prato
Publications
Prato, Italy

Dining in the Raw, Cooking with the Buff.
Rita Romano
Illustrations by Nancy Jolly
Graphic Design and Typesetting: JoAnn Lantz

Cover design by JoAnn Lantz
Cover photo by Jennifer Girard.

Film printed by microPRINT, Florence, Italy

Printed by

Nuova Castello snc, Florence Italy

**3rd printing
July 1996**

rato
ublications

Prato, Italy

ISBN 0-9634742-0-0

Library of Congress Cataloging-in-Publication Data

Romano, Rita
    Dining in the Raw, Cooking with the Buff
    Vegetarian Recipe book with nutritional information
    Foreword by Viktor Kulvinskas and Brian Clement

LCCC No. 92-96991
    1. nutrition   2. vegetarian recipes   3. raw foods

Rita Romano
P.O. Box 5893
Key West, Florida 33045
Telephone and FAX
1-500-449-4490

In memory of my mother Madeline who taught me to live every day to the fullest and to not be afraid to engage in life's opportunities and adventures. We never know when we'll pass this way again.

Rita Romano has had a unique interest in food as medicine for many years. What began as a hobby has become her life's work. Her creative ability and desire to nurture has resulted in an exciting new genre of life-giving recipes.

Rita's educational background includes a bachelor of arts degree from the State University of New York in Stonybrook and post-graduate nutritional studies at Hofstra University in New York. She is also a graduate of the Kushi Institute in Massachusetts where she studied nutritional food preparation, oriental medicine, shiatsu massage and visual diagnostic techniques. After co-owning and operating New Horizon' Natural Foods Restaurant in Key West, Florida, she went on to serve as the Executive Chef and Food Director at Hippocrates Health Institute in West Palm Beach, Florida.

For the past ten years she has been providing specially prepared meals as well as teaching theory and technique to a wide array of people ranging from those interested in maintaining health to the seriously ill. Her vast knowledge of different vegetarian styles and philosophies have helped her to satisfy just about anyone's palate.

After many years of observing the transformational effect of healthy diet, Rita has compiled her favorite recipes to share with others who are interested in optimum well-being. With her practical approach and educational background she has provided an international selection of recipes that represent the finest in health-enhancing cuisine.

I have dedicated the last ten years of my life to the study of the plant kingdom and how one can convert it into a pleasing meal. My intense and inspired interest in this particular subject entitles me to be described as a devotee, enthusiast or buff. Hence, **"Cooking with the Buff"**.

ACKNOWLEDGEMENTS

I'd like to thank all of my friends and co-workers for their encouragement, praise, assistance, and feedback.

Special thanks go to:

Wayne McCrossin for procuring major equipment to keep my kitchen running, donating many hours of service in the interest of good health and recipes, and supplying financial assistance for completion of this project.

JoAnn Lantz for her exquisite graphic design, painstaking typesetting, editing suggestions, overall creative assistance, cover design, and constant encouragement to finish this project.

Danny Erneston and his family for procuring and delivering beautiful organic produce daily.

JoAnna Ford and Katri Arcaro for their assistance in helping me to type and format the first draft of the book.

Suzie Thomas, Michelle Davis and Nancy Tucker for typing the first drafts of my recipes.

Lucy Chales and Lone Barlous for assisting me with laughter and love all day in the kitchen.

Kelly Kristopherson for always getting me the supplies I requested when I really needed them.

Brian Clement and Anna Maria Gahns Clement for giving me the reins and letting me run with them at Hippocrates.

Marilyn Willison for her assistance with editing and proofreading.

Viktoras Kulvinskas for answering all my questions about raw and living foods.

Nancy Jolly for her beautiful black and white illustrations of fruits and vegetables.

Jennifer Girard for her patience in producing the cover photograph.

Thanks to Jane Smith for inside cover photo.

Judy Lyman for retyping the edited work.

Joe Pecoraro for computerizing the food combining chart.

Edith Saunders for her sprout jar drawing created in the Hippocrates kitchen.

Blanche Edwards for her help in creating the title.

Laura Pallanti for her sketches of cutting techniques.

Ron, my brother, for all of his love and encouragement.

And last but not least, the many informative customers who passed through my restaurant in Key West as well as all of the guests and employees at Hippocrates who clearly let me know which dishes on the buffet table they liked best.

TABLE OF CONTENTS

FOREWORD

Each year hundreds of new recipe books join thousands of other recipe books on booksellers' shelves. Few of these are based on sound nutritional principles, but are instead often nothing more than thinly veiled dedications to the glories of what I call "the taste trip". These books are downright dangerous for human consumption. Alternatively, every few years a classic recipe book is released. The book in your hands is one of them.

Now, if for some unexpected reason I were exiled to a desert island (one with a fully equipped kitchen, I hope) and I were allowed to take two or three of my favorite recipe books - Rita Romano's <u>Dining in the Raw, Cooking with the Buff</u> would have to be one of them. Not only are her recipes absolutely delicious, but they are based on a mature balance of both scientific knowledge and intuitive nutritional wisdom.

Throughout this book Rita demonstrates that she deeply understands the practical needs of folks who are both health seekers AND lovers of good-tasting food. I also really appreciate Rita's thoughtful commentaries that accompany the recipes. I consider her ideas about food a valuable contribution to the advancement of the fields of diet and nutrition.

Rita's natural food preparation methods represent the best of live food and macrobiotic principles. Most importantly, she transforms these principles into fantastic raw and cooked entrées, soups, sauces, marinades, dehydrated crisps, salads, dressings and desserts. I first became acquainted with Rita and her fabulous cuisine for two delectable weeks at Hippocrates Health Institute in West Palm Beach, Florida, where she was Director of Food Services and Executive Chef.

For over thirty years, Hippocrates Health Institute has been a magnet for health seekers the world over. Hippocrates attracts a wide array of clientele from cosmopolitan jet-setters possessing the most refined gourmet tastes, to young adults with sprouting jars stuffed in their backpacks, to SAD (Standard American Diet) working couples looking for a better way to healthfully raise their kids. Also among Hippocrates's guests include those who have just left their hospital beds, and are fighting for their lives due to life-threatening illnesses.

For one less talented, preparing food at one common table for as diverse a group would be an almost insurmountable task. But Rita is a magician of sorts. No doubt divinely inspired, I am sure she consults with at least seven invisible kitchen angels who inspire her to create "miracles in serving bowls". As you'll find out, Rita pulls off similar wizardry in this book.

In my two-week stay, every meal was a delight to the eye, incredibly nutritious, easy-to-digest, properly combined, and delightfully seasoned with herbs, spices and fresh vegetables. For the salty taste Rita has often substituted Braggs liquid aminos in place of soy sauce, which is frequently used to excess in many otherwise excellent recipe books.

This is the type of book that leaves you plenty of space to expand your culinary skills and graduate to a place where you become a master in the kitchen instead of a slave to some formula-oriented cookbook. The only person who may not like this book is perhaps some restaurant owner somewhere who is hard-pressed to meet his or her overhead. This is because, now that this book is in your hands, there will be less reason to go out to restaurants to eat! Bon Appetit.

Love in service,
Viktor P Kulvinskas, MS
Lecturer and Author of
<u>Survival Into the 21st Century</u>

In all my years of work in the health field, I have yet to find a more dedicated professional than Rita Romano. The quality and aesthetic appeal of her cuisine are unsurpassed. She has taken her formal education and widened it through perfecting and improving the presentation of healthy food. I've watched hundreds of people enjoy the dishes that she has so carefully and classically prepared.

As we know, the physical aspect of food is one issue, but the emotional and spiritual aspects are equally important.

Through Rita's contributions in the kitchen, she helps manifest life, which is therefore transformed into health for the partaker. I've often thought of diet as the true pharmacy and of Rita as a precision pharmacist! When reading this book, please remember that these recipes come from depth of knowledge, a deep caring, and a genuine concern for her fellow humans on this planet.

At this time in our history, we must be fully responsible for each of our actions, and the most important is the act of choosing correct foods. This not only builds a strong person, but also helps to keep nature and the environment in balance. When it comes to a health-enhancing diet, there is no room for less than perfect choices. Your decision to purchase this book and prepare healthful dishes may be your first step in practicing what you believe. There is no doubt in my mind that your efforts will be rewarded with the greatest gift of vibrant, complete health.

Throughout history the people who ate predominantly raw vegetarian diets have flourished. The longest living people on earth today

share that experience. For my entire work life in the field of health, I have watched multitudes of people regain their strength through the simple act of ingesting the proper foods. <u>Dining in the Raw, Cooking with the Buff</u> will help you tastefully enjoy a life that abounds with energy, vitality and vigor.

Be well.
Brian R. Clement
Director
Hippocrates Institute

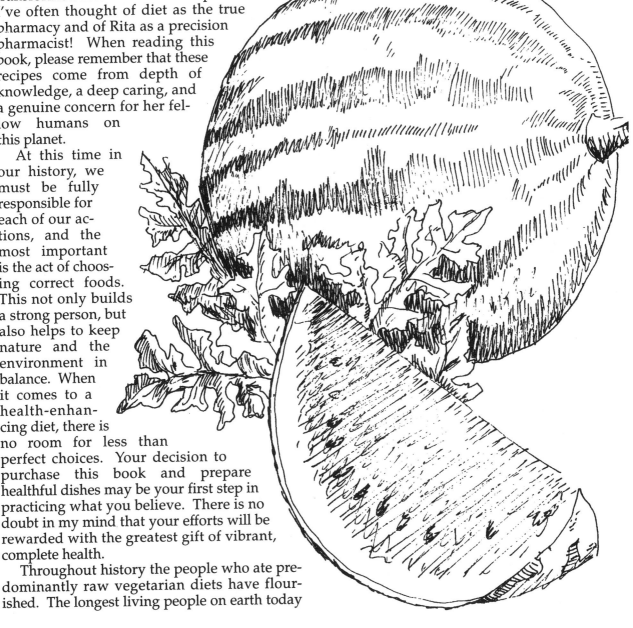

INTRODUCTION

I remember sitting in my grandmother's kitchen as a very young child helping her prepare meals everyday during my long visits. Fruits, vegetables, beans, and grains were on the daily menu. It was a quietly rewarding time in my life. We would go to the market together quite often to buy the freshest produce. Watching her in the kitchen was a wonderful experience. She carefully cleaned and cut the vegetables, slowly and gently cooked them and allowed them to come to room temperature before serving dinner. We also enjoyed raw fruit salads for breakfast and raw vegetable salads for lunch.

This training was very important for me, because several years later my mother lost her battle with cancer and I began cooking for my family at the age of 15. My father later remarried and I anxiously left home to go to college. In spite of my old-world knowledge, I went through five years of college eating all the fashionable junk food. I got fat and my health deteriorated. Ultimately, a life-threatening case of food poisoning landed me in the hospital for almost a month.

My ravaged insides begged for help. The doctors sent me home without a clue concerning after-care. It was then that my quest for renewed knowledge of food nourishment began. I proceeded to read, study and understand the usefulness of nourishing food as medicine. Six months of weekly visits to a naturopath in New York City broadened my awareness and brought me back to a state of balance and vibrant health.

The fact that I lost my health once, however, was not enough of a lesson. I found out, in my late twenties, that good health requires ongoing attention and maintenance. After graduating from S.U.N.Y. at Stony Brook, I moved to New York City to teach high school mathematics. I lived life in the fast lane, traveling and dining out quite often. I made the wrong food choices, eating sensually instead of intellectually. Gourmet food at too many social gatherings for too many years began to add up to another round of poor health. Eating out frequently is the American way of life, yet there was no doubt my health would continue to deteriorate. I realized it was important to go back to the beginning and start over again. I gave up teaching math, left N.Y.C. and moved to Long Island to open a small flower shop.

The decision to go back to school was an easy one. Attending the Hofstra University Health Sciences program, I studied the western philosophy of nutrition. At the same time I bought some vegetarian cookbooks and began eating the fresh produce with which I had grown up. It was hard at first, because I went through another period of detoxification and healing. Six months into my renewed healthy habits, I walked through the little town of Sea Cliff, where neighbors walked up to me and said, "Rita, you look so beautiful today. What have you done that's so different?" At that moment in time I knew I wanted to learn even more about nutrition and healing diets. I gave up floristry and moved to Boston to study macrobiotics and the eastern philosophy of nutrition at the Kushi Institute. While there, I cooked for my own macrobiotic study house daily. I was simultaneously teaching and being taught different ethnic cuisines. After graduating I moved back to New York for a short period and began cooking for people with serious illnesses. I spent my nights working in a natural foods restaurant where I learned how to incorporate the techniques of classic French cuisine with healthier ingredients.

In 1984, after a tour of the United States and Canada in a motor home, I settled in Key West, Florida. My great love of the sea brought me there and I soon opened a natural foods restaurant. I'll never forget the day one of my customers came back to the kitchen and said to me with great sincerity, "That was the most de-

licious veal cutlet I ever tasted!" We all laughed. When he began to understand that what he had eaten was not meat, he was amazed. The dish was prepared with whole wheat flour, vegetables, miso, and herbs that had become the restaurant's favorite, capturing his interest along with that of many other customers from all over the world. I received letters from afar thanking me for a wonderfully unique culinary experience which confirmed my belief that food can be both wholesome and delicious.

After two years of hard work I sold the restaurant and moved to Palm Beach County. The culmination of all my training has come to fruition at Hippocrates, combining the study of Japanese, Chinese, Asian, Mediterranean, and American styles to create a healing nouvelle cuisine for the twenty-first century.

To cook or not to cook, that is the question? How we feed our bodies is a lasting commitment toward creating and enjoying life. I am a culinary artist and a catalyst, whose main goal in this book is to help interested newcomers make the raw food connection in their daily diet. I don't want to bore you by listing all those highly processed foods we can so easily purchase in the nearest supermarket that shortchange us both nutritionally and financially.

What we put in our mouths strongly determines the daily and long-term quality of our lives. Like you, whether I'm working or playing, I want to have abundant energy and clarity of mind. Proper nutrition gives me the wherewithal to make that possible. You will find the feeling of individual power, strength and well being that result from a sensible diet more than justifies the time you spend preparing fresh foods.

Furthermore, a healthy body aids the deve-

lopment of our spiritual essence. As the years allow us to gather experience, knowledge, and wisdom, the quality of life should continue to grow. What a shame to reach our middle years and feel too sick to enjoy the rewards we've earned! And so we must realize it is beneficial to fulfill certain nutritional needs in order to go on with the rest of our rewarding adult lives. Eating sensibly is something you need to do on a daily basis - like bathing and exercising. There are many different theories, views, diets, and philosophies about proper health habits. Each one of us as individuals must decide on a nutritional program that is the most suitable.

Upon moving to hot, sunny Florida in 1984 I developed an appetite for more raw foods. Hippocrates Health Institute moved to West Palm Beach (from Boston) several years ago and so our paths crossed. After studying many different styles of cooking, raw food cuisine has become the icing on my professional cake. I used my knowledge and overall experience to recreate a whole new menu at Hippocrates. I also introduced a cooked-food menu, always staying within the guidelines of good health and proper food combining. Visiting guests as well as alumni from around the world have continually praised the excellent variety and gourmet style of both the raw and cooked cuisine I presented at the Institute.

I prepared mostly raw-food cuisine at Hippocrates, and that new adventure has inspired me to write this book. Consuming fresh fruit juices for breakfast and raw vegetable juice combinations for lunch helps to serve the purposes of rejuvenation, detoxification, and healing. Drinking nutrients is a blessing for many of us since in our fast-moving society we don't take the time to sit down and really chew our foods well. While we first cleanse and nourish our bodies with a diet of raw foods and juices, we may also have the pleasure of enjoying the benefits of cooked foods.

As a graduate of the Kushi Institute, I have spent over ten years teaching students how to prepare vegetarian cuisine. I have eliminated long, involved cooked-food recipes because too many ingredients often produce flatulence, indigestion, and intestinal putrefaction. In addition a plant-based diet provides the fiber we need; it has been said that disease starts in a dirty colon.

I have studied with many great vegetarian chefs over the years and worked toward developing my own style in the kitchen. Preparing fresh, alive foods seems to have become a lost art. Learning a few basic recipes can take you a long way and there are several factors that should be remembered when choosing foods. Consider your age, occupation, state of health, geographical location, climate, and local crop availability.

Other key factors are food rotation and variety of style. Proper equipment makes working in the kitchen a pleasure instead of a chore and is essential to the art of quality cuisine. By using various pieces of equipment you can create a whole plethora of unique taste experiences. I often use a juicer, a blender, and a food processor to prepare a wide assortment of meals. As you will see, many of the recipes in this book present food in a manner that is different than most traditional cookbooks.

If you follow the guidelines of live food preparation, weight control will never again be a main issue in your life and concerns about calories will become a thing of the past. The reci-

pes largely stay within the latest guidelines for food combining. Please note since vegetables vary in shape, size, variety and quality throughout the world it is difficult to measure ingredients exactly. I have tried to create recipe amounts that serve four to eight people. Overall, eating the highest-quality organic produce whenever possible, regular exercise, relaxation, proper rest and daily meditation are the right combination of ingredients for healthy living.

During tenure at Hippocrates Health Institute, I have experienced the great value of nutrient-rich, easily digestible sprouted foods. Eating a diet that consists of fruits, vegetables, grains, nuts, seeds, beans, sprouts and seaweed facilitates freedom of physical and mental expression. The aesthetic beauty of simply prepared, properly combined foods always shines through. I have tried to make these recipes simple yet exciting so that you will be inspired to tap your own inner creativity. An attractive meal is a wonderful gift you can give yourself and your family each and every day. It's one of the ways I show my love to all who enter my home.

My goal in this book is to help you learn more about living foods and their preparation. Moreover, the information presented in this book is based on my own personal experience and research. The following recipes do not claim to cure illness or disease but this is a good starting place to get some great ideas for your own health-enhancing food creations. I hope you find <u>Dining in the Raw, Cooking with the Buff</u> a rewarding experience.

Rita Romano

HIZIKI

DULSE

DIGESTION PROCESS

Understanding more about digestion will help you to know why it is important to make intelligent food choices. Moreover, the enzyme factor, the question of "to cook or not to cook?", and the theory of proper food combining are all inter-related. Individually and in connection with each other they play a vital role in maintaining good health.

Let's start with understanding a little bit about how enzymes work. They are catalysts that help other substances in the body to either combine or to break down. Enzymes are involved in, and important to, every bodily function. Specific digestive enzymes help break down foods so that the body can better utilize them. This is a fascinating process, since each enzyme has a different job and helps digest separate categories of food (i.e. starches, proteins, and fats). They also build upon each other in each stage of digestion. Enzymes are supplied naturally via two sources: our bodies produce and store them, and we get an abundance of enzymes from raw and living foods. Our goal for optimum health and longevity is to conserve the body's own enzymes for use in repairing and rebuilding rather than to deplete them during the process of digestion. This brings us to the discussion of the issue "To cook or not to cook?".

Good-quality raw and living foods that are appropriately chewed and properly combined provide us with necessary enzymes and nutrients. These enzyme-rich foods help the body digest as we eat. Consuming a diet of predominantly cooked food on a long-term basis creates an incredible demand for enzymes produced by the body because all the enzymes that naturally exist in food have been destroyed by heat (i.e. cooking). Premature aging, degeneration and disease begins when the body's enzyme reserves are constantly being over-taxed; the organ hit hardest is the pancreas.

Cooked and processed food high in protein, fat and refined carbohydrates generates acidity and toxins. Moreover, any nourishment will turn into poison in the body unless properly digested. Most food-related diseases have their origins in rich gourmet, overcooked, improperly combined meals consumed over a period of time. How long it takes before the body breaks down depends on several factors including age,

constitution and heredity. Humans are the only species on earth that try to exist on cooked enzymeless meals without the proper balance of raw and living foods. In addition, we live in a fast-food society that creates chemical (food) addictions and ill-health.

The human body can handle a lot more abuse at a young age, but as it gets older, it produces fewer enzymes and has accumulated more internal toxic waste. Excess fat is deposited as cholesterol and cellulite. Excess calcium helps create arthritis and excess sugar helps create diabetes. Undigested starch taxes the liver, kidneys and the skin, our largest organ of elimination. The skin will attempt to excrete undigested food and toxic fluids, often showing up in the form of all kinds of body rashes. Undigested protein rots in the digestive tract creating an incredible amount of acids and waste. Many believe this is the basis for allergy problems, something from which millions of Americans suffer. The heart, kidneys, blood vessels and body joints will also suffer from deposited toxic wastes. Undigested fats create obesity, skin disorders and heart disease. High-fat, high-protein and highly refined carbohydrates in cooked form create a body laden with toxic waste, dead cells, mucus, pain, poor elimination, overacidity, organ and capillary damage, poor absorption and fatigue, followed by formation of cysts and crystals as well as malnutrition.

Common sense tells us that cooked meals take a lot longer to pass through the system and create more work. Supplemental enzymes are controversial, yet many leading nutritionists believe they are helpful and important additions to a cooked meal. This will be discussed in more detail later in the book.

Let's talk about the actual process of digestion. Hopefully, we chew our foods well which allows them to be coated with starch-splitting salivary enzymes. A meal including sprouts and raw food provides plenty of outside enzymes. There is another school of thought that believes the stomach is divided into two parts as opposed to one main cavity. I base the following information on this premise. The food moves to the first part of the stomach where predigestion continues. Raw food enzymes and salivary enzymes break down the starch portion of the meal for up to one hour.

The food gradually moves to the lower part of the stomach where accumulating gastric juices take over and peptic digestion begins. We have now gone from an alkaline environment to a more acidic one that aids protein digestion. For vegetarians, the stronger acids called for to digest animal proteins are not necessary. The present acidic environment is not as intense. Salivary enzymes shut down, but food enzymes can continue to do their job in a moderately acidic stomach. The food moves from the lower stomach to the small intestines in the form of chyme. The pancreas secretes digestive enzymes to continue the process. Three enzymes to break down protein, one for fat, and one for carbohydrates enter through the duodenum. The liver also sends enzymes: four for carbohydrates, two for proteins, and one for fats. Bile is produced by the gall bladder and sent to break down fats if needed. Using the whole body as its enzyme reserve, the pancreas will round up what is necessary to help complete digestion. The nutrients are absorbed by the villi, millions of tiny little fingerlike projections in the small intestines, and enter the bloodstream.

At this point, we need to ask ourselves, "What happens when all of the foods at one meal are cooked and improperly combined?". For example, most American meals are based upon animal protein eaten with concentrated starches in cooked enzymeless form. The food is sent to the upper part of the stomach with only salivary enzymes to aid digestion. The starch and animal protein sit there together for approximately one hour. Minimal starch digestion proceeds while the protein begins to putrefy producing toxic waste. The food moves to the lower half of the stomach, where strong gastric juices take over. Upper stomach enzymes can no longer aid this process because of a highly acidic environment. The digestion of animal proteins is time consuming, greatly slows down the passage of starches into the small intestines, and causes further putrefaction. Fats are also held up and cannot be fully digested until they move to the small intestines. Protein often gets mutated into another indigestible form and the resulting toxic residues get released into the bloodstream to travel to different parts of the body. The pancreas, the intestines and the liver can become overworked and, ultimately, exhausted. The results are not beneficial and yet we ignorantly continue to abuse the incredible machine called the human body. Poor health and premature aging are inevitable.

This is why it is beneficial to understand how to help the body properly consume food. The importance of enzymes and how they work, the process of digestion, the theory of food combining and the significance of including raw and living food in our daily diets all fit together. Enzyme-rich, pre-digested sprouts and raw foods aid digestion giving the internal organs a rest. If we remain faithful to a vegetarian food regimen, even our worst sins of improper food combinations will have fewer repercussions on overall well being.

It is important to be cautious about eating fish, fowl, eggs, meats, and dairy products. These foods need a higher concentration of stomach acids to digest properly. They should only be consumed with high water content vegetables to allow passage through the system quickly.

To cook or not to cook is a personal choice one makes on a daily basis. We may still enjoy our cooked food if we have a better awareness of how the body works and what we can do to make the job of digestion and absorption a more complete and beneficial process. Cooked meals lacking in enzymes, mutated by high heat (especially proteins and oils) and hampered by improper combinations create a tremendous burden for the body to resolve. Learning how to combine foods, using more beneficial cooking techniques and eating meals that are at least 50% raw are a few basic guidelines being presented. Other suggestions are: Don't overeat. Don't eat under stress. Eat only when your stomach is empty. Minimize intake of acid-forming food. Realize the importance of proper food combining especially when eating animal food. Please remember to chew your food well. Understand that cooked food lengthens the process of digestion. Be aware of the fact that healing disease can be greatly hastened by reducing the amount of cooked food and increasing the amounts of raw and sprouted foods and their juices.

Improper eating habits are a major cause of skyrocketing health-care costs today. Take control of your own health by starting with a well balanced diet plan. In closing, your children are the leaders of the future, so don't leave them out. Learning how to feed their bodies properly must be part of their educational process. Try to introduce programs with current information about proper nutrition in your local schools.

NUTRIENTS

An easy way for our bodies to ingest foods without the use of heat is by the process of sprouting to release available nutrients. Germination (or sprouting) is accompanied by an intense enzymatic hydrolysis of plant protein. These proteins begin to break down into their component amino acids. The high content of complex carbohydrates in grains and legumes also breaks down into simple sugars high in vitamins A, B, C and K. Sprouts are said to contain a magic anti-aging substance called auxinon that is present in all embryos, as well as vitamin B_{17}, an anti-carcinogenic substance. Used before the process of photosynthesis takes place, sprouts can provide a tremendous amount of available, easily digested nutrients. They become counted as vegetables when allowed to become green, form leaves and are grown in dirt. Sunflower greens are a complete protein; they are high in chlorophyll and provide vitamin D. Buckwheat lettuce contains significant amounts of B vitamins, chlorophyll and lecithin to help remove deposits formed on the walls of our arteries. Wheatgrass is the star of all sprouts and grasses because of its many gifts from the earth. It is a rich source of vitamins A and C and contains many known mineral elements. It also contains significant amounts of vitamin B_{17}, which is said to destroy cancer cells. Wheatgrass has a composition of over 60% chlorophyll, which is the green pigment of plants and is often referred to as the "blood" of plants. Chlorophyll is also abundantly found in green algae.

As one of the main components of not only land but also sea vegetables, chlorophyll is interwoven with vitamins, minerals, oxygen, enzymes and other nutritional factors used by the body to remain healthy and strong. The structural resemblance that has been stated between chlorophyll in plants and the hemoglobin of human red blood cells leads one to believe that chlorophyll's place in human dietary needs is one of great importance. The use of green leafy vegetables along with a variety of sprouted and raw foods is an intelligent way to help satisfy our nutritional requirements. This eliminates the stressful job of having to digest cooked fish, meat, dairy and eggs.

Furthermore, a coalition of over 3000 medical doctors has requested that the FDA and Department of Agriculture eliminate meat and dairy from the four basic food groups. This fact strengthens the premise that we should be looking more closely at the use of plant sources to supply our proteins, fats and carbohydrates while reducing the risk of disease and premature death associated with the consumption of meat and dairy.

It is extremely beneficial to eat your green leafy vegetables raw whenever possible. They contain large amounts of chlorophyll and just about every known nutrient. Heating destroys vitamins and some nutrients are washed away in the cooking water. Minerals are lost and the ones left behind cannot always be assimilated. It is also essential to know that many greens form unwanted acids when cooked. For example, spinach forms oxalic acid and is best eaten raw. Another class of vegetables that create harmful acids when cooked are members of the "night shade" family, for example tomatoes, bell peppers and white potatoes (partial list). Eat them in moderation.

The following chart gives you a clear view as to how most all vitamins and minerals are found in green leafy vegetables.

Nutrient Source Chart

VITAMINS

Bioflavinoids:
apricots, cherries, citrus fruits, papaya and buckwheat.

Biotin (B Complex):
bananas, raisins, almonds, walnuts, legumes, mushrooms, whole grains.

Choline (B Complex):
seeds, nuts, legumes, especially soybeans and **green leafy vegetables**.

Folic acid (B Complex):
cantaloupe, beets, cabbage, asparagus, soybeans and **green leafy vegetables**, especially spinach.

Inositol (B Complex):
citrus fruits, sprouts, nuts, seeds and spinach, and **green leafy vegetables**.

Pantothenic Acid (B Complex):
cantaloupe, broccoli, carrots, cauliflower, legumes, mushrooms, wheat berries, walnuts, spinach, and **green leafy vegetables.**

Vitamin A:
apricots, cantaloupe, papaya, prunes, peaches, carrots, asparagus, broccoli, red pepper, winter squashes and **green leafy vegetables**, especially kale, collards, mustard, spinach, turnip, beet, and dandelion greens.

Vitamin B1 (Thiamine):
dried apricots, avocados, pineapple, asparagus, fresh peas, **green leafy vegetables**, especially spinach, as well as soybeans, millet, rye berries, sunflower seeds, sesame seeds and almonds.

Vitamin B2 (Riboflavin):
avocados, broccoli, asparagus, okra, mushrooms and **green leafy vegetables**, especially spinach and kale, as well as soybeans, lentils, garbanzos, buckwheat, sunflower seeds and almonds.

Vitamin B3 (Niacin):
prunes, dried figs, dates, mushrooms, legumes, avocados, asparagus, broccoli, cantaloupe, millet, wheat berries and **green leafy vegetables** especially kale, spinach and collard greens.

Vitamin B6 (Pyridoxine):
raisins, avocado, blueberries, bananas, cantaloupe, cabbage, mushrooms, soybeans, walnuts and **green leafy vegetables**.

Vitamin B$_{12}$ and B$_{17}$:
sprouts.

Vitamin C:
tomatoes, citrus fruits, mangoes, papaya, pineapple, cantaloupe, broccoli, asparagus, cauliflower, kohlrabi, sauerkraut, cabbage, **green leafy vegetables**, especially kale, spinach, collard and mustard greens, and alfalfa sprouts.

Vitamin E:
apples, strawberries, cherries, asparagus, broccoli, corn, parsnips, leeks and **green leafy vegetables**, especially spinach and turnip greens as well as rye berries, almonds, filberts, walnuts and sunflower seeds.

MINERALS

Calcium:
broccoli and **green leafy vegetables**, especially kale, watercress, collards, mustard and dandelion greens, legumes, sesame seeds, sunflower seeds, wakame, hiziki and dulse.

Chlorine:
green leafy vegetables, especially lettuce, dandelion, spinach and watercress as well as beets, celery, carrots, onions and parsnips.

Chromium:
apples, grapes, raisins, **green leafy vegetables**, mushrooms, legumes, nuts, wheat and rye berries.

Copper:
cauliflower, avocado, almonds, filberts, walnuts, buckwheat, millet, soybeans and whole grains.

Fluorine:
Brussels sprouts, cauliflower, cabbage, beet and **green leafy vegetables**, especially spinach and watercress.

Iodine:
asparagus, cabbage, cucumbers, sea vegetables, spinach and **green leafy vegetables**.

Iron:
dried apricots, prunes, raisins, winter squashes, brussels sprouts, asparagus, **green leafy vegetables**, especially spinach, kale and beet tops, as well as millet, wheat berries, garbanzos, soybeans, lentils, pumpkin seeds, sunflower seeds, almonds and hiziki.

Magnesium:
dried apricots, strawberries, cantaloupe, mangoes, avocado, bananas, pineapples, broccoli, corn, cauliflower, beets, parsnips, mushrooms and **green leafy vegetables**, especially collards,

Swiss chard, spinach, beet, and mustard greens as well as soybeans, lentils, almonds, filberts, pumpkin seeds, buckwheat, millet, wakame and dulse.

Manganese:
apples, apricots, pineapples, bananas, broccoli, carrots, celery, legumes, almonds, filberts, buckwheat and **green leafy vegetables**.

Phosphorus:
broccoli and **green leafy vegetables**, especially kale and collard greens as well as wheat and rye berries, buckwheat, soybeans, garbanzos, almonds, sesame seeds, pumpkin seeds, and dulse.

Potassium:
dates, bananas, cantaloupe, papaya, garlic, onion, winter squashes, avocado, Brussels sprouts, broccoli, and **green leafy vegetables**, especially spinach and Swiss chard, legumes, sunflower seeds, buckwheat.

Selenium:
broccoli, cabbage, asparagus, garlic, onions, mushrooms, whole grains.

Silicon:
apples, grapes, strawberries, asparagus, beets, celery, parsnip and **green leafy vegetables**, especially lettuce, spinach, and Swiss chard.

Sodium:
celery, **green leafy vegetables**, especially Swiss chard, beet tops, dandelion greens, spinach, watercress and sea vegetables.

Sulphur:
asparagus, garlic, onions and **green leafy vegetables**, especially watercress and Swiss chard.

Zinc:
mushrooms, onions, legumes, especially soybeans, nuts, sunflower seeds, pumpkin seeds and spinach, a **green leafy vegetable.**

GERMINATION

By converting the proteins and starches during the sprouting process, a higher-quality protein source develops. Here is a list of some vegetarian sources of complete proteins: alfalfa, chickpeas, clover, buckwheat, sunflower seed, mung bean, soybean, sesame seed, millet, lentil, quinoa, almond and pumpkin seed. By unleashing their full potential, sprouted foods increase their original protein content. During the germination process, amino acids are released from their protein structures and new proteins are synthesized. If there is a complete protein present in the seed, it should be present in the sprout. Sprouts are so readily digestible because of their high quality and content of available enzymes. Tests have indicated that other nutrients in sprouts can increase from 50 to 400% when germinated. For example, millet and wheat contain over five times the amount of vitamin C when sprouted. Vitamin B content also grows substantially with germination. If you want to enrich the vitamin C as well as chlorophyll in your sprouts, expose them to sunlight near the end of germination. These pre-digested foods rich in activated enzymes enhance the body's own internal enzyme activity. As we know, food enzymes are present to help break down protein, starches and fats. Therefore, the digestibility of sprouted foods is unsurpassed. The fatty acids, amino acids and simple sugars produced by this process provide the body with an easy job of digestion. In addition, tests have shown that man's ability to absorb proteins when cooked dramatically decreases. This is another reason why soaking and sprouting is a superior way of ingesting our protein sources for complete assimilation.

Furthermore, it is no longer a necessary practice to combine foods at one meal for the sole purpose of achieving a complete protein. It is an incorrect assumption that our bodies are only able to use ingested complete proteins. The Wendt doctrine describing 30 years of research debunks this theory. We have the ability to store proteins in our cells, and also convert these proteins into amino acids that can move freely throughout the body; excess moves to deficient areas. This makes combining different foods to achieve a complete protein unneccessary because our bodies have the ability to shift and combine stored amino acids internally to create what is needed.

The Wendt doctrine also shows the damaging effects of excess concentrated protein. It clogs the system, creates acids, and depletes the cells of oxygen along with other nutrients. Recent studies show that our bodies do not require more than 30 grams of protein and even less if we are consuming a raw, living diet. All in all, sprouted foods provide us with ample amounts of quality protein that are better suited for the human digestive system.

The following pages explain and direct those of you who want to grow your own sprouts. Apart from the satisfaction of being self-sufficient, it is financially beneficial because commercial sprouts are usually expensive.

ENZYME INHIBITORS

Enzyme inhibitors are nature's way of preserving the life force for the purpose of future plant reproduction. They are present in cereal grains, legumes, tree nuts and seeds. They were recently discovered in the 1940's and it is necessary to remove them from our plant foods for proper digestion. The addition of supplemental enzymes will inactivate these inhibitors and enhance enzyme activity. Cooking will also destroy these inhibitors but the enzymes will be destroyed as well. Another way we can accomplish the same goal is sprouting. These enzyme rich foods lay dormant until activated by water. As the enzymes come to life, they inactivate the inhibitors and begin to sprout.

Therefore, in order to healthfully consume substantial amounts of raw nuts, seeds, grains and beans, it is necessary to germinate them first or supplement with external enzymes. Scientific studies have documented serious physical degeneration in small animals when fed large quantities of raw foods containing enzyme inhibitors over a period of time. Dr. Howell applied this research to the process of human consumption. Overall, it is more beneficial to eat cooked foods without enzymes, than raw foods with inhibitors intact.

Research with laboratory animals further indicates specific harmful effects from ingesting inhibitors. They include gastrointestinal problems, an extremely enlarged pancreas, excretion of large quantities of wasted enzymes and a condition of overall poor health. In addition, the total loss of pancreatic enzymes will lead to death.

In conclusion, it is most important to soak or sprout your nuts, seeds, grains and beans or eat them with supplemental enzymes or cook them to avoid the harmful effects of enzyme inhibitors.

Germination Chart

	Plant Variety	Soaking Hours	Daily Rinses	Approx. Sprouting Length in inches	Growing Time in Days	Quantity	Yield Estimation
1.	Alfalfa	4-6	4	1-2	3-5	3 tbsp.	3 cups
2.	Amaranth	4-6	3	0-$^1/_4$	2-3	3 tbsp.	$^3/_4$ cup
3.	Anise	4-6	5	1	2	3 tbsp.	1 cup
4.	Most Beans	8-10	3	1	3-5	1 cup	3-4 cups
5.	Barley	8-10	3	0	3	$^1/_2$ cup	1 cup
6.	Buckwheat	4-6	2	$^1/_2$	3	1 cup	2-3 cups
7.	Cabbage	4-6	2	1-2	3-5	1 tbsp.	1 $^1/_2$ cups
8.	Chickpeas	10-12	3	$^1/_2$	3	1 cup	3 cups
9.	Chia	4-6	5	$^1/_4$	2-3	1 tbsp	1 $^1/_2$ cups
10.	Clover	4-6	2	1 $^1/_2$	4-5	1 tbsp.	2 $^1/_2$ cups
11.	Corn	8-10	3	$^1/_2$	3	1 cup	2 cups
12.	Flax	5-7	5	1-2	4	1 tbsp.	1 cup
13.	Fenugreek	4-6	4	2-3	3-5	4 tbsp.	1 cup
14.	Green Peas	10-12	3	$^1/_2$	2-3	1 cup	2 cups
15.	Lentils	6-8	3	$^1/_4$-$^1/_2$	3-4	1 cup	3-4 cups
16.	Millet	6-8	3	0-$^1/_8$	2	1 cup	1 $^1/_2$ cups
17.	Mung Beans	8-10	2	1-2	3-5	1 cup	3-4 cups
18.	Mustard	4-6	2	1 $^1/_2$	4	1 tbsp.	1 cup
19.	Most Nuts	8-12	2	0	1	1 cup	1 $^1/_2$ cups
20.	Onion	4-6	3	1-2	3-5	1 tbsp.	1 cup
21.	Oats	8-10	2	0-$^1/_4$	3	1 cup	2 cups
22.	Radish	4-6	2	1	3-5	1 tbsp.	1 cup
23.	Rye	8-10	4	0-$^1/_4$	3-4	1 cup	2 $^1/_2$ cups
24.	Rice	8-10	3	0	3	1 cup	1 $^1/_2$ cups
25.	Pumpkin Seeds	6-8	3	0-$^1/_8$	1-2	1 cup	1 $^1/_2$ cups
26.	Sesame Seeds	4-6	4	0	1	1 cup	1 $^1/_2$ cups
27.	Sunflower Seeds	6-8	2	0-$^1/_8$	1-2	1 cup	1 $^1/_2$ cups
28.	Soybeans	10-12	5	$^1/_2$-1	3-4	1 cup	2 $^1/_2$ cups
29.	Watercress	4-6	4	1	3-5	1 tbsp.	1 $^1/_2$ cups
30.	Wheat	10-12	4	0-$^1/_8$	2-3	1 cup	2 $^1/_2$ cups
31.	Quinoa	4-6	4	0-$^1/_{16}$	2-3	1 cup	1 $^1/_4$ cups

Remember that the final yield is an estimation. Sometimes it will be a little more or a little less.

The following list of helpful comments corresponds by number to the Germination Chart above.

Please note: Nuts, seeds, grains and beans require at least 24 hours to totally dissipate enzyme inhibitors.

HELPFUL COMMENTS

1   Alfalfa sprouts are high in protein, vitamins, and minerals. They have a very clean, refreshing taste and are easy to sprout. Place in the sun for leaves to appear at the end of sprouting.

2. Sprouted amaranth has a mellow flavor and the sprouts smell like corn silk. Try sprout-

ing this grain like you would chia sprouts listed below.

3. Anise has a very strong flavor when sprouted and should be used sparingly or mixed with other sprouts.

4. Bean sprouts are a good source of fiber and they are high in protein. Aduki sprouts, for example, are high in iron and calcium. To keep the sprouts tender, do not germinate for more than three days. (See mung beans.)

5. Sprouted barley has a chewy character and does not have a sweet aftertaste.

6. We purchase and eat the roasted hulled groats (kasha). To sprout buckwheat without soil use the raw hulled seeds. The raw unhulled and hulled buckwheat are both used for growing in soil; the unhulled works better and is more resistant to rotting.

7. Cabbage sprouts are high in vitamins A and C, and a good source of minerals.

8. Chickpeas, also called garbanzos, are high in nutrients and are easy to sprout.

9. Chia sprouts have a strong flavor. They tend to be difficult to sprout because they are gelatinous. Try sprouting them on screens covered with undyed paper towels; sprinkle instead of rinse with water.

10. Clover is high in protein and has a unique flavor. It grows well with alfalfa.

11. It is sometimes hard to locate untreated corn kernels for sprouting. They are sweet and chewy.

12. Flax is high in protein, fiber and rich in essential oils. Sprout them the same as you would chia because they are also gelatinous. If you expose them to sunshine, leaves will grow.

13. Fenugreek is known for being an internal deodorizer. It has an exotic flavor, rich in vitamin A and iron. It will get bitter if you let the sprouts germinate too long.

14. Sprouted peas are a good source of vitamins B and C and minerals. The sprouts taste almost like fresh peas.

15. Sprouted lentils have an overall excellent flavor. They are protein rich, contain minerals and B vitamins and are very easy to sprout.

16. Millet is a complete protein and is the most alkaline grain. You need the unhulled variety for sprouting. Try sprouting it like you would flax seed or chia.

17. Mung beans are easy to sprout. They like to be rinsed in very cold water and weighted down with a heavy dish when sprouting. Grown in the dark, they are rich in vitamins A, B, and C and minerals. Aduki beans are sprouted the same way. Be sure to get the sprouting variety of adukis.

18. Mustard sprouts have a strong, penetrating flavor and should be mixed with other sprouts.

19. Germinated nuts have high-quality fats and - protein; they swell, but rarely sprout tails.

20. Onions in any form are therapeutic. The sprouts have a potent oniony flavor and taste great mixed with tossed salads or other sprouts.

21. Unhulled oats must be used for sprouting. Too much water can make the oats rot so be careful. They are a good source of fiber and vitamins.

22. Radish sprouts are high in vitamin C and potassium. They have a hot radish flavor yet, if they are allowed to grow longer, they get sweeter. They are good mixed with other sprouts.

23. Rye is easy to sprout. It has a sweet, chewy texture and it makes great dehydrated crackers. Make sure to rinse it often because it tends to rot in warm weather.

24. The only variety of rice that will sprout is the whole-grain brown rice. It is a good source of fiber and B vitamins.

25. Pumpkin seeds are high in quality fats. The hulled seeds are best for sprouting.

26. Only the unhulled sesame seeds will sprout. A good source of fats, vitamins and minerals, these sprouts turn bitter if left too long.

27. Sunflower seeds have a delicious flavor. Rich in nutrients, sprouted sunflower seeds become bitter if left too long. They are grown in soil either hulled or unhulled. Like buckwheat, it is better to use the unhulled.

28. Soybeans are difficult to germinate. You must frequently rinse them to prevent fermentation. They are rich in proteins and fats.

29. Watercress has a strong pungent flavor. It is a gelatinous seed of the mustard family and sprouted like chia or flax.

30. Wheat is easy to sprout. It is a very sweet, chewy food that may be used in place of bulghur in cracked wheat salads.

31. Quinoa is high in protein and has a nutty flavor. Get the unhulled variety and sprout it like flaxseed or chia.

ALKALINES AND ACIDS

It is worthwhile to discuss the concept of alkaline and acid and how it relates to the food we eat. At least 80% of the food we consume should produce alkaline compounds when digested, while 20% is left for acid-forming food. Some alkaline-forming elements, for example, are calcium, potassium, sodium, magnesium, and iron. They are changed into mineral salts in the body. Some acid forming elements are phosphorus, chlorine, sulphur, silicon, and iodine. They are changed into strong acids in the body. Let's see how alkaline-forming elements tie into body function. To start with, human blood should be slightly alkaline in nature, yet the typical SAD (Standard American Diet) is predominantly acid forming. Furthermore, we are constantly producing acid compounds in our bodies just through normal daily human functions. It is necessary to eat an abundance of alkaline forming foods and limit the rest in order to maintain a healthy acid-alkaline balance. On a scale of 0 - 14, 7 is neutral. Our blood needs to be around 7.4 to maintain proper alkalinity. Body cells are highly sensitive to over acidity and will not function well. Iron-containing hemoglobin in our blood helps to neutralize acids. The kidneys produce alkaline compounds that are released into the blood to also help neutralize acids, while they filter out acidic compounds produced by protein digestion. Eating too much protein overworks the kidneys. The lungs also aid the alkalinizing process by removing carbon dioxide from the body. Deep breathing, rest, happy thoughts, relaxation, as well as fresh air and exercise help keep the body in balance through the process of continued alkalization. Specific types of food we eat do the same.

The ability to understand food properties is also important. For example, people are often confused by the issue of acid fruits being alkaline forming. Although they are acidic tasting upon entering our mouths, they are metabolized in the body to release alkaline compounds. Most ripe fruits and most of the vegetables create an alkaline ash with some exceptions. For those of you who have studied chemistry, these foods create substances like sodium hydroxide and carbon dioxide, as well as other compounds during the process of digestion. Here is the easiest example to understand: When sodium hydroxide (NAOH) combines with hydrochloric acid (HCL) found in the stomach, we are left with a neutral salt and water by-product that is eventually eliminated through the kidneys. (NAOH + HCL → NACL + H2O). Tree-ripened lemons, for example, contain organic acids that oxidize into carbon dioxide and water. They do not create an acid system, but instead contribute to the alkaline mineral reserve. Furthermore, predigested nuts, seeds, legumes and whole grains (which are normally acid-forming) become alkalizing. Again we see the importance and significance of sprouting our food for longevity.

Acidosis is often times a contributing cause of drug addiction. The nicotine in tobacco and the caffeine in coffee, for example, are alkaloids, or alkalizing substances, that neutralize acids in the body. Yet as a whole, tobacco and coffee are acid forming. The more acidic our bodies become, the more addicted we get to these alkaloids. Other examples of alkaloid containing substances are cocaine, marijuana, morphine, amphetamines and heroine. A properly balanced alkaline diet can perhaps help eliminate addictive behavior.

If the body cannot neutralize excess acids successfully, these acids will be placed in the joints and tissues creating pain and disease. Common sense dictates a correlation between highly acid forming diets and crippling arthritis.

If we continually eat foods that produce acids, we must neutralize them with alkaline-forming elements. Therefore, it is important to eat enough alkaline forming foods to maintain balance. This proper balance is part of supporting a powerful immune system. A strong internal alkaline reserve protects our bodies from unexpected conditions and emergencies.

The important point to remember is this: An acidic body contains excess hydrogen. In order to make balance, it must combine with available oxygen to form water, a harmless compound, thereby neutralizing the excess. The result is a constant depletion of internal oxygen. Other necessary metabolic processes are unable to function properly without sufficient oxygen and this leads to degeneration.

Finally, in an oxygen-rich internal enviroment, disease is unable to grow. Remember to limit acid-forming foods in your diet.

Acid Forming Foods

all meats
all fish
poultry and eggs
commercial nut and seed butters
pasteurized and processed milk
all commercial dairy cheeses, ice cream
all grains except millet
breads, cereals, crackers
flours, pastas, noodles
most legumes, especially
lentils and peanuts
commercial olives
many preservatives and additives
white sugar
dried coconut
ungerminated nuts and seeds
carob
candy and chocolate
commercial soda and alcoholic beverages
megavitamin consumption
coffee and commercial tea
rancid food
drugs and tobacco
undigested food
blueberries, cranberries, plums and prunes
unripe fruits
sugar-processed fruits
Brussels sprouts, rhubarb and asparagus
all chemically processed and pickled foods
all sugar-containing foods
commercial vinegars and dressings

Alkaline Forming Foods

most raw vegetables
most ripe raw fruits, especially melons
all kinds of raw milk
sundried olives
lima beans
avocados
sprouted whole grains
sprouted legumes
soaked or sprouted nuts and their by-
products
especially almonds, hazelnuts,brazil nuts
and pignoli nuts
soaked or sprouted seeds and their by-
products
especially sunflower, sesame,and pumpkin
bee pollen
royal jelly, honey
chestnuts
herbal teas
wheatgrass and other sprouted grasses
algaes and sea vegetables
fresh coconut
enzymes

FOOD COMBINING

The lines between the blocks of categories indicate compatibility, the higher the number the better the combination. I have included three blocks of categories for predigested foods, (protein rich sprouted legumes, sprouted grains, and predigested nuts, seeds, and algae). I have not included meat, fish, poultry, eggs, or dairy in the chart because this book is dealing with plant foods, although I will discuss their limited compatibility in the following information. This chart explores the realm of possibilities available to us with the specific use of vegetarian sources. Soaking and sprouting increases the number of acceptable food combinations and digestion takes place with more speed and grace.

• Food combining is a useful technique to help us understand and create healthier meals. Different types of foods need a certain amount of time for digestion, for specific enzymes to do the job, and for a particular acid or alkaline PH to finish the process completely. It would be wise to understand some basic concepts and also be aware that we each have different constitutions. Listen to your body, experiment and find out what works best for you.

• To start with, raw fruit is considered a predigested food in its own right. It contains its own digestive enzymes and passes through to the intestines more quickly than most other foods. Melons are the most easily di-

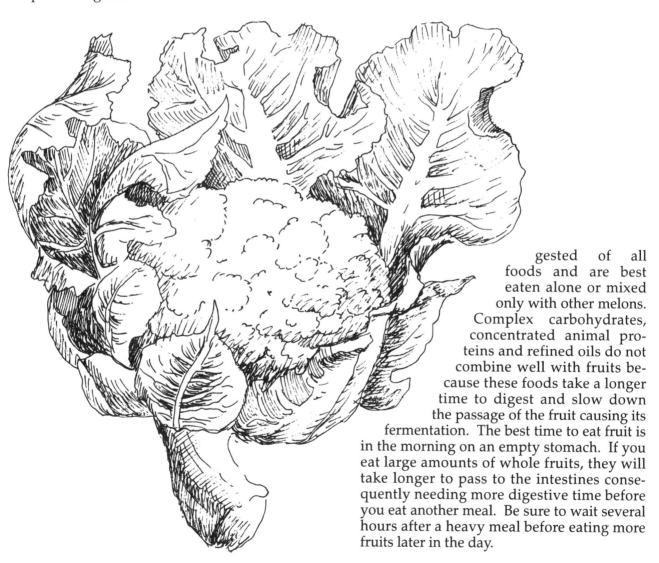

gested of all foods and are best eaten alone or mixed only with other melons. Complex carbohydrates, concentrated animal proteins and refined oils do not combine well with fruits because these foods take a longer time to digest and slow down the passage of the fruit causing its fermentation. The best time to eat fruit is in the morning on an empty stomach. If you eat large amounts of whole fruits, they will take longer to pass to the intestines consequently needing more digestive time before you eat another meal. Be sure to wait several hours after a heavy meal before eating more fruits later in the day.

- In the special fruits category, lemons and papayas combine well with all plant foods. This means that lemons and papayas can be used as ingredients in dressings, soups, sauces and any other recipes. Lemons easily replace all types of vinegar. Papayas are used less often in this book because of price and availability. Avocados and tomatoes combine well with acid and sub-acid fruits and high water content vegetables, especially leafy greens. Avocados and sundried olives can be combined because they are both high-fat fruit proteins. Apples, unlike most other fruits, combine well with vegetables when they are all in juice form.

- Nuts and seeds do not combine well with starchy foods or refined oils.

- Concentrated sugars like honey, as well as acidic foods like vinegar, and fruits all block predigestion of starchy foods in the mouth by restricting the secretion of ptyalin, a starch-splitting enzyme in saliva. (Activities in the mouth and in the stomach are considered stages of predigestion.)

- Refined oils, concentrated sugars, acidic foods, and fruits will inhibit the flow of gastric juices hindering protein predigestion in the stomach.

- There is the ability to make the combination of raw nuts and seeds with acid fruits. Since nuts and seeds have a high oil content, they do not decompose as rapidly as other types of food in the stomach, but receive their strongest breakdown in the intestines. The oil in nuts and seeds and the sugar in fruits both inhibit the gastric juices in the stomach. They must move together to the intestines where the digestive process is completed. The combination of fruits, nuts and seeds do well eaten as a separate meal. Predigested nuts and seeds gain strong compatibility with sub-acid and sweet fruits.

- Refined oils combine well with vegetables and starchy foods. There are enough oils in whole foods to satisfy our dietary requirements, so refined oils are best used sparingly.

- By sprouting legumes and grains they gain compatability with soaked nuts and seeds. Sprouted grains also gain compatability with sweet fruits.

- High water content vegetables combine well with just about everything except fruits. One acid or sub-acid fruit like tomatoes may be added to a salad that does not include starchy foods, refined oils, concentrated proteins or cooked foods.

- If you are going to eat meat, fish, poultry, dairy or eggs, they combine well only with high water content vegetables and especially leafy greens. Since these vegetables do not inhibit salivary enzymes and gastric juices the animal protein can easily move to the intestines for final breakdown.

- Most vegetarians consume soybeans and their by-products, so a special category block has been included. Many have allergies to this legume and some soybean products are not necessarily healthful. Make your own decisions and use what is best for you.

- Vegetables with an asterisk are technically classified as fruits. We commonly refer to them as vegetables and they will be treated as such in the chart.

- It is beneficial to the process of healing a serious disease to limit intake of refined oils and carbohydrates, salts, spices, concentrated sweeteners, desserts, and animal foods.

With the above information in mind, proper food combining can help us maintain good health. Excess weight, toxemia, fatigue, water retention, pain, emotional irritability and ultimately disease can be avoided through education and discipline. Moreover, it is important to stop poisoning your own personal environment. Excess alcohol, white sugar, caffeine and tobacco are all legal narcotics that are destroying the health of our nation. Learn to make the right choices.

I've tried to make this chart easy to read and understand. It is a guideline and not an absolute, unbending set of rules. Don't be neurotic. There are times to let loose and enjoy in moderation.

VEGETARIAN FOOD COMBINING CHART

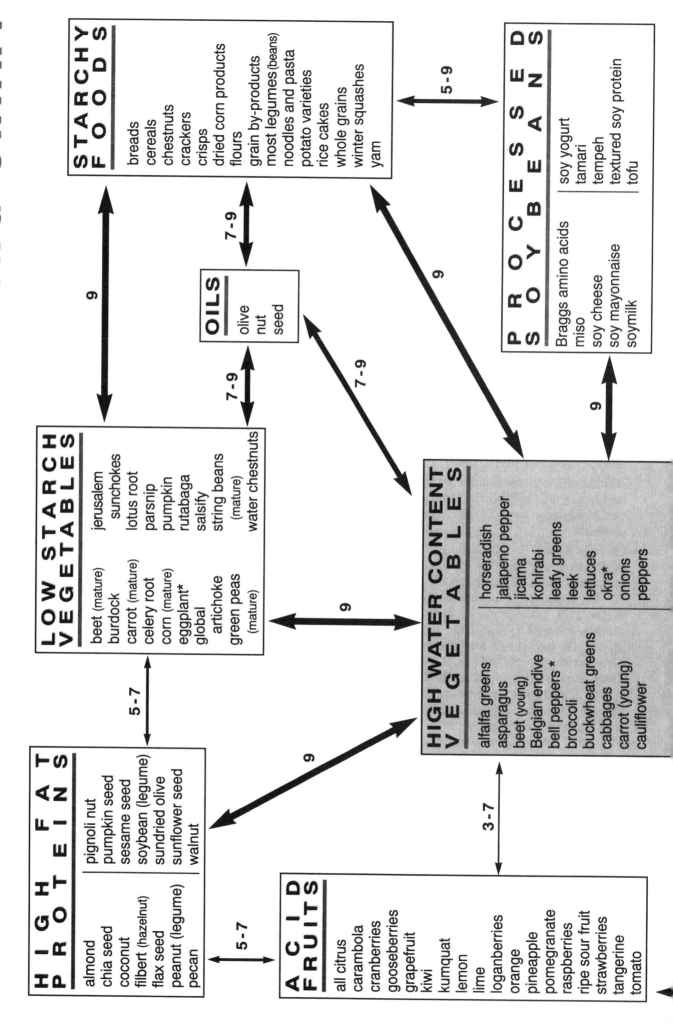

STARCHY FOODS

breads
cereals
chestnuts
crackers
crisps
dried corn products
flours
grain by-products
most legumes (beans)
noodles and pasta
potato varieties
rice cakes
whole grains
winter squashes
yam

PROCESSED SOYBEANS

Braggs amino acids
miso
soy cheese
soy mayonnaise
soymilk

soy yogurt
tamari
tempeh
textured soy protein
tofu

OILS

olive
nut
seed

LOW STARCH VEGETABLES

beet (mature)
burdock
carrot (mature)
celery root
corn (mature)
eggplant*
global artichoke
green peas (mature)

jerusalem sunchokes
lotus root
parsnip
pumpkin
rutabaga
salsify
string beans (mature)
water chestnuts

HIGH WATER CONTENT VEGETABLES

alfalfa greens
asparagus
beet (young)
Belgian endive
bell peppers *
broccoli
buckwheat greens
cabbages
carrot (young)
cauliflower

horseradish
jalapeno pepper
jicama
kohlrabi
leafy greens
leek
lettuces
okra*
onions
peppers

HIGH FAT PROTEINS

almond
chia seed
coconut
filbert (hazelnut)
flax seed
peanut (legume)
pecan

pignoli nut
pumpkin seed
sesame seed
soybean (legume)
sundried olive
sunflower seed
walnut

ACID FRUITS

all citrus
carambola
cranberries
gooseberries
grapefruit
kiwi
kumquat
lemon
lime
loganberries
orange
pineapple
pomegranate
raspberries
ripe sour fruit
strawberries
tangerine
tomato

9

5 - 9

7 - 9

7 - 9

9

9

5 - 7

9

9

5 - 7

3 - 7

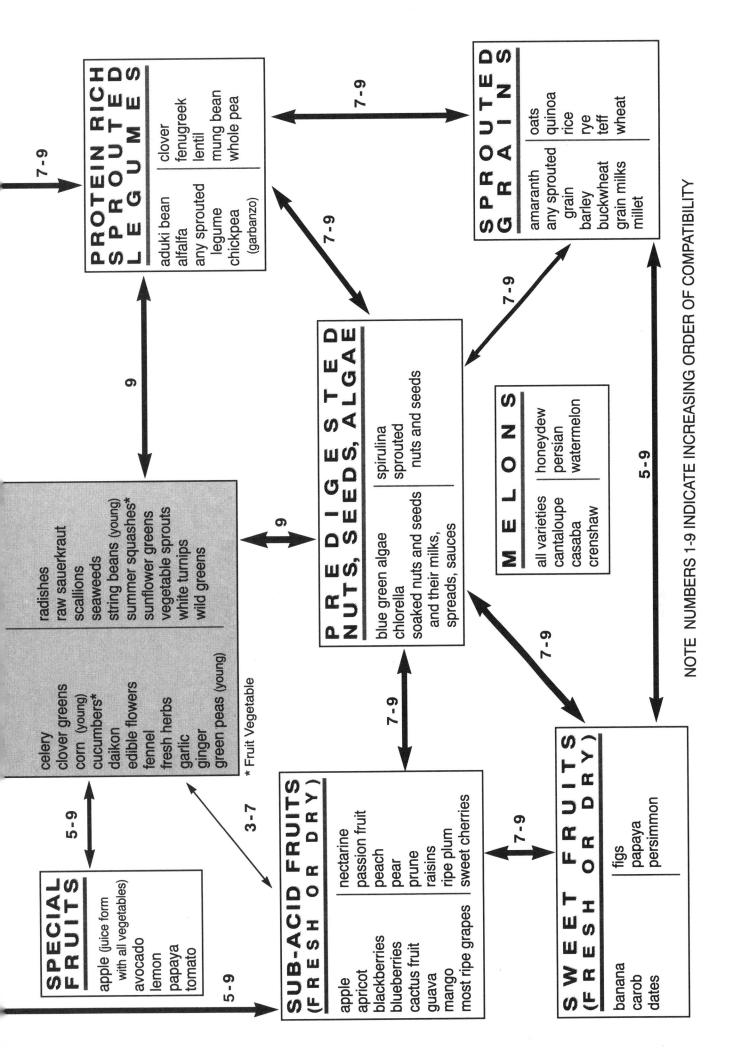

PROTEIN RICH SPROUTED LEGUMES

aduki bean	clover
alfalfa	fenugreek
any sprouted	lentil
legume	mung bean
chickpea	whole pea
(garbanzo)	

SPROUTED GRAINS

amaranth	oats
any sprouted	quinoa
grain	rice
barley	rye
buckwheat	teff
grain milks	wheat
millet	

7 - 9

9

7 - 9

7 - 9

7 - 9

5 - 9

PREDIGESTED NUTS, SEEDS, ALGAE

blue green algae	spirulina
chlorella	sprouted
soaked nuts and seeds	nuts and seeds
and their milks,	
spreads, sauces	

MELONS

all varieties	honeydew
cantaloupe	persian
casaba	watermelon
crenshaw	

9

7 - 9

7 - 9

celery
clover greens
corn (young)
cucumbers*
daikon
edible flowers
fennel
fresh herbs
garlic
ginger
green peas (young)

radishes
raw sauerkraut
scallions
seaweeds
string beans (young)
summer squashes*
sunflower greens
vegetable sprouts
white turnips
wild greens

* Fruit Vegetable

5 - 9

3 - 7

SPECIAL FRUITS

apple (juice form
with all vegetables)
avocado
lemon
papaya
tomato

5 - 9

SUB-ACID FRUITS
(FRESH OR DRY)

apple	nectarine
apricot	passion fruit
blackberries	peach
blueberries	pear
cactus fruit	prune
guava	raisins
mango	ripe plum
most ripe grapes	sweet cherries

7 - 9

SWEET FRUITS
(FRESH OR DRY)

banana	figs
carob	papaya
dates	persimmon

NOTE NUMBERS 1-9 INDICATE INCREASING ORDER OF COMPATIBILITY

FORETHOUGHTS

The word nutrition has usually focused on describing a physical, chemical law of life. We should learn to look past the conventional concept of nutrition into a new understanding of the multiple forces of complete nourishment. The life force of food not only affects us on the physical, chemical level but also affects our minds and spirits. This goes beyond the concepts of proteins, carbohydrates, fats, vitamins, etc. We are soaking up the consciousness and cosmic energy of that which we eat. These energy forces are somehow transferred to human form and directly link together physical and spiritual health. Our level of energy depends upon our total ability to assimilate the multi-dimensional micro-nutrients found in living plant foods, pure water, fresh air and sunlight.

For thousands of years, different groups of people have understood and described the life force in relation to subtle forms of energy travelling throughout the body as well as the presence of energy fields in the plant kingdom. The Essenes, the Orientals, and the Eastern Indian cultures have written about the aura surrounding the human body, the energy chakras located at different points in the body, and the meridians of energy travelling within the body. The concept of yin/yang, which describes the expanding and contracting energy forces of foods is another example of this phenomena. Through Kirlian photography, we have been able to photograph the human aura and the energy fields of plants. It is necessary to understand the importance of living foods and how they rejuvenate our physical bodies and spiritual energy. Properly nourished, we may enjoy unlimited, inherent strength and power.

Foods that nourish our bodies resound with universal, infinite vitality and allow us to become directly linked to a higher spiritual consciousness. What we are talking about here are the omnipresent laws of nature. If we consistently stress-out our life force, energy reserves,and internal physical organization by the use of tobacco, drugs, alcohol and chemi-calized, processed foods, the likely outcome will be physical and mental disorder followed by premature death. Improper foods disrupt the flow of energy to our systems, and deter our ability to activate and rejuvenate. Instead of rejuvenating, we are busy fighting degeneration and poor enzymatic ability.

The ability to know intuitively what your daily requirements are and to be able to satisfy them describes the fundamental goal of physical and spiritual nutrition. Every beam of sunlight, every breath of fresh air, every drink of pure water, and every taste of living plant food takes us closer to the truth. These essential nutrients contribute to the full circle of body, mind, and spirit. We have now gone beyond the dinner table as our main source of nutrition. Understanding some basic facts about these other forms of nourishment helps tie together the information discussed in this book.

Sunlight charges our human batteries and helps regulate body functions and cycles. There has been a lot of controversy recently about the negative effects of exposure to the sun. Daily outdoor activity for small periods of time has a positive effect on overall health. I remember the joy of romping outdoors as a child for a couple of hours each day. How nice it was to soak up the sunlight and inhale deeply while at play. Many of us have enjoyed the pleasure of walking through a pristine forest and absorbing the strength and sustenance of clean air passing through our lungs. Clean air filled with oxygen is especially important to the brain. Deep breathing techniques are commonly used to create mental calmness. The good news is that living plant foods contain the energy forces of both sunlight and oxygen. Another major duty of oxygen is to combine with the foods we eat to create energy for maintaining the life process. This connects the significance of eating a diet rich in alkaline-forming foods. Acid-forming foods will consistently deplete the body of oxygen creating an imbalance in the system. The available oxygen must combine with the excess hydrogen produced by acid

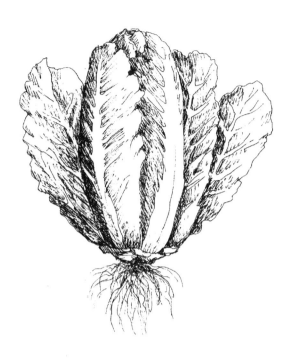

by-products while using up the internal oxygen supply. Sprouted grains, legumes, and fresh greens are the highest-quality energy sources and are the easiest to digest. Correct amounts of sunlight, clean air, pure water, and living foods combined with the ever-present forces of our earth's electro-magnetic energy and the cosmic energy of the universal heavens lead to an exciting full circle of life-giving elements.

Understand that what we each individually require is in constant flux. As we grow older, our consumption of physical food should be kept to a minimum. The most important rule to remember and practice is to undereat, not overeat physical foods; everything in moderation. Our aging bodies require more energy sources that are less condensed.

Raw foods are not only a less-condensed form of nourishment, they are full of enzymes. Dr. Edward Howell, Ann Wigmore, and Viktor Kulvinskas are all forerunners in the movement to popularize the importance of internal enzymatic activity as the major essential factor holding together all physical internal functions to maintain life. It is important for us to understand that cooking destroys enzymes, reduces the availability of digestible proteins, reduces the quantity and quality of important nutrients, and disrupts the subtle energy fields of food. Furthermore, the chemicals and pesticides used to protect our crops from bugs and fungus can combine together to form new, more toxic compounds within the body after they are heated and ingested. When we eat only cooked foods, we miss out on the major function of external food enzymes needed to enhance pre-digestion in the stomach. Our internal enzyme store as described by Dr. Howell, is a finite supply. Hence, we are constantly depleting our lifetime supply of internal enzymes by eating only cooked foods.

Germinating dramatically increases protein, enzyme and vitamin content, removes enzyme

forming foods to form water, a neutral substance. Many nutritionists believe that the central cause of disease is directly connected to a constant depletion of the internal oxygen supply. Sprouts, algae supplements, and wheatgrass juice are healthful because they contain a high concentration of this life-sustaining oxygen.

Interestingly enough, pure water also contains a high concentration of oxygen and is obviously important for maintaining good health. The foods that are high in water content and therefore high in oxygen are raw fruits and vegetables followed by sprouted grains, beans, seeds, and nuts. It is wise to limit our overall intake of concentrated proteins and fats, especially meat, fish, eggs, and dairy. These foods contain the smallest amount of available oxygen. Furthermore, fats harbor the toxins in our bodies as well as deplete the oxygen supply. This is not to say we should eliminate all fats from our diet because the body does require small amounts of essential fatty acids for proper functioning. They also transport the fat soluble vitamins like A, D, and E. Sesame seeds and avocados are examples of foods containing quality essential fatty acids.

Fats and all concentrated proteins are the densest food form, are also the hardest to digest, and require the most oxygen to break down. Eating them to excess creates poisonous

inhibitors, promotes an alkalizing effect on the body and augments the overall existing life force. Raw fruit and vegetables take second place to the power and majesty of nutrient-packed living sprouts. To improve the digestion of cooked foods, try to eat equal amounts of raw as well as sprouted foods. In addition, reduce cooking time as much as possible and use lower temperatures. One of the many benefits of sprouting is that it enables you to cook grains and beans quickly. Taking quality enzyme supplements with cooked foods aids pre-digestion and conserves internal enzymes. Know that eating foods that are either too hot or too cold will disturb enzymatic function. Finally, produce that is picked before maturity, shipped, stored for long periods of time, and then forced to ripen has a minimal life force. Try to eat locally grown produce.

Eating to live in harmony is your assignment. What, how, when and where are all up to you. Prepare your food with love and care, give thanks for each meal, and enjoy eating in relaxed atmosphere. Remind yourself to reflect upon life, share love and joy, understand and improve present surroundings and care for your body.

In order to function in this world, it is not necessary to become overly compulsive about living the right life. We will all continually go through cleansing and renewing processes until we die. Practice enough self-awareness to understand proper balance in relation to your daily and long-term care. Life is to be enjoyed, so take time to play and be happy.

In the last few years, I have concentrated on a program of raw and living foods together with cooked foods to create a very satisfying, restorative diet. In fact, for many leading nutritionists, the ultimate healing diet consists of 100% raw plant foods and their juices at least until the body is balanced and internally organized enough to handle cooked foods. The people who inspired me the most to learn and

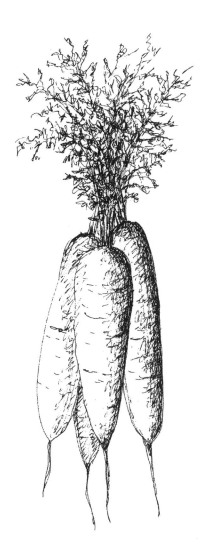

understand the true value of dining in the raw are Dr. Gabriel Cousens, Dr Edward Howell, Dr. Norman Walker and Dr.Humbart Santillo. Ann Wigmore and Viktor Kulvinskas, co-founders of Hippocrates and Brian Clement* have also inspired me along with all the wonderful teachers who have passed through the doors at the Hippocrates Institute.

Graduation from a predominantly cooked vegetarian diet to a combination of raw and cooked plant foods, together with a new appreciation of the many other forms of less-tangible nourishment, has taken me to a place where I am truly able to understand living the good life.

The overwhelming acceptance and praise consistently expressed by a worldwide clientele has made it a pleasure for me to prepare a written guideline for exciting, healthful, well-balanced, totally vegetarian meals.

DINING IN THE RAW

Life is an ever-changing continual cycle. Just as summer turns into winter and day turns into night, everything is in motion. Consequently, our diets must also be flexible as our needs change. There is one basic fact to remember: Four major elements of our existence are combined into one form, the vegetable kingdom. Water, soil, air, and sunlight are used to grow the food we eat and that food can be used to not only sustain life, but also to heal. While eating in harmony with the environment, we must also pay attention to the process of evolution and the laws of humanity. As the world becomes more complex, the environment more toxic, and our produce questionable, one should learn to consume increasing amounts of living foods that can be sprouted at home.

Economically and nutritionally, sprouts are a wonderful addition to anyone's diet. Raw vegetables and living sprouts are the rejuvenating factors missing from today's modern meal. These highly alkaline foods provide the necessary nutritional factors that are destroyed in improperly cooked or highly processed foods. Enzymes, vitamins, minerals, hormones, chlorophyll, and oxygen are the true ingredients needed in our recipes. Fruits, vegetables, sprouts, and their juices all have different nutritional gifts and therapeutic qualities; hence variety is important. Juicing removes the strain of continual digestion, separation, and elimination. Drinking the liquid essence of food with all its vitamins, enzymes and minerals intact gives the body an almost immediate absorption of nutrients. There is more time and energy available to be used for healing instead of digestion. That "inner vacation" for the body is what raw juice meals are all about.

When eating our meals, preparation and presentation are also significant because it is necessary for food to appeal to the senses of sight, smell, and taste. A variety of shapes, textures, flavors, and colors all play a role in the desire to satiate hunger, both mentally and physically.

As I mentioned earlier, sun, water, air, and soil all work together to create plant foods to nourish our bodies and promote regeneration. All the nutrients necessary to sustain life must be present and in proper proportion to help us

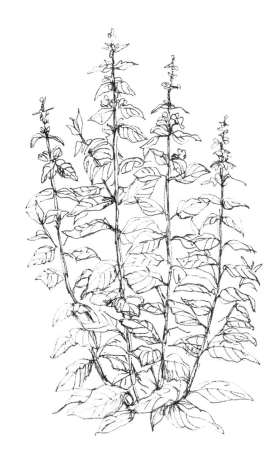

remain in balance and free of disease. In its raw state, the vegetable kingdom provides all these essential elements. I believe the health of America is currently in a state of crisis because this fundamental truth has been lost. The high incidence of disease and premature death tells the tale. Take the time to learn more about fruits, land and sea vegetables, legumes, grains, nuts and seeds and discover what they offer you. Here is helpful information about some of the ingredients used in the following chapters. A better understanding of plant foods will allow you to make intelligent food choices and prepare a more balanced meal for your family.

One special food I'd like to mention first is raw cultured vegetables, better known as sauerkraut. Its advantages have been studied since the early 1700's. The name sauerkraut was coined by the Austrians, but it has been around for thousands of years. It has been said that this food was a staple of the Orientals who built the Great Wall of China. It was also a principal food during the days of the Roman Empire. It was used through the centuries by sea captains and leaders of great armies to keep their men healthy. A Russian scientist named Metchnikoff did a study that concluded the lactobacillus found in sauerkraut not only created large amounts of friendly intestinal bacteria but also provided the body with easily absorbed vitamin C. A group of Russians who Metchnikoff studied had incredible longevity; a lifespan of 100 years or more was not uncommon. He concluded that a diet high in lactobacillus was one very important factor in their abundant good health.

The process of grinding up cabbage leaves and leaving them to ferment at room temperature creates an environment for wholesome microorganisms to grow, converting starches and sugars into lactic and acetic acids. This process of rapid fermentation will continue until you refrigerate the kraut. It will still continue to ferment, but at a much slower rate. The lower the temperature, the less breakdown. Do not heat the culture, as that will destroy it. Acetic acid is also a natural preservative. Eating these raw cultured vegetables every day with meals adds a tremendous contribution to the process of proper digestion. Consequently, candida yeast overgrowth is unlikely because of the high count of lactobacilli. Chewing kraut produces the same conversion in your mouth that is found in the intestines. The friendly lactobacilli bacteria in these cultured vegetables are full of enzymes and this gives the body

more time to let its own enzymes rejuvenate. So renew an old tradition and help extend your life-span.

A special food also presented in this book is the avocado, which has several nicknames. Its most popular is alligator pear. It can be traced back to ancient times. Artifacts and paintings displaying avocados have been found in the Indian ruins of the Mayans, Peruvians, and Aztecs. First introduced to Florida in the early 1800's, there are approximately sixty different varieties in Southern Florida alone. Avocados have a noted amount of calcium, magnesium, phosphorus, iron, and lesser amounts of many trace minerals. They contain vitamins A, B complex, C, E and are particularly abundant in thiamin, niacin and riboflavin. Low in saturated fat and sodium, the Florida avocado is also the lowest in calories of all domestic varieties. Avocados contain high quality unsaturated fatty acids necessary for good health. A one-cup serving has approximately two grams of protein, thirteen grams of carbohydrates, and seventeen grams of fat, totaling about 200 calories. Avocados should be eaten when soft to the touch. They do not do well when heated as a very bitter taste occurs because of the tannic acid present. The best way to use avocado is raw – in soups, dressings, salads and desserts. If you wish to freeze them, you must purée them first for use at a later date in dips, fillings or molds. Avocado purée makes a great facial mask. Scoop out the flesh nearest the skin and mash. Cover your face after a hot bath or shower. Let it sit on your face for about fifteen minutes before removing with tepid water. It nourishes the skin and keeps it looking young. This is a beauty secret given to me many years ago by a friend who has the most beautiful complexion.

The great potential of nuts and seeds has been long overlooked in our present diet; now they are primarily considered a snack food. In reality, however, they are a highly concentrated powerhouse of nutrients and sustainers of life . They are substantial in protein and are less likely to hold impurities and pollution. A good source of B vitamins and minerals, they are high in essential fatty acids. Nuts and seeds are best eaten raw. Soaking awakens these precious nuggets from their dormant state, removes enzyme inhibitors, alkalizes them and makes them more digestible. Almonds, filberts, sunflower, pumpkin and sesame seeds are most often used in this book. Sesame seeds are by far my favorite because they are so versatile. They contain vitamins A, B complex, C, D, E, and K as well as lecithin. They are high in calcium and are used in every section of my book from soups to desserts. Pumpkin and sunflower seeds are high in iron. Almonds and filberts carry the most calcium in the nut family and also contain vitamin E and various minerals. Experimenting with the recipes will help you gain a new respect for these so-called "snack foods." Try to purchase organic nuts and seeds whenever possible because commercial growers sometimes bleach and fumigate before shipping.

In addition to nuts and seeds, sprouted legumes are another important food source. Mung bean, aduki bean, pea, lentil and chickpea sprouts are among my favorites. Think about the fact that you can grow sprouts any place, in any climate and any time of year! You do not need soil or sunshine, and there is no waste or chemical residue. No fertilizer is needed. Your sprouts mature in three to five days. You don't need acres of land, yet can produce high-quality sources of protein, carbohydrates, enzymes, vitamins and minerals. The nutritional value of sprouts is incredibly higher than their ungerminated counterparts, and they are a lot easier to digest. In addition, some beans like sprouted chickpeas and lentils supply all the essential amino acids, which makes them a complete protein. Chickpeas are rich in minerals; lentils contain B vitamins and mung beans are high in vitamin C. Combining different sprouts at one meal produces a strong team for quick energy with quality protein that is easily digested.

One of my most exciting discoveries, aside from the delicious capabilities of sprouted legumes, is the incredible taste of sprouted grains. The two grains I sprout with great ease are wheat and rye berries. Grains have a nutty sweet flavor, and are great additions to any salad. They are a good source of B vitamins, minerals and dietary fiber. Eating sprouted grains really satisfies anyone's desire for a wonderfully chewy food. Try the sprouted grain recipes. You'll be pleasantly surprised. This food provides quality carbohydrates and protein for maintaning energy and vitality.

The perfect complement to a meal of raw foods and living sprouts is seaweed. Also called sea greens or sea vegetables, they have been widely used and eaten in many everyday

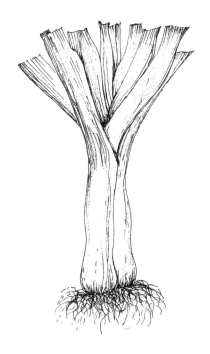

products. Among the most ancient forms of life, their potential as a daily food source has not been realized. Utilized in folk remedies to augment healing, they are most commonly prepared in Japan and China, and just coming into use in America.

Seaweeds are known to bond with radioactive substances, heavy metals, and stagnated poisons to help the body eliminate these toxins. The daily consumption of small amounts of sea greens increases the metabolic rate, purifies the blood, aids in body cleansing, dissolves fats and mucous, strengthens the endocrine and nervous systems and provides important vitamins (like B12) and minerals (like iron and calcium). The Japanese believe that everyday usage of sea greens beautifies their hair and overall complexion and is the secret to eternal youth. People of the British Isles and the South Pacific also regularly consume sea greens. Rich in protein, sea vegetables have an alkalizing effect on the blood because they contain ten to twenty times the minerals of land plants. They are indeed a buried treasure and a mandatory addition to anyone's diet.

I'd also like to talk about dehydrated foods. Drying is one of the oldest methods of food preparation. When seasonal fruits and vegetables are in abundance, drying is an inexpensive easy way to preserve them for future use. Drying preserves more of the nutrients in foods than cooking because of a lower heat exposure. There is no question about what's in

your food when you process it yourself at home. Dehydrating is a way of preserving without additives or chemicals. These foods take up a minimum of storage space and are great for traveling because they need no refrigeration. Lightweight dried foods have been used by man for hundreds of years to survive sea and land voyages. Food preservation became a large-scale operation during WWI, the Depression and WWII. The supermarkets today are full of dried foods packaged for the sake of convenience. Too bad most of them are poisoned with unpronounceable multi-syllabic additives and preservatives. By investing in an inexpensive dehydrator, anyone can eat real food wherever and whenever necessary. Most importantly, the flavor of dried foods is sustained or even improved. The natural sugar in fruit becomes concentrated when dried, making it a great sweet snack. Vegetables can be preserved and eaten as is, or used in soups and salads. With a dehydrator, make your own crackers, nut or seed patties, and cookies. Dried herbs from your own garden add flavor to any meal. Food never has to be wasted, for, if dried properly, it has a fairly long shelf life. Don't be afraid to experiment. For example, after soaking your nuts and seeds,

dehydrate them one day to get that toasted flavor. This method is a great alternative to high-heat roasting. Do not buy a dehydrator unless it has a temperature gauge. You will want to keep it around or below 105° to preserve the enzymes and other nutrients. There are many different ways to dry food, but for the sake of ease and success, it makes sense to buy a quality dehydrator.

Last but not least are the end-of-the-meal desserts that many of us look forward to. Desserts are a separate meal. When making sweets, it's sometimes hard to remain within the guidelines of proper food combining. Sweet snacks seem to be a habit for many of us, so if you must indulge, avoid refined sugar as well as highly refined white flour. They will cloud your complexion, decrease your vitality, and increase the possibility of depression, fatigue, emotional upset, and chemical imbalance. The use of whole and dried fruits, their juices, nuts, seeds, carob powder, fresh coconut and natural flavorings produce quite a wide selection of healthier creations in the realm of raw desserts. The recipes are fast and easy. With the addition of psyllium seed husks to congeal the ingredients without heat, gourmet delights are only a moment away. These husks are an excellent source of fiber and are quite often taken in a glass of water or juice to cleanse the intestinal tract. This auxiliary use is a bonus for all. Whoever thought you could eat dessert and cleanse your colon at the same time! So take heart and enjoy.

Now you're familiar with some of the key ingredients about to be combined in the following pages. Let's go on to some exciting new recipes.

Please note throughout the book:
• **The garlic in all recipes is peeled before using.**

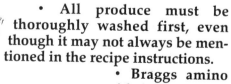

• **All produce must be thoroughly washed first, even though it may not always be mentioned in the recipe instructions.**
• **Braggs amino acids is sometimes abbreviated to Braggs.**
• **Please refer to the germination chart for information.**

CONTENTS
RAW SOUPS, DRESSINGS AND SAUCES

Raw Soups, Dressings and Sauces

Raw soups can easily be converted to salad dressings in many of the following recipes. Use your discretion and imagination. I have repeatedly found that once you establish a good-tasting combination, the exact amounts in most raw food recipes are not seriously important. You can vary the quantities of each ingredient and still end up with a tasty creation. The instructions for preparation often suggest substitutions for the sake of variety and appeal. For example, lemon juice and fresh ginger juice are interchanged . Remember that nuts are soaked and legumes are sprouted.

It is important to use the freshest produce for the best final result. Since you are working with raw foods, there is no way to mask the poor quality of old produce. Green leafy vegetables and sprouts must be perfectly fresh. The size of each bunch, head or pound of usable vegetable will vary and change the final yield. My recipes tend to produce larger portions due to the fact that I have consistently prepared meals for over fifty people at a time while kitchen testing and creating. I've scaled down the amounts for the average family, but you still might want to cut the recipe in half to get a better idea of final yield.

The dressings and sauces in this section are what really makes any combination of unadorned, raw vegetables or sprouts become tasty, attractive and unique. These recipes can also be used to complement cooked foods. I hope you will find them interesting and delicious.

RAW SOUPS

Curried Red Pepper Soup

4	red peppers, seeded and chopped
1/2	cup tahini
	juice of 1 small lemon
2	cloves garlic, minced
	pinch cayenne
1 1/2	tsp. curry
3	scallions, minced
	Braggs amino to taste

Blend all ingredients except scallions. Add enough water to make a smooth soup consistency. Add less water for a delicious salad dressing. Chill and garnish with scallions.

Sweet Gazpacho Soup

4	sweet red peppers
2	yellow squash
1	red onion
1	cucumber, minced
1/4	cup fresh parsley, minced
1/4	cup fresh cilantro, minced
1	large garlic clove, minced
	juice of 1 lemon
	Braggs amino to taste

Clean and shred first three ingredients. Marinate garlic, peppers, squash, and onion (covered with enough Braggs to coat) overnight in refrigerator. Add finely minced cucumber, herbs, lemon juice and enough water to create a thick soup consistency. Chill and serve.

Smooth Carrot Soup

3	cups fresh carrot juice
1	cup walnuts or pignoli nuts
1	yellow squash, chopped
1	garlic clove
1	yellow pepper, chopped (optional)
1	tbsp. fresh ginger juice
	Braggs amino to taste
2	scallions, minced

Blend all ingredients until creamy and add enough water to make soup consistency. Garnish with minced scallions and chill. Try substituting $3/4$ cup tahini for nuts.

Minted Cucumber Soup

4	cucumbers, peeled and chopped
2	shallots
$1/4$	cup tahini
$1/4$	cup fresh mint
	Braggs amino to taste
2	scallions, minced

Blend all ingredients and add enough water to make a thick soup. Garnish with scallions and chill. Remove cucumber seeds for easier digestion.

Creamy Corn Soup

4	cups corn, decobbed
$1/3$	cups tahini
$1/4$ -$1/2$	tsp. pumpkin pie spice
	Braggs amino to taste
4	scallions, minced

Blend corn and tahini with enough water to make a thick soup. Add spice to taste. Garnish with scallions and chill. Use any herb or spice that you prefer instead of pumpkin pie spice. This calls for very fresh seasonal sweet corn in order to create a good taste.

Cream of Asparagus Soup

4	cups asparagus, chopped
6	large mushrooms
6	scallions, minced
$1/2$	cup tahini
	Braggs amino to taste
$1/2$	cup fresh parsley, minced

Blend all ingredients together, saving $1/4$ cup parsley for the garnish. Add enough water to make a soup consistency. Chill.

Yellow Squash Soup

6	small yellow squash, chopped
8	scallions, chopped
2	stalks celery, chopped
2	tbsp. fresh or 2 tsp. dried tarragon
1	garlic clove, minced
	Braggs amino to taste
$1/3$	cup fresh basil, minced

Blend all ingredients together and add water to create soup consistency. Garnish with basil and chill.

Minestrone Soup

1	cucumber, peeled
1	cup mushrooms
1	red pepper
1	cup spinach
1	cup stringbeans
$1/2$	cup mung bean sprouts
4	scallions
1	carrot, shredded
$1/2$	cup tahini
2	cups water
	juice of 2 lemons
1	garlic clove
	Braggs amino to taste
$1/4$	cup fresh parsley, minced

Blend tahini, water, lemon juice and garlic. Finely chop remaining vegetables. Mix with shredded carrot. Combine all ingredients and add Braggs to taste. Garnish with parsley and chill.

Nutty Dulse Soup

3/4	cup dulse
1	cup pignoli nuts
3	cups water
1	tbsp. extra virgin olive oil
2	shallots, minced
1	tsp. fresh tarragon, minced
	dash rosemary
	dash cayenne
2	tbsp. fresh parsley, minced

Blend nuts and dulse with water until creamy. Combine all. Garnish with parsley. If necessary, add more water.

Dilled Zucchini Soup

4	cups zucchini
1	cup cucumber
1	cup celery
1	cup yellow pepper
1	bunch dill
1	bunch scallions
1	garlic clove
	Braggs amino to taste
1/2	cup fresh parsley, minced

Blend all ingredients and add enough water to create desired soup consistency. Garnish with chopped parsley and chill.

Beet Soup

4	medium beets, peeled and chopped
1/2	cup tahini
1/2	red onion, sliced
2	stalks celery, chopped
1/2	cup fresh dill, minced
1	date, pitted (optional)
	Braggs amino to taste

Blend all ingredients and add enough water to make a creamy soup. Chill. The quality of the beets will make the taste of this soup vary greatly.

Celery Soup

1	head celery
1/2	cup tahini
1	garlic clove
	juice of 1 lemon
4	scallions
	dash cayenne
	Braggs amino to taste
1/4	cup fresh parsley, minced

Blend all ingredients, adding enough water to make a creamy soup. Garnish with parsley.

Butternut Squash Soup

1	butternut squash, peeled, seeded and sliced
1	yellow pepper
4	stalks celery
1	red onion
1/2	cup tahini
1	tbsp. curry
1/2	tsp. nutmeg
	Braggs amino to taste
2	scallions, minced

Blend all ingredients well and add enough water to create proper consistency. Garnish with minced scallions and chill.

Cream of Mushroom Soup

1	lb. white mushrooms
3/4	cup tahini
	juice of 2 lemons
1	garlic clove
1	yellow (or red) pepper, chopped
	pinch cayenne
1	tsp. cayenne
	Braggs amino to taste
2	scallions, minced

Blend all ingredients until creamy and add enough water to make a thick soup. Garnish with minced scallions and chill. Substitute one tbsp. fresh ginger juice for lemon juice. Make sure mushrooms are very fresh.

Sprouted Pea Soup

3	cups sprouted peas
1 or 2	cloves garlic
1/4	cup dulse
4	shallots
	Braggs amino to taste
1/4	cup fresh parsley, minced

Blend all ingredients together adding enough water to obtain soup consistency. Garnish with parsley. Add some extra virgin olive oil for a richer taste. You can also add some shredded carrot for color.

Cream of Spinach Soup

2	lbs. spinach, washed well
1	large ripe avocado, peeled and seeded
	juice of 2 lemons
	Braggs amino to taste
1/2	cup fresh parsley, minced
2	cloves garlic

Blend all ingredients together and add enough water for a thick soup consistency. Chill. Fresh dill or cilantro is a good substitute for parsley. Herbs completely change the taste of this soup. My favorite is fresh dill.

Sea Vegetable Soup

1	sheet nori
1/4	cup dulse
1/4	cup ginger juice
1/2	cup tahini
4	cups water
1	cup mung bean sprouts, minced
1	cup spinach, finely chopped
2	cloves garlic
1/4	cup almonds, chopped
1/2	cup mushrooms, finely chopped
	Braggs to taste
3	scallions, minced

Blend together seaweeds, ginger juice, tahini, garlic and water. Add remaining ingredients and chill.

Vegetable Soup

1	bunch broccoli florets, finely chopped
2	shallots
2	cloves garlic
2	stalks celery, chopped
2	carrots, shredded
6	mushrooms, sliced
1	cup almonds
1/4	cup tahini
	dash nutmeg
	Braggs to taste
1/4	cup fresh parsley, minced

Blend almonds in four cups water. Strain out pulp. Blend liquid with shallots, garlic, celery and tahini. Add broccoli, mushrooms and carrots. Add seasonings, mix well and chill. Mushrooms can be optional, garnish with parsley.

Cream of Broccoli Soup

1	bunch broccoli florets
1	large or 2 small ripe avocados
1	cucumber
	juice of 2 lemons
1	large garlic clove
	Braggs to taste
1/4	cup each fresh parsley and cilantro, minced

Set aside some broccoli florets. Blend all remaining ingredients until creamy and add enough water to create a thick soup consistency. Chop the remaining broccoli florets and add to soup. Mix well. Chill and serve. Instead of herbs, add one tbsp. curry for a completely different taste.

Spinach and Sunflower Cream

1	lb. spinach, washed well
2	tbsp. tahini
1	garlic clove
1/4	cup fresh dill
1/2	cup sunflower seeds
1/2	cup fresh dill, minced
	Braggs to taste

Blend all ingredients except seeds to create a thick creamy soup. Blend seeds separately with Braggs to create a seed cream. Swirl the two mixtures together in a bowl and serve chilled with a minced dill garnish.

Zucchini Carrot Soup

3	medium zucchini, shredded
1	carrot, shredded
1	bunch scallions, minced
1/4	cup basil, minced
1	garlic clove, pressed
1/3	cup tahini
2	cups water
	Braggs to taste
1/2	tsp. paprika

Blend tahini and water. Mix all ingredients together and garnish with paprika. Chill.

Iceberg Lettuce Soup

1	head iceberg lettuce
2	carrots
1	avocado, peeled and seeded
1/4	cup lemon juice
4	scallions
1	garlic clove
	Braggs to taste
1/4	cup scallions, minced

Shred lettuce and carrots. Set aside. Liquify remaining ingredients, adding water to make a soup consistency. Mix in lettuce and carrots. Garnish with minced scallions.

Borscht

1	lb. beets, peeled and chopped
1	cup carrot juice
1	cucumber, peeled and diced
1	cup almonds
4	scallions, minced
1/4	cup fresh dill, minced
	dash cayenne
	Braggs to taste

Blend almonds in three cups water. Strain out pulp. Blend liquid with beets until creamy. Add carrot juice, cucumber, scallions, dill and seasonings. Chill and serve. Carrot juice should be sweet and fresh.

Cucumber Avocado Soup

4	medium cucumbers, peeled and chopped
1	garlic clove
1/2	large red onion, chopped
1	ripe avocado, peeled and seeded
	juice of 2 lemons
	Braggs to taste
1/2	cup fresh dill, minced

Blend all ingredients together and add enough water to create thick soup consistency. Mix in dill and chill. This would taste great served with a dollop of red pepper salsa. Remove cucumber seeds for easier digestion.

Potato Corn Soup

2	russet potatoes, peeled and chopped
1	ear corn, decobbed
2	shallots, chopped
1/2	cup fresh parsley
	cold water and Braggs

Liquify potatoes in blender with shallots, parsley and enough cold water to make a creamy soup. Add corn kernels and Braggs to taste; serve immediately.

Almond Mushroom Soup

1	cup almonds
1	garlic clove
1/2	lb. mushrooms, sliced
1	cucumber, peeled and sliced
1/2	cup fresh dill, minced
1	tsp. lemon rind
6	scallions, minced
	dash nutmeg
	dash cayenne
	Braggs to taste

Blend almonds with three cups water, cucumber and garlic. Strain out pulp, if desired. Combine liquid with sliced mushrooms and remaining ingredients. Chill before serving. Mushrooms must be very fresh.

Flaxseed Buttermilk Soup

3	cups "Buttermilk Dressing"
1/4	cup scallions, minced
1/4	cup red peppers, minced
1	cucumber, peeled, seeded and chopped
1/2	cup black olives, sliced

Combine all and serve. See dressing section for recipe to complete this soup.

Mixed Fruit Soup

4	very ripe pears, cored and peeled
2	cups fresh apple juice
1	cup fresh orange juice
1	ripe mango, peeled and pitted (optional)
1	tsp. vanilla extract
	mint leaves (optional)

Liquify the fruits and the juices, adding water if necessary to create a thick creamy soup. Garnish with mint leaves after it has been chilled at least one hour. For a party, garnish the soup with some chopped nuts or seeds.

Raspberry Peach Soup

6	ripe peaches, peeled and pitted
1	pint raspberries
	juice of 1 lemon
2	cups fresh apple juice
1/2	cup almonds, blanched

Blend peaches with one cup apple juice and lemon juice until puréed. Blend almonds with one cup apple juice and one cup water. Combine together. Purée raspberries. Chill all. Pour peach soup into bowl. Top with puréed raspberries. Swirl through soup and serve. (Blanch almonds by dropping in boiling water fo several seconds. Remove from water and skins will wash off easily.)

Winter Fruit Soup

2	cups mixed dried fruit, pitted
2	cups water
1	cup fresh orange juice
1	tsp. orange rind
2	cinnamon sticks
2	whole cloves
	juice of 1 lemon
1	tsp. Braggs

Soak fruit in water for eight hours and chop. Save the soaking water and heat it to a boil with the cinnamon sticks, cloves and orange rind. Turn off heat and leave for 1/2 hour. Remove cinnamon and cloves. Purée one cup fruit. Combine all ingredients. Serve hot or cold.

Luscious Strawberry Soup

3	pints ripe sweet strawberries, stemmed
1	lb. sweet seedless grapes
2	ripe pears, cored and chopped

Liquify all ingredients in blender. If this is not gratifying enough for you, add a few pitted medjool dates to add more sweetness. Chill and serve.

Apricot Soup

1	cup dried apricots
4	cups water
$1/3$	cup raisins
1	ripe pear, cored and chopped
	dash cinnamon

Soak apricots in four cups of water overnight. Soak raisins separately overnight. Keep both in refrigerator. Blend apricots in the four cups of soaking water. Drain raisins and add to apricots. Add chopped pear. Mix well and serve with dash of cinnamon.

Three Melon Soup

$1/2$	honeydew
$1/2$	crenshaw
$1/2$	muskmelon (cantaloupe)
	mint leaves

Peel and seed melons and blend together. Use any combination of melons to create different flavors. The melons must be ripe! Garnish with mint leaves, if desired.

Cantaloupe Soup

1	cantaloupe, peeled, seeded and sliced or cut into large chunks
	dash cinnamon

Blend with approximately six ice cubes until light and creamy. Pour into a bowl and garnish with a dash of cinnamon.

Tasteful Tomato Soup

8	ripe tomatoes
2	stalks celery, finely minced
$1/4$	cup fresh basil, minced
	pinch cayenne
	Braggs to taste
2	scallions, minced

Peel and quarter tomatoes. Try to remove the seeds as best you can. Blend them in two cups water or enough to make a thick creamy soup. Add remaining ingredients and top with minced scallions.

RAW DRESSINGS

Basic Tahini Dressing

8	oz. tahini
	juice of 2 lemons
2	cloves garlic
$1/4$	tsp. cayenne
	Braggs to taste

Blend all ingredients together and add enough water to make a thick dressing. By interchanging different herbs and spices, this basic recipe has many variations. Substituting red or white onions, scallions, shallots, leeks or elephant garlic creates different flavors. The amount of water you add depends on how thick or thin you like your dressing. Substitute two tbsp. ginger juice for lemon juice.

Sweet Tahini Dressing

8	oz. tahini
	juice of 2 oranges
2	pitted dates (optional)
$1/2$	tsp. cinnamon

Blend together tahini with orange juice to desired consistency. Use sweet spices for different flavors like nutmeg or five spice powder. Add water as needed.

Buttermilk Flaxseed Dressing

1/2	cup flaxseeds
2	cups water
1/4	cup lemon juice
1/2	cup pignoli nuts
1	garlic clove
	Braggs to taste
2	tbsp. fresh dill (optional)

Soak flaxseeds and pignoli nuts overnight with two cups water. Combine with remaining ingredients. Blend until smooth, adding more water for desired consistency. Leave out the garlic for a plain buttermilk to enjoy as a drink. Add herbs of your choice and interchange garlic with onions. This is a versatile recipe. Flaxseed is very soothing to the digestive tract and is a good source of protein as well as unsaturated fatty acids. It is also an aid for correcting constipation.

Lime Mint Dressing

1/2	cup tahini
	juice of 2 limes
4	sprigs mint, stems removed
2	stalks celery, sliced
1/8	tsp. cayenne
1/8	tsp. paprika
	Braggs to taste
3	scallions, minced

Blend ingredients together and add water as needed. Garnish with scallions and chill.

Spinach Squash Dressing

1	lb. spinach leaves
1	yellow squash, chopped
4	oz. tahini
	juice of 2 lemons
1	garlic clove
1/8	tsp. cayenne
	Braggs to taste

Blend all ingredients adding enough water to make a thick dressing. Chill.

Olive Dill Dressing

1/2	cup tahini
1/2	cup cured black olives, pitted
1/2	cup fresh dill
1	tbsp. basil
1/8	tsp. cayenne
	Braggs to taste
4	scallions, minced

Blend all ingredients together adding enough water to reach desired consistency. Garnish with scallions.

Italian Dressing

2	red peppers, seeded and chopped
3	stalks celery, sliced
1	cucumber, peeled and chopped
2	cloves garlic
	juice of 2 lemons
3	tbsp. tahini or extra virgin olive oil
1	tbsp. Italian seasoning
	Braggs to taste
1/2	cup parsley, minced

Blend all ingredients together and add water as needed to make a dressing. Garnish with parsley and chill. Remove cucumber seeds for easier digestion.

Cucumber Raita

2	cups pignoli nuts
	lemon juice to taste
	dash cumin
	dash coriander
1/2	onion, minced
	dash cayenne (optional)
2	cucumbers
	fresh mint (optional)

Peel and remove seeds from cucumbers. Shred them and set aside. Put pignoli nuts in a blender and add enough water to create a very thick creamy sauce almost the consistency of sour cream. Add lemon juice to taste, spices, onion and cucumber. Mix well. Add cayenne if desired. Add some fresh minced mint to this recipe for another variation.

Gingered Pumpkin Seed Dressing

2	cups pumpkin seeds
2	tbsp. fresh ginger juice
2	cloves garlic
1	tsp. oregano
1/4	tsp. cayenne
	Braggs to taste
4	scallions, minced

Blend all ingredients together with enough water to obtain a smooth creamy dressing. Garnish with minced scallions and chill. Substitute four tbsp. lemon juice for ginger juice.

Sprout Dressing

1	cup sunflower sprouts
1	cup buckwheat sprouts
1/2	cup tahini
1	cup green cabbage, shredded
2	tbsp. fresh ginger juice
1/2	cup fresh dill
2	cloves garlic
	Braggs to taste
3	scallions, minced

Blend all ingredients and add water as needed. Substitute two cups mung bean sprouts for sunflower and buckwheat. Leave out the Braggs and add 1/4 cup dulse. Garnish with minced scallions.

Pignoli Beet Dressing

1 1/2	cups pignoli nuts
1/2	cup beet juice
1	date, pitted (optional)
1/2	red onion
1	garlic clove
	Braggs to taste
1/4	cup fresh dill, minced

Blend all together, adding water as needed. Garnish with dill. Leave out the beet juice and add water. Add poppy or toasted sesame seeds for a different taste.

Walnut Thyme Dressing

2	cups walnuts
4	cloves garlic
2	tbsp. ginger juice
1	tbsp. powdered thyme
1/2	tsp. cayenne
1/4	cup dulse

Blend to creamy consistency with desired amount of water. Use lemon juice instead of ginger juice for a variation.

Cauliflower Dressing

1	head cauliflower, chopped
2	tbsp. tahini
1	yellow pepper, chopped
1	garlic clove
	juice of 2 lemons
	Braggs to taste
4	scallions, minced

Blend all ingredients adding water until you reach desired consistency. Garnish with minced scallions. Add more tahini for a creamier, richer dressing.

Sesame Seed Dressing

1	cup sesame seeds, hulled
1/2	cup tahini
2	cloves garlic
1	tsp. oregano
1/2	tsp. paprika
1/4	tsp cayenne
2	tbsp. fresh ginger juice
	Braggs to taste
3	scallions, minced

Blend all ingredients together and add enough water to create a dressing. Garnish with scallions. Substitute two tbsp. orange peel for oregano and paprika, or add lemon juice instead of ginger juice.

Sunflower Dressing

2	cups sunflower seeds
1	small beet
1	carrot
2	cloves garlic
2	inch piece of ginger, peeled
1	tsp. dried basil
1/4	cup dulse
1/4	cup fresh basil, minced

Blend all ingredients together with water to desired consistency. Garnish with fresh basil. For variation, substitute one tsp. orange peel for the basil, one tsp. poppy seed for the dulse, and add Braggs to taste.

Jicama Dressing

1	large or 2 small jicama
1	small onion, chopped
1	inch piece ginger, minced
1/2	cup tahini
	Braggs to taste

Peel and chop jicama. Blend all ingredients, adding water to desired consistency. Peel ginger before mincing.

Coconut Dressing

1	cup fresh coconut, grated
1/2	cup tahini
1	small onion
	juice of 1 lemon
	dash cayenne
	dash nutmeg
	dash coriander
1	tbsp. ginger juice
	Braggs to taste

Blend all ingredients, adding water to desired consistency. Add more ginger juice for stronger flavor.

Almond Dressing

2	cups almonds
1	tsp. coriander
1	tsp. cumin
	Braggs to taste
1/4	tsp. cayenne

Pour boiling water over almonds to loosen skins. Remove skins and place almonds in a blender with remaining ingredients and three cups water. Liquify and adjust seasonings to taste.

Almond Mayonnaise

Chill all ingredients first!

1	cup almonds
1	cup water
	juice of 2 large lemons (1/4 cup)
2	tsp. herbamare or 2 tbsp. Braggs
1/2	tsp. cayenne
1 - 1 1/2 cups canola oil or extra virgin olive oil	

Soak and blanch almonds. Combine all ingredients in blender except oil. Liquify on high speed. Very slowly drizzle in oil. It will get thicker and thicker. You can use one cup of oil or add as much as 1 1/2 cups, depending on how tight you want the mayonnaise. Keep adding oil until all is used. Use this in place of mayonnaise. This is a party food that is very high in fat. Almond mayo is not recommended for people on a restricted diet.

VARIATIONS:

Mix any of the following with 1/2 cup almond mayonnaise:

1	tbsp. capers
1	tbsp. pimento
1	tbsp. lemon rind
1	tbsp. whole grain mustard
2	tbsp. chopped chives
2	tbsp. chopped parsley
1	tbsp. pressed garlic

Cucumber Avocado Dressing

2	ripe avocados, peeled and pitted
1	garlic clove
2	cucumbers, peeled and chopped
	juice of 1 large lemon
1/2	cup fresh dill
	Braggs to taste
2	scallions, minced

Blend all ingredients and garnish with scallions. Add water if dressing is too thick and chill before serving.

Basic Avocado Dressing

2	ripe avocados, peeled and pitted
2	cloves garlic
	juice of 2 lemons
1/2	cup fresh parsley
	Braggs to taste
4	scallions, minced

Blend all ingredients together and add water as needed. Garnish with scallions and chill. Good substitutes for parsley are fresh cilantro, dill or oregano. Basil is sometimes bitter and doesn't seem to taste good with avocado dressing. Garlic and onions are easily interchanged to create different flavors. Using bermuda onions instead of garlic makes a sweeter dressing. Lime juice is another nice addition.

Carrot Avocado Dressing

2	ripe avocados, peeled and seeded
1	garlic clove
3	cups fresh carrot juice
	Braggs to taste
1	tsp. oregano
2	scallions, minced

Blend all ingredients. Chill and garnish with scallions. This dressing is very sweet because of the carrot juice and is one of my favorites.

Watercress Dressing

1	cup almond mayonnaise
1	bunch watercress
	juice of 1/2 lemon
1/2	tsp. dry mustard
1/4	tsp. dried tarragon
	Braggs to taste
2	scallions, minced

Blend all ingredients together to create dressing. Adjust seasonings and garnish with scallions. Chill before serving.

Avocado Tomato Dressing

2	ripe avocados, peeled and pitted
1	small red onion, peeled and chopped
2	ripe tomatoes, stems removed
	juice of 2 lemons
1	tsp. caraway seeds
2	stalks celery, chopped
	Braggs to taste

Blend all ingredients together, adding water to create desired consistency.

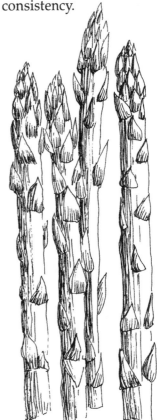

RAW SAUCES

Pignoli Sauce

2   cups pignoli nuts
1/2   tsp. lemon rind
1/4   tsp. nutmeg
1   tbsp. fresh ginger juice
1   garlic clove
        Braggs to taste

Blend all ingredients together and add e-nough water to make a sauce. Lemon juice can be used instead of ginger juice.

Sweet and Sour Sauce

2   beets, peeled
3   dates, pitted
        juice of 1 lemon
2   inch piece of fresh ginger, peeled
1   small jicama, peeled and chopped
        Braggs to taste

Blend all ingredients, adding water to make a thick sauce. If jicama is not available, add a small piece of daikon root. Peel and chop the daikon as you would the jicama. You can eli-minate the jicama and still have a tasty recipe.

Italian Sauce

2   cups carrot juice
1   cup red pepper juice
1   stalk celery
1   red onion
4   cloves garlic
1   cup pignoli nuts
1   tbsp. Italian seasoning
        Braggs to taste
6   mushrooms, sliced

Blend all ingredients except mushrooms into a thick sauce. Mix in the sliced mushrooms. Substitute one cup tahini for pignoli nuts.

Pesto Sauce

1   cup pignoli nuts
3   cloves garlic
1/2   cup basil leaves
1/2   cup parsley
1   cup spinach
        juice of 1 lemon
        Braggs to taste

Blend all ingredients and add enough water to make a sauce. Substitute walnuts for pignoli nuts. You can also substitute cilantro for basil for a different pesto. Remove stems from herbs and spinach.

Arugula Pesto

1/2   cup pignoli nuts
1/2   cup extra virgin olive oil
1 1/2   cups arugula
1/4   cup parsley
2   cloves garlic
        Braggs to taste

Blend all ingredients, adding water to desir-ed consistency.

Parsley Almond Pesto

1/2   cup almonds, blanched
2   cups fresh parsley
2   cloves garlic
2   scallions, minced
1/4   cup fresh basil
1/2   cup extra virgin olive oil
        Braggs to taste

Blend all ingredients together, adding e-nough water to make a sauce. Remove stems from parsley and basil. They sometimes leave a bitter aftertaste.

CONTENTS
FLAVORFUL SALADS

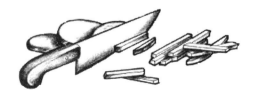

Flavorful Salads

Many people have asked me to say a few words about Braggs liquid amino acids since a large number of raw recipes contain this ingredient. It is made of soybeans and water only. There are no additives, preservatives, chemicals, coloring agents or added sodium. Braggs is not fermented or heated and is easily digestible. In this secret process soybeans are converted into a liquid vegetable protein. Amino acids, our body builders, are the foundation of this protein. Dr. Bragg firmly believed that it is necessary to replenish our bodies with protein rich amino acids in order to keep feeding the process and production of new cells. He introduced this formula to aid formation and interaction of all body functions necessary to sustain and rejuvenate every tissue, organ and muscle. Braggs amino contains all eight essential amino acids and is free of cholesterol and uric acid. Years ago, nutritionists believed that protein could not be stored in the body but it has since been proven otherwise. Although we do have stored protein in our cells that is converted into amino acids when and where needed, replacing amino acids daily as they are depleted helps to maintain a healthy body and ward off unnatural degeneration of cells. Dr. Bragg has described his product as "life-renewing". By adding Braggs to your daily diet, you are receiving not only a dose of nourishing liquid protein but also a natural source of sodium with quality flavor.

I prefer to use Braggs in many of my preparations and especially with raw food cuisine. It is salty yet delicate. Braggs does not mask, but only complements the wonderful characteristic tastes of "fresh" vegetables and sprouts. If Braggs is not available in your area, or you choose not to use it, any choice of seasalt or other favorite salty condiment is easely substituted. Some may prefer to use no salt at all. The decision is yours.

EDIBLE FLOWERS

Whenever I serve a salad that is full of the brilliant colors of fresh flowers, my guests are always pleasanty anxious to taste what is in the bowl. Adding edible flowers to your presentation of any meal creates a special gourmet touch. It is extremely appealing to the eye and the senses. The following is a partial list of edible flowers to complement your salads.

Chamomile
Chrysanthemum
Fuschia
Geranium
Gladiola
Lavender
Marigold
Nasturtium
Orange and Apple Blossoms
Pansy
Rose Petals
Rosehips
Squash Flowers
Strawberry Blossoms
Violet

FLAVORFUL SALADS

Beautiful Beet Salad

4	large beets
1	rutabaga
1	red onion, minced
1/4	tsp. caraway seeds
1/2	cup basic tahini dressing
	Braggs to taste

Peel and matchstick beets and rutabaga. Add remaining ingredients and serve.

Hot Dilled Beans

1	lb. string beans
1	large garlic clove, minced
1	tsp. dried jalapeño pepper flakes
1/2	cup fresh dill, minced
	Braggs to taste
2	tbsp. lemon juice

Clean and cut beans into 1/2 inch pieces. Add remaining ingredients and serve.

Stimulating Pepper Salad

2	red peppers, cut into chunks
2	yellow peppers, cut into chunks
1	medium red onion, chopped
1	stalk of celery, chopped
4	tbsp. Italian seasoning
	juice of 1 lemon
1	tsp. coriander
1/2	tsp. cayenne
1/4	cup tahini
2	cloves garlic
1	tbsp. orange peel
	Braggs to taste

Blend tahini, garlic, orange peel and spices with 1/2 cup water. Combine with remaining ingredients.

Hazelnut Salad

1/2	cup hazelnuts
1/2	head radicchio
1/4	head romaine lettuce
1	belgian endive
2	large mushrooms, sliced
	juice of 1 lemon
2	tbsp. extra virgin olive oil
	Braggs to taste
	dash cayenne

Coarsely chop hazelnuts. Set aside. Clean and chop all leafy vegetables. Combine all ingredients together and serve.

Almond Coconut Salad

1	head broccoli, broken into small florets
1	cup almonds, chopped
4	scallions, minced
1/2	cup fresh coconut, grated
1	cup water
1/8	tsp. cayenne
	juice of 1 lemon
	Braggs to taste

Combine broccoli, almonds and scallions. Liquify coconut, water and remaining ingredients. Combine all and adjust seasoning.

String Bean Surprise

1/2	lb. string beans, stemmed and chopped
1/2	head cauliflower, chopped
3	red peppers, seeded and sliced
3	cloves of garlic
	juice of 2 lemons
2	tbsp. tahini
1/8	tsp. cayenne (optional)
	Braggs to taste

Blend garlic, lemon juice, tahini and 1/2 cup water. Pour over vegetables and add Braggs amino. Mix well and serve.

Sweet Jicama Fascinations

1	large jicama
1	large carrot, shredded
	juice of 1 orange
	Braggs to taste
1/2	tsp. anise seed
1/8	tsp. cinnamon

Peel and dice jicama. Combine all ingredients and serve. Omit spices if you prefer a simpler taste.

Variation I:

1	large jicama
2	beets
1/2	red onion
	Braggs to taste

Peel and shred jicama and beets. Blend Braggs and onion. Mix all ingredients together and serve.

Variation II:

1	large jicama
1	red pepper, minced
1/4	cup fresh cilantro, minced
1	scallion, minced
1/2	tsp. cumin
	Braggs to taste

Peel and slice jicama. Combine all ingredients and serve.

Delectable Daikon

1	medium daikon, shredded
2	large carrots, shredded
6	radishes, shredded
4	stalks celery, minced
1/2	bunch scallions, minced
1/2	cup parsley, minced
2	tbsp. tahini
	Braggs to taste

Thin out tahini with 1/4 water. Combine all ingredients and mix well. Add more tahini for a richer salad.

Cucumber Caper

3	cucumbers, thinly sliced
2	cups mung bean sprouts
1	small head bok choy, minced
1/4	cup tahini
	juice of 1 lemon
1	red pepper
1/4	red onion
	Braggs to taste

Toss together first three ingredients. Blend tahini, lemon, pepper, onion and Braggs. Pour over vegetables and mix well before serving. Peel the cucumbers if they are not organically grown.

Garden Gastronomy

1	head green cabbage
10	radishes
1	red onion
4	stalks celery
2	red peppers
	dash cayenne
1	tbsp. savory
4	tbsp. tahini
	juice of 2 lemons
	Braggs to taste

Clean and dice all the vegetables. Blend tahini with lemon juice. Mix all ingredients together and serve.

Mushroom Salad

1	lb. mushrooms, sliced
1	carrot, shredded
1	cup mung bean sprouts
1	tsp. marjoram
1/8	tsp. cayenne
1	tbsp. lemon juice
	Braggs to taste

Mix all ingredients together and serve.

Belgian Endive Attraction

6	endives, sliced
1	cup snow peas, stems removed
10	red radishes, minced
1/2	cup fresh parsley, chopped
1	red onion, peeled and sliced
1/2	cup basic tahini dressing
	Braggs to taste

Combine all. Mix well and serve. You can marinate the onions first for a different twist.

Sunflower Seed Satisfaction

1/2	head iceberg lettuce, shredded
1/2	lb. spinach, cleaned and chopped
1/2	cup sunflower seeds
1	carrot, shredded
3/4	cup basic tahini dressing
	Braggs to taste
1/4	cup fresh dill, minced

Mix well and serve.

Brussels Sprout Salad

1/2	lb. Brussels sprouts
1	carrot
2	scallions, minced
	basic tahini dressing
2	tbsp. fresh dill, minced

Clean and shred Brussels sprouts and carrot. Combine with scallions, dill and enough dressing to coat the vegetables as desired.

Curious Cauliflower

1	head cauliflower
1/2	cup cured black olives, pitted
1	red pepper, chopped
1	garlic clove, pressed
1/2	cup scallions, minced
1	tsp. dried oregano
	juice of 1 lemon
	Braggs to taste

Clean, remove stem and chop cauliflower. Combine all ingredients and serve over sprouts or lettuce. Fresh oregano is wonderful in this recipe.

Broccoli Mushroom Marvel

1/2	bunch broccoli, stemmed and chopped
1	cup mushrooms, sliced
2	stalks celery, minced
1	cup basic avocado dressing
2	scallions, minced
1	tsp. curry
	Braggs to taste

Mix all together and serve. For variation, substitute one cup basic tahini dressing for avocado dressing and one tsp. Italian seasoning for curry. Add more curry for an even richer taste.

Zippy Zucchini and Carrots

2	zucchini
3	large carrots
1/2	cup fresh parsley, minced
1/2	tsp. nutmeg
1/8	tsp. cayenne
2	tbsp. tahini
	Braggs to taste

Julienne zucchini and carrots and mix with parsley. Combine remaining ingredients in a blender with 1/2 cup water. Pour over vegetables, mix well and serve.

Wilted Bok Choy

1	small head bok choy
1	red pepper, sliced
1/2	cup marinated onions
1/4	cup cured black olives, pitted
1/2	cup snow peas

Remove stems from snowpeas. Set aside. Wash and slice bok choy into 1/2 inch pieces. Pour boiling water over leaves. Drain and combine with remaining ingredients. Use your favorite dressing or enjoy as is.

Watercress Salad

2	bunches watercress
1/2	cup pignoli nuts
1/2	red onion, minced
2	stalks celery, finely chopped
6	red radishes, sliced

Clean and chop the watercress. Mix all together and coat with your favorite nut or seed dressing.

Jerusalem Artichoke Salad

1	lb. artichokes (sunchokes)
2	carrots
4	stalks celery, minced
1	tsp. fresh ginger, grated

Peel and grate artichokes and carrots. Add celery and ginger. Top with favorite dressing.

A Chinese Design

1/2	napa cabbage, shredded
1	cup mung bean sprouts
2	cups snow peas, stemmed
1	carrot, shredded
4	scallions, minced
1	cup almonds chopped
	Braggs to taste

Slice snow peas in half lengthwise. Combine all ingredients and mix well before serving. Add tahini dressing for variation.

Snappy Snow Peas

1/2	lb. snow peas
2	red peppers
2	carrots, julienned
1	cup mushrooms
2	tbsp. toasted sesame seeds
1	sheet nori, slivered
4	scallions, minced
	Braggs to taste

Remove stems from snowpeas. Clean red peppers removing the stem and seeds. Thinly slice the peppers and mushrooms. Mix all ingredients and toss well before serving.

Appetizing Asparagus

1	lb. asparagus
1	cup snow peas, sliced in half
1	large carrot, julienned
4	scallions, minced
1/2	cup basil, chopped
1	tbsp. dried lemon peel
	Braggs to taste
	juice of 1 lemon

Cut asparagus in small pieces. Combine all ingredients and serve.

Heavenly Spinach

1	lb. spinach
1	garlic clove
	juice of 1 lemon
1/2	tsp. cumin
4	scallions, minced
	Braggs to taste
2	tbsp. tahini
1	small carrot (optional)

Purée all ingredients in food processor with S blade. Add a peeled, shredded carrot for extra flavor, color and texture.

Spiced Cabbage Concoction

1	small head red cabbage, shredded
1	carrot, shredded
2	stalks celery, finely minced
4	scallions, minced
2	parsnips, shredded
1	cup mung bean sprouts
1/2	tsp. cinnamon
1/4	tsp. each nutmeg and cloves

Combine all ingredients and coat with choice of dressing or Braggs to taste. Peel the carrot and parsnip if you prefer.

Broccoli and Olives

1	bunch broccoli, chopped into florets
1	cup cured black olives, pitted
1	cup basic tahini dressing
4	scallions, finely minced
1	red pepper, seeded and stemmed
1	garlic clove
	Braggs to taste

Liquify red pepper and garlic. Combine all ingredients. For a variation, substitute one cup fresh corn kernels for the pitted olives.

Summer Squash Salad

2	yellow squash
2	carrots
2	stalks celery, finely chopped
4	scallions, minced
1/4	cup toasted sesame seeds
	Braggs to taste
	juice of 1 orange or lemon

Julienne the squash and carrots. Mix together with the remaining ingredients and serve. The orange gives it a unique flavor.

Radicchio and Fennel

1	head radicchio
1/2	head iceberg lettuce
1	bulb of fennel
1	cup basic tahini dressing
	Braggs to taste

Radicchio looks like a head of lettuce with reddish purple leaves. Cut it in half and slice half-moon style. Do the same with the iceberg lettuce. Clean outer bulb of fennel and chop. Mix all together and coat with dressing. This salad has a very unique flavor.

Stuffed Cucumbers

3	cucumbers
2	cups celery, finely minced
1/2	cup cured black olives, pitted
1	zucchini, chopped
2	red peppers, chopped
4	scallions, chopped
2	tbsp. fresh basil
1/2	cup tahini dressing
	Braggs to taste
2	tbsp. parsley, minced

Peel cucumbers and cut in half lengthwise; remove seeds with spoon. Place remaining ingredients, except parsley, in food processor with S blade. Process until combined. Stuff cucumbers. Garnish with parsley.

Mushrooms Florentine

1	lb. mushrooms, stems removed
1	lb. spinach, washed well
1	tbsp. dried dill
1/4	tsp. nutmeg
	dash cayenne
2	tbsp. lemon juice
1/2	cup basic tahini dressing
	Braggs to taste

Clean mushroom caps and set aside. Break down a few spinach leaves at a time in a food processor using the S blade. When all of the spinach is finely chopped, add remaining ingredients. Stuff the mushrooms and serve.

Combination Salad

2	cups mung bean sprouts
1/2	cup cured black olives, pitted
1/2	cup spinach, chopped
4	mushrooms, sliced
1	cucumber, cubed
1	carrot, julienned
4	scallions, minced
1/2	tsp. dried garlic flakes
1/2	tsp. dried lemon peel

Mix all ingredients and serve with your favorite dressing. Peel the cucumber if desired. Use fresh garlic and lemon peel instead of dried. I use the dried form to create a different variety of flavor and intensity.

String Bean Filbertine

1	lb. string beans
1	cup basic tahini dressing
3/4	cup filberts, finely chopped
1/2	tsp. dried marjoram
2	shallots or scallions, minced
	Braggs to taste

Stem and slice string beans lengthwise or french style. Combine all ingredients and serve. Substitute almonds or sunflower seeds for filberts. When using sunflower seeds, substitute one tsp. poultry seasoning for marjoram. This is a tasty variation.

Stuffed Belgian Endive

3 or 4	large Belgian endives
4	carrots, finely shredded
	several leaves of red leaf lettuce
1	cup olive dill dressing

Separate the leaves of the endive by cutting off the stem. Rinse leaves and drain. Arrange lettuce leaves on a platter. Arrange endive leaves like flower petals. Combine carrots with dressing. Stuff leaves with carrot mixture. Use any choice of dressing or even almond mayonnaise to vary this recipe.

Escarole Ecstacy

1	head escarole, finely chopped
4	scallions, minced
1/2	cup parsley, minced
1	tbsp. fresh or 1 tsp. dried tarragon
2	bulbs fennel, chopped
1/2	cup basic tahini dressing
	Braggs to taste

Clean and discard tough outer leaves of the escarole before chopping. Mix all ingredients well and serve. You can add one tsp. fennel seeds instead of fresh fennel.

Carrot Aspic

2	cups fresh carrot juice
3	tbsp. agar flakes
1/2	cup water
2	large carrots, peeled and shredded
2	stalks celery, minced
1/2	tsp. pumpkin pie spice
	parsley garnish

Dissolve agar in 1/2 cup water by gently heating over low heat for several minutes. Combine all ingredients, pour into one quart mold and chill for two hours or until set before serving. Garnish with parsley.

Carrotuna

8	medium carrots
1	yellow pepper, minced
2	shallots or scallions, minced
2	stalks celery, minced
1/2	tsp. oregano
1/4	cup tahini
1	tbsp. fresh lemon juice
	Braggs to taste

Place carrots in food processor with S blade. Process until puréed. Add tahini, lemon juice and Braggs until well combined. Mix in remaining ingredients and serve. (You can also use leftover carrot pulp from juicing your carrots.)

Carrots Rouge

2	large carrots, shredded
2	beets, peeled and grated
1/4	cup basic tahini dressing
	Braggs to taste
2	tbsp. fresh parsley, minced

Peel carrots if skin is bruised. Mix all ingredients well and serve.

Casablanca Carrots

4	carrots, shredded
2	scallions, minced
	juice of 1 lemon
1	tsp. dried orange peel
1/4	tsp. cumin
	dash cayenne
1	tbsp. extra virgin olive oil
	Braggs to taste

Combine all ingredients. Mix well and serve.

Carrot Sprout Salad

4	large carrots, shredded
1	cup sprouts of your choice, chopped
1/4	cup basic tahini dressing
	Braggs to taste
1	tbsp. dried orange peel

Mix all ingredients well and serve. Lentil, mung or aduki bean sprouts are good choices for this recipe.

Sweet Rutabaga Salad

1	small rutabaga
2	carrots
1	parsnip
	Braggs to taste

Peel and shred rutabaga, carrots and parsnip. Mix all together and serve.

Dandelion Salad

1   lb. young dandelions
1   garlic clove, pressed
        juice of 1 lemon
2   tbsp. extra virgin olive oil
        Braggs to taste

Try to use young tender dandelion leaves. Dandelion is a great liver cleanser. Wash well and remove all stems. Cut into small pieces and add remaining ingredients.

Shoots and Kernels

1   cup mung bean sprouts, chopped
2   cups alfalfa sprouts, chopped
1   cup celery, minced
2   scallions, minced
1/2   cup almonds, chopped
1/2   cup sunflower seeds

Mix all ingredients together and serve with favorite dressing.

Mung Bean Buds

4   cups mung bean sprouts
1/2   cup basic tahini dressing
2   scallions, minced
1   stalk celery, minced
1   carrot, shredded
        Braggs to taste

Pour very hot water over sprouts and follow with cold water. Drain well. Mix together all ingredients and serve.

Crunchy Walnut Cabbage

1/2   head white cabbage, shredded
1/2   head red cabbage, shredded
1   cup walnuts, chopped
1   red onion, minced
1   cup parsley, chopped
        Braggs to taste

Combine all ingredients. Mix well. Serve with or without dressing.

Hot Sprout Salad

2   cups mung bean sprouts
1   small jicama
2   scallions, minced
1   jalapeño pepper, minced
2   tbsp. fresh cilantro, minced
1   tbsp. extra virgin olive oil
        juice of 1 lemon
        Braggs to taste

Peel and shred jicama. Combine all ingredients. Mix well and serve. Be sure to remove all seeds from jalapeño before mincing. This is delicious stuffed in an avocado.

Tomato Aspic

1 1/2   cups fresh ripe tomato juice
2   tbsp. agar flakes
1/2   cup boiling water
1   tsp. lime juice
1/4   cup fresh basil, finely minced
        Braggs to taste
1/8   tsp. cayenne
        minced scallions garnish

Dissolve agar in 1/2 cup water over very low heat. Mix in remaining ingredients and chill in a two cup mold. Remove from mold and garnish with minced scallions.

Fennel Slaw

2   heads fennel, finely sliced
1   head red cabbage, shredded
4   stalks celery, chopped
6   scallions, minced
4   tbsp. poppy seeds
        Braggs to taste

Combine all ingredients. Mix well. Serve with or without dressing. Be sure to remove any inedible parts of the fennel bulb. Sometimes the outer part is very tough and should be discarded.

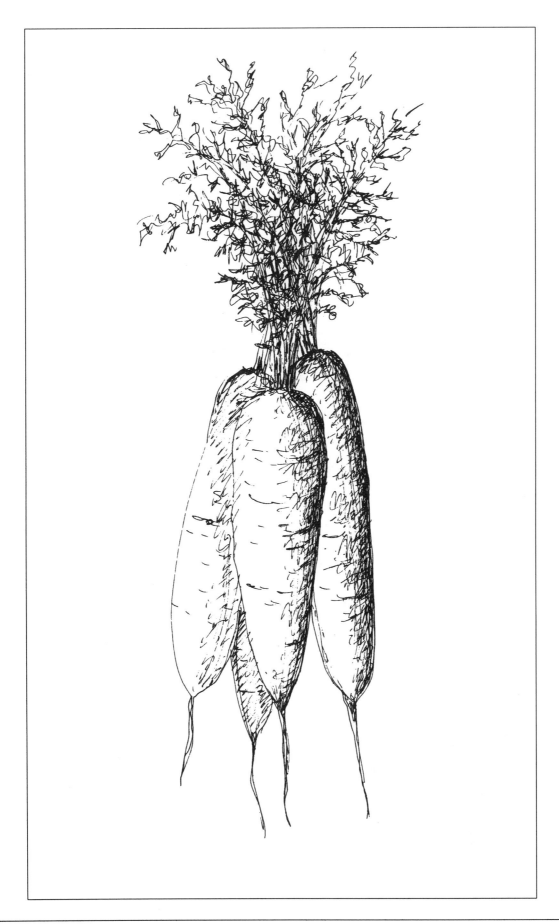

CONTENTS
MARINATED DELIGHTS

Marinated Delights

IMPORTANCE OF ENZYMES

The importance of enzymes has long been overlooked and ignored, but now their involvement in daily bodily functions is becoming a major issue in circles of clinical nutritionists. For many, the question of vitamins and minerals is no longer the main issue. The enzymatic content present in our bodies is directly related to the quality of our health and longevity. Increasing age, smoking, eating only cooked foods, stress, environmental pollutants, drugs and physical abuse continually deplete our internal enzyme supply.

There are three known enzyme groups: digestive, metabolic, and food source. Metabolic enzymes are present in every part of the body right down to every cell and tissue. They act as catalysts to help boost the immune system, repair damage, prevent disease and retard the aging process, just to name a few functions. Our bodies also produce digestive enzymes to break down the foods we eat. We can greatly assist this process by eating living foods that contain rich sources of food enzymes. Uncooked, marinated and dehydrated foods have the highest enzymatic potential, especially sprouted grasses, grains and legumes, soaked nuts and seeds, wild weeds and herbs, raw sauerkraut and bee pollen. Since meat and dairy are rarely eaten in their raw,high-enzyme state, their consumption is not recommended. Most fruits and vegetables do not contain high concentrations of enzymes as do the sprouts. Some fruits rich in food enzymes are pineapple, figs, dates, grapes, mango, papaya, avocado and banana. Spas and clinics around the world are prescribing diets high in enzymes to establish optimum health.

An interesting study done in the 1930's revealed that eating cooked food immediately increased the white blood cell count travelling in the bloodstream. Consuming the same food in its raw state did not cause any change in the blood chemistry. This phenomenon is called leucocytosis. Enzyme-rich leucocytes or white blood cells are part of the body's defense system. Their job is to digest foreign matter and destroy disease-causing organisms entering the body. These leucocytes are pulled away from their really important job of protection to help digest cooked foods that they treat as foreign matter. Eating only cooked foods for long periods of time leads to a chronic condition of leucocytosis and an immune system that cannot work at its peak. Switching to a raw and living plant-food diet eliminates this condition. If this is not a choice you wish to make, you are able to minimize leucocytosis by eating a diet that is at least 50% raw. Tests have shown that this 50/50 ratio of raw and cooked foods eliminates leucocytosis. You take the burden off the pancreas, white blood cells and all the other organs that are called upon for reserve enzymes.

When consuming cooked foods, it is helpful to take enzyme supplements. Some recent studies have been done showing the ineffectiveness of various supplemental enzymes. The University of California at Berkeley currently reported ineffectiveness but did not make it clear in their monthly newsletter what enzyme sources were studied. Dr. Howell, who wrote Enzyme Nutrition, did studies with papain and animal-derived enzymes. He clearly found them ineffective. After many studies, he concluded the aspergillus plant, a fungus or mushroom, to be a concentrated source of effective supplemental digestive enzymes.

The Orientals have used fungi for thousands of years to produce enzymes to aid the process of predigestion and for making cultured soybean products like tempeh and miso. Aspergillus Oryzae is a commonly used healthful variety that is cost effective and not highly expensive to market. Dr.Howell started researching enzymes in the 1930s. He was able to develop a compound from this plant to aid the process of predigestion in the mouth and stomach where he felt the body needed the most assistance. Therefore, these enzyme supplements should be taken before or during the meal. (There is an enzyme company listed in the appendix.)

It is evident to me that more research regarding enzymes is inevitable and the benefits of enzyme-rich foods will become clearer. Increase your longevity and contribute to your daily health. Eat it raw, sprouted, dehydrated or marinated. In this chapter try marinating as an alternative to cooking. You will discover how easy it is. The use of salt and time in the process of marination actually cooks the vegetables without heat, preserving the enzymes and nutrients. If you ever use too much Braggs or salt in the marinating process, you can rinse it off with cold water to eliminate the excess.

MARINATED DELIGHTS

Escarole and Zucchini

1	head escarole
2	small zucchini, julienned
4	red radishes, shredded
1/2	red onion, minced
2	cloves garlic, minced
1	tsp. Italian seasoning
1/2	cup basic tahini dressing
	Braggs to taste

Discard outer escarole leaves. Clean and slice escarole into thin strips. Add radishes and zucchini. Combine all ingredients and mix well. Let marinate one hour before serving.

Marinated Mustard Greens

1	bunch mustard greens
4	tbsp. toasted sesame seeds
2	tbsp. fresh ginger juice
	Braggs to taste

Wash and chop mustard greens. Remove the stems of the greens if they are tough. Combine all ingredients and let sit one hour before serving.

Beet Greens

1	bunch beet tops
2	scallions, minced
1/4	cup basic tahini dressing
	Braggs to taste

Slice beet tops and discard all tough stems. Marinate in Braggs one hour. Add scallions and dressing. Mix well and serve.

Pickled Mushrooms

1	lb. mushrooms, sliced
1	garlic clove, minced
2	tbsp. extra virgin olive oil
	juice of 1 lemon
1	tsp. pizza seasoning or oregano
1/4	cup parsley, minced
	Braggs to taste

Mix all ingredients together and let sit one hour before serving. Mushrooms tend to soak up a lot of Braggs, so be advised.

Herbed String Beans

1	lb. string beans
1	tbsp. dried onion flakes
1	garlic clove, minced
2	stalks celery, minced
1	tsp. dried rosemary
1/4	cup fresh basil, minced
1/2	cup basic tahini dressing
	Braggs to taste

Remove stems from beans and slice. Combine all ingredients and let sit one hour before serving.

Marinated Daikon

1	lb. daikon, peeled
3	tbsp. fresh parsley, minced
	Braggs to taste
1	scallion, minced

Peel the daikon if the skin is damaged. Shred the root and add remaining ingredients. Braggs sweetens the taste of the daikon which tends to be pungent. Also try adding a shredded yellow squash or a large peeled, chopped cucumber. Let sit 20 minutes before serving. Another nice combination is daikon, fresh dill, dried orange peel and Braggs to taste.

Marinated Collard Greens

2	lbs. young collard greens
6	scallions, minced
	juice of 1 lemon
1	tsp. oregano
1/2	cup basic tahini dressing (optional)
	Braggs to taste

Wash and cut out all collard stems and chop. Add remaining ingredients, mix well and marinate for one hour before serving. Add tahini dressing after marination.

Marinated Turnips

4	white turnips
	juice of 1 lemon
	Braggs to taste
1	scallion, minced
1/4	cup fresh dill

Clean turnips and cut off ends. Slice paper thin or shred. Coat with lemon juice, Braggs and minced dill. Marinate one hour before serving. Mix in scallion just before serving.

Sesame Red Cabbage

1/2	head red cabbage
1	zucchini
1	small red onion
1/2	bunch fresh dill, minced
1/4	cup toasted sesame seeds
	juice of 1 lemon
	Braggs to taste

Shred the first three ingredients. Mix all ingredients together and marinate two hours . Chill.

Minted Cucumbers

4	cucumbers, sliced thinly
3	shallots, minced
	juice of 1 lemon
1	tsp. fresh mint, chopped
	Braggs to taste

Combine all ingredients and coat with Braggs. Let sit one hour before serving.

Pickled Sweet Peppers

4	red peppers
2	yellow peppers
2	stalks celery
	juice of 1 lemon
2	tbsp. dry mustard
1	tsp. tumeric
	Braggs to taste

Remove stems and seeds and slice peppers thinly. Blend remaining ingredients and coat peppers. Let sit one hour before serving.

Cinnamon Beets

4	beets
1	large cucumber
1	parsnip
1	tsp. cinnamon
2	tbsp. tahini
3	tbsp. fresh orange juice
	Braggs to taste

Peel and shred beets, cucumber and parsnip. Blend remaining ingredients and coat the vegetables. Let sit 1/2 hour before serving. For a different taste substitute one tsp. chives for the cinnamon and add one tsp. dry mustard.

Fresh Peas and Carrots

2	cups shucked peas
1	carrot, finely shredded
1/4	cup tahini
1/2	cup water
1	tbsp. fresh mint
	Braggs to taste

Blend last four ingredients to make a sauce. Mix with peas and carrots. Let sit 1/2 hour.

Spinach Pie

2	cups walnuts
1	inch piece of ginger, peeled
4	cups spinach, minced
1/4	cup tahini
	juice of 1 lemon
1	cup mushrooms, sliced
1/4	tsp. nutmeg
	Braggs to taste
2	tbsp. psyllium seed powder

Process walnuts and ginger with S blade to a finely chopped consistency. Press into a 10" pie plate. Quickly process remaining ingredients in food processor. Press into crust. Top with sliced mushrooms in a nice design. Let sit 1/2 hour before serving.

Sesame Rutabagas

2	small rutabagas
1/2	cup tahini
2	tbsp. minced bermuda onion
	Braggs to taste
1	tbsp. toasted sesame seeds
1/4	cup water

Peel and shred rutabaga. Combine remaining ingredients in food processor. Coat rutabaga with dressing and let sit one hour or more before serving.

Marinated Eggplant

1	young eggplant, peeled and diced
	juice of 2 lemons
1	red onion, chopped
1	garlic clove, minced
1	red pepper, diced
4	large mushrooms, sliced
1/4	cup fresh basil, chopped
2	tbsp. fresh parsley, chopped
	Braggs to taste

Combine all, coat with Braggs and let marinate about two hours before serving. Eggplant requires a lot of Braggs. Be careful when choosing eggplants for raw preparation. Ones with a lot of seeds inside tend to be bitter. Remove excess seeds when possible. For variation, marinate eggplant separately, squeeze out and discard juice. Add to recipe.

Raw Potato Salad

14	medium sized potatoes
1	red onion
2	tbsp. extra virgin olive oil
	juice of 1 lime
	Braggs to taste
1	bunch fresh cilantro, minced

Peel and shred potatoes. Peel and dice onion. Combine all ingredients. This dish is best eaten the same day otherwise the potatoes will turn color overnight. Cut the recipe in half to experiment. Let marinate 1/2 hour before serving. This has a most unusual taste.

Jerusalem Artichoke Amazement

6	artichokes, peeled and sliced
1	large cucumber
1/2	red onion
1	small jicama
1	tbsp. tahini blended with 1/4 cup water
	Braggs to taste

Peel and chop the cucumber, red onion and jicama. Mix all ingredients and let sit one hour before serving

Eggplant Ganoush

1	eggplant
3/4	cup tahini
2	cloves garlic
	juice of 2 lemons
	Braggs to taste
1/2	cup fresh parsley, chopped

Peel and chop eggplant. Coat it with Braggs and let sit one hour. Drain and wash eggplant. Combine eggplant, tahini, garlic and lemon juice into blender, adding more Braggs if necessary. Blend to creamy consistency. Mix in chopped parsley and serve. This dish depends on the quality of eggplant. Add cumin and paprika for extra flavor.

Fennel Delight

2	bulbs fennel
2	stalks celery
1	large carrot
4	scallions, minced
	juice of 1 lemon
1	tsp. fennel seeds
1	tbsp. fresh mint (optional)
	Braggs to taste

Clean and dice first three vegetables and combine with remaining ingredients. Let sit one hour before serving.

Pickled Cucumber Slices

3	cucumbers
1	red onion
2	tbsp. lemon juice
2	tbsp. fresh parsley, minced
1/4	tsp. tumeric
	dash cayenne
1	garlic clove, minced
	Braggs to taste

Peel cucumbers and onion. Slice them as thinly as possible. Add remaining ingredients and let sit 1/2 hour before serving.

Marinated Onions

3	onions of your choice
	Braggs to taste
	herb, seed or spice of your choice

This is an open-ended recipe where you may use any type of onion. I use red, Bermuda, white or green onions, as well as leeks. You need to slice them as thinly as possible so the Braggs can marinate them easily. Once marinated (for about one hour), add any number of flavorings. My favorites are fresh parsley, basil, dill or mint. I also use poppy, caraway, sesame or fennel seeds. Try adding a little curry or cinnamon. You can also add a little tahini for another dimension. For example, tahini and mint make an interesting combination.

Hot Celery

1	head celery
1	red pepper
4	jalapeño peppers, seeded
1	red onion
1	yellow squash
1	garlic clove
1/2	cup parsley, chopped
	Braggs to taste

Mince all vegetables and coat with Braggs. Let sit one hour before serving. Garnish with parsley.

Marinated Garlic

2	whole bulbs garlic
1	cup Braggs amino

This is a great way to have peeled garlic on hand whenever you need it. Peel all the garlic, put into a jar and add Braggs to cover all the garlic. Let marinate in the refrigerator. The garlic takes on a sweeter flavor for raw or cooked dishes. Use the garlic-flavored Braggs to season your foods and then add more Braggs to the jar.

Jicama Sprout Salad

2	cups jicama, shredded
2	cups mung bean sprouts
2	scallions, minced
2	tbsp. fresh cilantro, minced
$1/2$	tsp. dried jalapeño peppers
2	tbsp. extra virgin olive oil
	juice of 1 lemon
	Braggs to taste

Peel the jicama before shredding. Combine all ingredients and let sit for at least one hour before serving.   It is delicious!

Marinated Red Chard

1	bunch red chard
2	cups snow peas
	juice of 1 lemon
1	tsp. oregano
4	shallots, minced
	Braggs to taste

Remove snowpea stems. Cut the stems out of the chard and chop finely. Mix all ingredients and let sit one hour before serving. Substitute one head of red cabbage for Swiss chard.

Pressed Lettuce

1	head iceberg lettuce, shredded
2	small carrots
5	red radishes
1	stalk celery
2	scallions (green part only), minced
$1/2$	cup fresh dill, minced
	juice of 1 lemon
	Braggs to taste

Wash and slice hard vegetables into very thin pieces. Place layers of vegetables and lettuce into a large pickle press or large bowl, sprinkling a layer of Braggs over each level. Add dill, scallions and lemon to the top and apply pressure. If you use a bowl in place of a press, put a plate on top of the vegetables with a weight to hold it down. Press for two hours. This is a great warm weather dish. Chill the salad before serving.

Mexican Salad

1	head red cabbage
2	tbsp. tahini
1	onion, shredded
2	tsp. chili powder
1	tsp. cumin
1	large garlic clove, minced
	Braggs to taste
	juice of 1 large lime

Shred the cabbage. Combine all ingredients and let sit one hour before serving. I use my hands to work the tahini and spices around the shredded cabbage.

Marinated Chicory

2	heads chicory
2	tbsp. fresh ginger juice
2	cloves garlic
2	tbsp. fresh or 1 tbsp. dried tarragon
1	tbsp. curry
$1/2$	cup basic tahini dressing
	Braggs to taste

Clean chicory and chop into small pieces. Blend remaining ingredients together and pour over chicory. Let sit one hour before serving.

Marinated Celeriac

1	large celeriac (celery root)
$1/2$	head white cabbage
1	large carrot
	juice of 2 lemons
$1/2$	cup almond mayonnaise
1	tsp. dry mustard
1	tsp. dried tarragon
3	tbsp. fresh parsley, minced
	Braggs to taste

Clean and peel celeriac, cutting away all inedible parts. Shred the celeriac, cabbage and carrot. Put this mixture into a bowl with lemon juice and Braggs to coat. Let marinate for one hour. Combine remaining ingredients and add to the mixture. Mix well and serve. Use the mayonnaise of your choice.

Carrot Salad

4 large carrots, shredded
3 scallions, minced
   juice of 1 lemon
1 tsp. orange rind
1 tbsp. extra virgin olive oil
3 tbsp. fresh parsley, minced
1/4 tsp. cayenne
1/2 tsp. cumin
   Braggs to taste

Combine all ingredients, toss well and let marinate for at least one hour before serving.

Caraway Cabbage Creation

2 cups green cabbage, shredded
1 cup red cabbage, shreddeed
1 cup green beans, sliced
1 cup carrot, grated
4 scallions, minced
1 cup almonds, chopped
1 tsp. caraway seeds
1 cup basic tahini dressing
   Braggs to taste

Combine all ingredients and let sit one hour before serving.

Cauliflower L'Orange

1 head cauliflower, finely chopped
4 small carrots, shredded
2 cloves garlic
1/2 cup fresh dill
1/4 cup orange juice
1/2 avocado, peeled
   Braggs to taste

Blend garlic, dill, juice, avocado and Braggs to make dressing. Mix cauliflower, carrots and dressing together. Let sit one hour before serving. Instead of chopping the cauliflower you can cut it in half. Slice each half into thin slices and then coat with dressing.

Hot Zucchini Salad

3 zucchini
1/4 cup dried onion flakes
1/4 cup poppy seeds
1 tbsp. hot chili pepper flakes
   Braggs to taste

Clean and slice zucchini into very thin strips. Add remaining ingredients and mix well. Let sit about 30 minutes before serving.

Bonvivant Bok Choy

1 small bunch bok choy
1 small daikon, julienned
1/2 cup fresh basil, minced
1 yellow pepper, minced
   juice of 1 lemon
   Braggs to taste

Peel the daikon if necessary. Clean and slice the bok choy into thin pieces. Mix all ingredients well and marinate 1/2 hour.

Cauliflower Pecan

1 head cauliflower
1/2 cup pecans
1 carrot, peeled and shredded
1/4 cup fresh parsley, minced
   Braggs to taste

Clean and break cauliflower into small florets and marinate in Braggs 1/2 hour. Use just enough to coat cauliflower. Chop pecans. Combine all ingredients, mix well and serve.

Fresh Shitake Mushrooms

1 lb. shitake mushrooms, stemmed
1 large carrot, shredded
2 tbsp. fresh ginger, peeled and grated
1 scallion, minced
   Braggs to taste

Wash and slice. Combine all ingredients and coat with Braggs. Let sit 1/2 hour before serving.

Red Sauerkraut

4	heads red cabbage
2	apples, quartered and cored
	several strips of dried wakame

There are different methods to prepare sauerkraut; this is the one I find easiest. You need a food processor with an S blade. Clean the cabbage and remove three or four outer leaves from each head. Chop two heads of cabbage very fine. Take the other two heads and cut into pieces small enough to fit into the food processor and process the cabbage into a fine mush. If you don't have a processor, you can put the same two heads of cabbage through the champion juicer with the blank blade. Mix the four heads together and place into a crock. (If you don't have a ceramic crock, use a strong plastic bucket, a large glass jar or a deep ceramic bowl.) Push the apples down into the cabbage and cover the top with wakame strips. Line the inside with the whole cabbage leaves you set aside. Wipe down the sides of the crock to the cabbage to prevent spoilage. Fill a plastic bag with about three quarts of water and tie tightly. Place over top of cabbage to seal. Cover with a towel and let sit three to five days to ferment in a cool dark place. When sauerkraut is done, remove water bag and throw away top layer of cabbage leaves. Take out wakame, slice it, and serve as a side dish. Move kraut into another container and keep refrigerated. It will stay fresh for several weeks if properly stored. To make variations in the taste of the kraut, the additions I like the best are a few caraway or fennel seeds, shredded carrot, minced dill or chopped scallion. Sauerkraut (in the raw) aids in digestion at any meal. It is a good source of vitamin C and B-complex. It introduces friendly bacteria into the intestinal tract and helps satisfy cravings. It is an aid in the control of yeast overgrowth in your system. It can be purchased in some health food stores, but is very expensive so try to learn to make it yourself.

Hippocrates Sauerkraut Nouveau

2	cups red sauerkraut
1	stalk celery, minced
1/2	red onion, minced
1/8	tsp. cayenne

Mix together and let sit 1/2 hour before serving. Red cabbage makes a raw sauerkraut that is even more delicious than white cabbage kraut. Add different minced raw vegetables to your homemade kraut for varied taste and texture. Try to use organic cabbage whenever possible. It is said that cabbage grown conventionally and not organically may harbor many pesticides and chemical fertilizers.

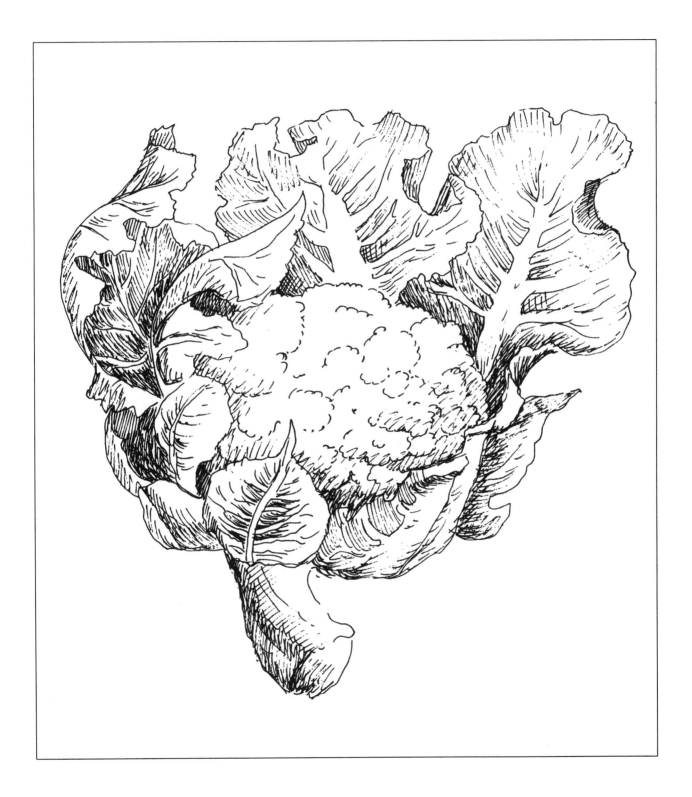

CONTENTS
AVOCADOS, NUTS, SEEDS AND SPROUTS

Avocados, Nuts, Seeds and Sprouts

PROTEIN ALTERNATIVES

The belief that a diet high in concentrated animal proteins is healthful has become obsolete. They are difficult to digest and their composition is altered when cooked decreasing the amount of available protein that the body can absorb. Serious toxic waste is a by-product that must be eliminated, and high water consumption is recommended when eating large amounts of animal foods. In fact both water and oxygen are needed to purify the body. It seems like a high price to pay and a lot of work in more ways than one.

What about cooked plant foods as a protein alternative? Cooked legumes can certainly provide the body with enough protein and create less toxic waste than animal food. To avoid confusion, the words bean and legume are interchangeable. Most beans are members of the leguminous family along with peas and pulses. Even though legumes are considered a protein source, it is interesting to note they contain a higher concentration of starches. Technically speaking, the ratio of starches to protein is approximately three to one in most beans. The fat content is relatively low. Soybeans are the exception. They contain approximately equal amounts of protein and starch with a relatively high concentration of fats. Tofu is different. It contains a much higher concentration of protein to starch, three to one.

It is also interesting to note that there are more calories as well as more starch, fat, and less available protein in a cup of cooked beans versus the same cup of sprouted beans. This brings us to the discussion of the superiority of sprouted foods. Germinating, also called sprouting, benefically changes the overall composition, concentration of nutrients, and their ratio figures. It actually increases the protein, water, and oxygen content while decreasing the starches and fats. By adding sprouts to your diet, you are theoretically able to absorb more nutrients with fewer calories and a minimum amount of digestive work for the body. This is truly the way to eat light and still get the greatest benefit from your food. This is not to say we must only eat our meals in this manner. This information is meant to better inform you about the advantages of germination. Sprouting also helps to eliminate problems like intestinal gas, heartburn, heaviness and unpleasant odors in the bathroom. In addition, legumes and grains are much easier to digest when sprouted before they are cooked.

The use of sprouted grains is also amazingly beneficial. They provide us with substantial amounts of protein even though they are thought of as a starchy food. There is a list of specific grains (as well as beans) that potentially provide all essential amino acids in the germination section. The high concentration of complex carbohydrates in grains along with their available protein is broken down into starches, simple sugars and more readily absorbed amino acids. Rich in food enzymes, they are easily digested and make an even better combination with sprouted legumes.

Raw nuts and seeds are yet another source of available protein. They are much different in composition compared to legumes and grains. The concentration of fats is extremely high at 60 to 70%. The remaining 30 to 40% is not quite equally divided between protein and carbohydrates. Seeds have a slightly higher ratio of protein. It is interesting to note that nuts and seeds are described as protein sources by many, yet their main component is fat. Soaking and sprouting these foods breaks down the fats into fatty acids. The protein and starch is also broken down into simple sugars and amino acids. Again, by sprouting you are able to absorb more nutrients with fewer calories.

The process of cooking nuts destroys enzymes and makes digestion more difficult. Nuts and seeds are best eaten sprouted. They are more beneficial when mixed with cooked foods after the heating process is over. It is important to note that eating unsoaked nuts and seeds on a long-term basis puts a tremendous strain on the pancreas and may cause digestive problems in the future. It is necessary to remove the enzyme inhibitors that block the breakdown of these foods, otherwise the internal organs have a serious chore to accomplish. Germination is essential.

Peanuts and cashews are not included in this book for several reasons. Cashews are cooked in their processing for commercial sale even though they may be labelled raw. Cooking makes them hard to digest and nutrient poor. They are often heavily treated with chemicals before entering the country for distribution. If you really love cashews, eat them as a special treat and not as a regularly stocked item. Peanuts are a legume and they may contain a known carcinogenic substance called aflatoxin which is a dangerous mold that often grows on the peanut. Improper storage and distribution create this problem. Again, if you love peanuts, eat them as a special treat. For these reasons I avoided the use of the above and have concentrated on more beneficial choices.

Please note:

Remember to soak your nuts and seeds, otherwise the following recipes will not be tasty or nutritious.

AVOCADOS

Avocado Kaleidoscope

2	avocados, peeled and diced
1	cucumber, peeled and diced
1	small jicama, peeled and diced
1	red pepper, chopped
1	small carrot, shredded
1	small red onion, chopped
1/2	bunch cilantro or parsley, chopped
	juice of 1 lemon
	Braggs to taste
1	garlic clove, minced
1/2	tsp. cumin
1	sheet dry nori, slivered

Combine all ingredients and mix well before serving. Use avocado that is still firm and not overly ripe.

Guacamole

4	avocados, ripe
	juice of 3 small limes
2	stalks celery
1	red onion
1	cucumber, peeled
1	red pepper, seeded
2	jalapeño peppers, seeded
	Braggs to taste
1	tsp. cumin
1/2	bunch fresh cilantro, chopped

Peel and mash avocados adding lime juice. Mince all the vegetables and mix together. Add cumin, cilantro, and Braggs. Mix all ingredients and chill. Substitute dill for the cilantro for a variation.

Avocado and Nori

2	avocados, ripe but firm
1	cup daikon, shredded
1	cucumber, shredded
	juice of 1 lemon
	Braggs to taste
1/2	cup parsley, minced
	lettuce leaves for garnish
1	sheet nori, slivered

Peel whole avocado and carefully slice into rounds. Slide off pit. Arrange on a platter covered with lettuce. Combine daikon and cucumber. Coat with Braggs and lemon juice and let sit 1/2 hour. Squeeze out liquid and add parsley. Stuff avocado rounds. Top with slivered nori before serving. Add some sliced red peppers for a decorative garnish.

Avocado Nori Rolls

2	avocados
1	red pepper, seeded
1	carrot
	juice of 1 lemon
1/4	cup parsley, minced
2	scallions, minced
	alfalfa sprouts
	nori sheets
	Braggs to taste

Peel and slice firm avocados. Thinly slice red pepper. Cut the carrot into slivers. Coat sliced avocado with lemon juice, parsley and Braggs. Place avocado on sheet of nori with sprouts, red pepper, carrots and some scallions. Roll up, seal and serve immediately.

Leafy Avocado Salad

2	avocados, ripe but firm
1/2	bunch spinach
1/2	bunch watercress
1	head Bibb lettuce
1	bunch scallions, green part only
2	sprigs fresh mint, minced
4	red radishes, minced
	juice of 1 lemon
	Braggs to taste

Cut avocados in half, remove pit and cut into balls with a melon ball cutter. Use a firm avocado! Clean and chop greens. Mince scallions. Combine all ingredients together, tossing with lemon juice and Braggs.

Avocado Pâté

2	avocados, mashed
1	jalapeño pepper, seeded
2	yellow squash, sliced
4	stalks celery, sliced
1/2	tsp. cumin
1	garlic clove
1	red pepper, minced garnish
	Braggs to taste

Process all except avocados and red pepper with S blade until minced. Mix with avocado and press into a loaf form. Chill. The mashed avocado should hold pâté together. Garnish with minced red pepper.

Avocado Shish Kebab

2	firm avocados, peeled and cut into chunks
10	small mushroom caps
2	carrots cut in round, thin slices
10	radishes
1	red pepper, seeded and cut in chunks
1	head Iceberg lettuce, cut in chunks
	wooden shish kebab sticks
	dressing of your choice
	sprouts

Skewer vegetables in rotation on a wooden stick and serve on a bed of sprouts with dressing on the side.

Avocado Salad

2	avocados, ripe but firm
6	mushrooms, sliced
1	cup snow peas, stemmed
2	tbsp. fresh basil, minced
6	red radishes, sliced
	juice of 1 lemon
	Braggs to taste
1/2	tsp. cayenne

Peel and slice avocados. Gently mix in remaining ingredients and adjust seasonings.

Sweet Avocado Delight

2	ripe avocados
1	head fennel
1	small jicama
6	scallions, minced
	Braggs to taste

Peel and halve avocados. Clean fennel and mince. Peel and mince jicama. Combine them. Mix in scallions and Braggs to taste. Stuff the avocado and serve.

Lettuce Rolls

1   head leaf lettuce
1   avocado, peeled and sliced into strips
2   scallions, minced
1   red pepper, minced
     alfalfa sprouts or onion sprouts

Clean lettuce. Cut out the core. Separate leaves. Place one or two strips of avocado onto a leaf. Top with some minced scallions and a few pieces of red pepper. Add some sprouts and roll the leaf carefully. Secure with a toothpick and continue the process with the remaining ingredients. Serve with a tasty dressing.

Avocado Stuffed Tomatoes

4   large ripe tomatoes
2   ripe avocados
     juice of 2 lemons
1   garlic clove, pressed
2   scallions, minced
2   tbsp. fresh cilantro, minced
     Braggs to taste
     lemon slices

Cut off tomato tops and scoop out seeds and pulp. Peel and mash avocados. Add remaining ingredients to avocado. Stuff tomatoes with avocado mixture. Serve on a bed of sprouts. Garnish with lemon slices.

Avocado with Tomato Sauce

2   avocados
3   ripe tomatoes
1   garlic clove, minced
1   shallot, minced
2   tbsp. parsley, minced
     juice of 1 lemon
     Braggs to taste
1   tbsp. fresh basil

Peel and remove pits from avocados. Slice into quarters. Liquify remaining ingredients in blender. Serve avocados on a bed of lettuce along with some extra minced parsley. Top with tomato sauce. You can convert this into an avocado tomato salad by chopping the tomatoes and avocados together. Use an extra tomato if they are small.

Sprout-Stuffed Avocados

3   small avocados, peeled and halved
2   cups alfalfa sprouts, chopped
4   scallions, minced
1/4   cup fresh lime juice
2   red peppers, sliced in rounds
1   large garlic clove
2   stalks celery, minced
1   cucumber, sliced in rounds
       parsley or scallion garnish
       Braggs to taste

Combine alfalfa, scallions and celery. In blender, mix lime juice, one avocado, garlic, Braggs and enough water to make a thick dressing. Stuff the remaining halves with sprout mixture. Put on serving plate surrounded with red peppers and cucumbers. Top with dressing or serve dressing on the side. Garnish with some scallions or parsley.

Red and Green Novelty

2   avocados, ripe but firm
1/2   head red cabbage, shredded
1/2   red onion, thinly sliced
       juice of 1 orange
1/4   cup fresh dill, minced
       red leaf lettuce
       Braggs to taste

Peel and slice avocado. Gently add remaining ingredients and serve on a bed of lettuce.

Variation I:

2   avocados, ripe but firm
1   grapefruit, sectioned and seeded
1/2   red onion, diced
1   small ripe papaya, puréed
       romaine lettuce leaves

Slice avocados. Combine remaining ingredients and serve on a bed of romaine lettuce.

Avocado and Olives

3	avocados, ripe but firm
1/2	cup black cured olives, pitted
3	stalks celery, minced
1/2	cup radishes, minced
	juice of 2 lemons
1	tsp. oregano
	Braggs to taste
1/2	cup parsley, minced
1/2	cup watercress, minced garnish
2	Belgian endives

Peel, pit and slice avocados. Combine remaining ingredients except endives and gently toss to coat and chill. Clean and separate endive leaves. Use as a bed for the avocado salad and stuff each individual leaf. Top with watercress.

Avocado Vegetable Aspic

1	large ripe avocado, peeled and chopped
	juice of 1 lemon
1	garlic clove
1	cucumber, peeled, seeded and diced
2	cups carrot juice
2	tbsp. fresh cilantro
	Braggs to taste
5	tbsp. agar
	scallion garnish

Dissolve agar in one cup of water by heating gently for five minutes. Blend all ingredients together. Turn into an oiled mold and chill overnight. Unmold and garnish with scallions.

NUTS, SEEDS AND SPROUTS

Sprouted Pea Patties

2	cups sprouted peas
1	large carrot, chopped
1/2	cup tahini
1	cup pignoli nuts
1/2	cup parsley
1/2	red onion
	Braggs to taste

Process peas and carrot until finely minced using S blade. Set aside. Process remaining ingredients. Combine all, add Braggs and form into patties.

Protein Patties

1 1/2	cups sunflower seeds
1/2	cup walnuts
4	cups alfalfa sprouts
1/4	cup scallion, minced
1/4	cup fresh parsley, minced
	Braggs to taste

Process seeds and nuts with S blade into a fine paste. Process alfalfa just enough to mince. Combine all ingredients together. Press into patties. Serve on a bed of lettuce with your favorite dressing.

Nutty Nori Rolls

1	cup almonds
1	cup filberts
1/2	cup tahini
1	red pepper, chopped
1	stalk celery, chopped
1	large carrot, chopped
2	cloves garlic
1/2	cup fresh parsley
1	tsp. each dried basil and oregano
	Braggs to taste
	alfalfa sprouts and nori sheets

Mince nuts with S blade. Add tahini, red pepper, garlic and herbs to produce a thick paste. Put into a bowl. Then process carrot and celery until finely minced. Mix together, adding Braggs. You use a special mat obtained in Oriental stores to roll the nori but it can be done by hand. Press nut mixture onto 1/3 of the sheet of nori . Top with approximately 1/2 cup alfalfa sprouts. Place a little tahini with your finger on the binding edge of the nori sheet. Roll tightly to hold together. For variation, add red pepper strips and green scallion strips to the roll. Leave nori rolls whole or slice into pieces.

Hot Chickpeas with Tahini Sauce

2	cups sprouted chickpeas
1/2	lb. spinach
2	jalapeño peppers, minced
1	red pepper, chopped
1	cup mushrooms, sliced
4	scallions, minced
	tahini dressing

Wash and finely chop spinach. Combine all ingredients and coat with tahini dressing. Be sure to remove all seeds from the jalapeño peppers.

Italian Style Chickpea Hummus

3	cups sprouted chickpeas
3/4	cup tahini
1/2	cup lemon juice
3	cloves garlic
6	scallions, sliced
1/2	cup fresh parsley
1/2	cup fresh basil
6	stalks celery, chopped
1/4	tsp. cayenne
	Braggs to taste

Combine chickpeas, tahini and lemon juice in food processor to a paste consistency, adding a little water only if necessary. Set aside. Then process the garlic, scallions, parsley and basil together. Combine with chickpea mixture. Next, process celery with cayenne until very finely minced. This is all done with the S blade. Combine all ingredients together and add Braggs. Chill and serve.

Carrot Hummus Loaf

3	cups raw chickpea hummus
2	large carrots, finely shredded
1	stalk celery, minced
	minced parsley

Combine hummus, carrots and celery to form a loaf. Garnish with minced celery.

Sprouted Chickpea Hummus

3	cups sprouted chickpeas
1/2	cup tahini
1/2	cup lemon juice
2	large cloves garlic
1/2	tsp. cumin
1/2	tsp. cayenne
1	tsp. oregano
1	tsp. paprika
1/4	cup toasted sesame seeds (optional)
	Braggs to taste

Process all ingredients with S blade, adding water only if necessary to make a thick pâté. Serve with fresh vegetable slices. Depending on the size of your processor, you may need to do this in steps.

Sesame Pâté

1	cup tahini
1	cup hulled sesame seeds
1	carrot, sliced
1	stalk celery, sliced
4	scallions, sliced
2	tbsp. lemon juice
1	tsp. dried basil
1/2	tsp. dried dill
1/4	cup fresh parsley
1/2	cup raw white sauerkraut
	Braggs to taste

Place all ingredients in food processor with S blade and blend into a fine creamy pâté. Serve with vegetable sticks. Add more sauerkraut for a richer taste. This recipe is delicious with homemade white cabbage kraut, but you can substitute commercial kraut.

Walnut Onion Pâté

2	cups walnuts
1/2	cup pignoli nuts
1	cup marinated onions
1	tbsp. Italian seasoning
1/4	cup fresh basil

Process all with S blade to make a rich creamy pâté. Add Braggs if necessary. You can make a thinner pâté by adding more water.

Mushroom Pâté

1	lb. mushrooms, sliced
1	cup pignoli nuts
1	small onion, chopped
1	garlic clove
2	tbsp. tahini
1/2	tsp. thyme
1/4	cup fresh parsley
1/4	tsp. nutmeg
	Braggs to taste

Process all with S blade. Mushrooms must be fresh. Form into loaf and chill. Use different varieties of mushrooms for variation.

Exotic Almond Pâté

3	cups almonds
1	pepper, seeded (red or yellow)
1	stalk celery, sliced
1	small red onion, sliced
1	large carrot, sliced
2	tbsp. dried tarragon
1	tsp. caraway seeds
1/2	tsp. cumin
1	tsp. curry
1/4	tsp. cayenne
	Braggs to taste

Process vegetables and nuts through Champion juicer with blank blade or process in food processor with S blade until creamy. Add seasonings and mix well. Form into a loaf. Chill before serving.

Filbert Corn Loaf

2	cups filberts
3	ears corn, decobbed
1/2	cup parsley, minced
1	cup thick sunflower dressing
	Braggs to taste

Put filberts through Champion juicer with blank blade. Mix processed filberts with corn-kernels and minced parsley. Add Braggs. Form into a loaf and serve with sunflower dressing. For variation, process filberts and the dressing first with S blade to a fine paste. Add corn and parsley. Form into a loaf and serve.

Rainbow Nut Loaf

1	cup almonds
1	cup filberts
1	inch piece ginger, peeled
1	red pepper
1/2	head cauliflower
1	yellow squash
4	stalks celery
2	carrots
4	mushrooms
1/2	tsp. coriander
1	tsp. marjoram
1	garlic clove
	Braggs to taste

Clean and cut vegetables into small pieces. Put all ingredients through Champion juicer using blank blade. Alternate vegetables with nuts to avoid overloading the motor. Add Braggs and form into a loaf.

Almond Filbert Loaf

1 1/2	cups almonds
1	cup filberts
1/2	cup tahini
1/2	small red cabbage, chopped
4	stalks celery, chopped
1/2	red onion, sliced
2	tbsp. poultry seasoning
1	tsp. caraway seeds
	Braggs to taste

Process nuts and tahini with S blade to a fine paste, adding a little water if necessary. Process remaining ingredients until finely minced. If you have a small food processor, you will need to do one vegetable at a time. Combine all ingredients. Form into a loaf. Dried nuts have a different consistency and using them without soaking will result in a totally different taste and texture as well as create digestive discomfort.

Zesty Sprouted Lentils

2	cups lentil sprouts
1	red pepper, diced
1	bunch fresh oregano, minced
1	carrot, shredded
4	scallions, minced
1	garlic clove, minced
1	tsp. grated lemon peel
	Braggs to taste
$^1/_4$	tsp. cayenne
1	cup basic tahini dressing

Remove tough stems from fresh oregano before mincing. Combine all ingredients. Toss well and serve.

Stuffed Celery

Variation I: Amandine

1	head celery
1	cup almonds
1	cup pignoli sauce
	Braggs to taste
$^1/_2$	cup fresh parsley, minced

Cut the bottom off the celery and clean the stalks. Set aside. Chop the almonds with the pignoli sauce in a food processor with the S blade to make a thick chunky filling. Stuff the celery stalks and serve garnished with parsley. Substitute filberts for almonds.

Variation II: Sunflower Sage

1	cup sunflower seeds
1	tbsp. fresh sage
1	tbsp. lemon juice
	Braggs to taste
$^1/_2$	cup pignoli sauce
	minced scallion garnish

Process all ingredients except scallions with S blade. Stuff celery. Garnish with green part of scallions only.

Combination Loaf

$^1/_2$	cup each walnuts and filberts
$^1/_2$	cup each sunflower and pumpkin seeds
4	scallions, chopped
1	carrot, sliced
1	zucchini, sliced
1	garlic clove
$^1/_2$	bunch fresh dill or parsley
1	tbsp. dried orange peel
	Braggs to taste

Process all ingredients alternately through Champion juicer with blank blade. Add Braggs and form loaf. You can also use a food processor with an S blade. If you do, add a little tahini to the nuts and seeds to produce a sticky consistency in order to form a loaf. Process the nuts and seeds to a very fine meal and then add the tahini.

Herbed Pumpkin Seed Loaf

2	cups pumpkin seeds
1	cup walnuts
1	cup fresh parsley
$^1/_2$	cup fresh basil
$^1/_2$	cup basic tahini dressing
	Braggs to taste

Process seeds with tahini dressing using S blade. Then process walnuts to a fine paste. Finally, process herbs together until finely minced. Mix all ingredients together to form a loaf adding Braggs to taste. You can often interchange the use of the Champion juicer and a food processor to prepare nut and seed dishes. Remember to use the blank blade with the Champion; this technique produces a creamier loaf.

Fiesta Chili

2	cups sprouted chickpeas
2	cups lentil sprouts
1	cup sprouted green peas
2	carrots, finely grated
4	stalks celery, minced
2	jalapeño peppers, minced
1	zucchini, chopped
2	tbsp. chili powder
1/2	tsp. cayenne
	Italian sauce

Combine all ingredients and coat with Italian sauce to taste. Marinate two hours before serving. Instead of the Italian sauce, try using tahini dressing with the blended addition of one red pepper.

Basic Seed Cheese

2	cups sunflower seeds
1	cup pignoli nuts
1	inch piece ginger, peeled
2	cloves garlic
1	tsp. dried oregano
1/4	cup fresh basil
	Braggs to taste

Combine all in a blender with enough water to cover. Start blender, adding more water to produce a very thick creamy liquid. Pour into a sprout bag and squeeze out liquid. You are left with the cheese. (The remaining liquid becomes a dressing with the addition of fresh minced herbs and a little more Braggs amino. To thicken the dressing blend in some tahini.) The yield varies, so double or triple the recipe to meet your needs. Use this cheese as stuffing for celery, mushrooms, cucumber boats, etc.. If you have a small blender, cut recipe in half to accommodate its size. Make this into a sweet cheese by eliminating last five ingredients and adding dates with cinnamon instead.

Seed Cheese Pie

2	cups seed cheese of your choice
1/2	cup mung bean sprouts
4	cups alfalfa sprouts
1/2	cup each cauliflower and carrots
1	cup walnuts, garnish
1/2	cup scallions, minced
	Braggs to taste

In a 10" pie plate, first layer two cups alfalfa sprouts then smooth over one cup seed cheese with a knife. Process mung bean sprouts, cauliflower and carrots individually with S blade until finely minced. Coat each vegetable with some Braggs. Layer each one and then top with another layer of seed cheese. Add layer of scallions. Finish with last two cups of alfalfa sprouts. Turn pie plate upside down onto platter, garnish with walnuts and chill. Use any minced vegetables for the center stuffing. Fresh corn kernels are a nice addition.

Pumpkin Seed Cheese

2	cups pumpkin seeds
1	cup pignoli nuts
1	stalk celery, chopped
3	shallots or garlic cloves
	juice of 1 lemon
1/2	cup fresh basil
	Braggs to taste

Follow the basic seed cheese process. Pignoli nuts, walnuts or pecans combined with sunflower or pumpkin seeds make numerous combinations.

Sunflower Walnut Cheese

1 1/2	cups sunflower seeds
1 1/2	cups walnuts
1	small red onion, chopped
	juice of 1 lemon
1/2	cup fresh dill
	Braggs to taste

Follow basic seed cheese process.

Pumpkin Pecan Cheese

1 ¹/₂   cups pumpkin seeds
1 ¹/₂   cups pecans
1   bunch scallions, chopped
1   inch piece ginger, peeled
         Braggs to taste
¹/₂   cup fresh parsley

Follow basic seed cheese process.

Seed Cheese Loaf

2   cups seed cheese
1   red pepper
2   stalks celery
¹/₄   cup fresh parsley
¹/₂   red onion
1   carrot
         lettuce leaves

Mince the pepper, celery, onion, and parsley. Finely shred the carrot. Mix together all ingredients and press into a loaf. Serve on a bed of lettuce.

Pignoli Nut Mold

3   cups pignoli nuts
1   pkg. agar flakes (1 oz.)
1   cup bermuda onion, minced
1   cup red peppers, minced
¹/₂   cup celery, minced
         Braggs to taste

Dissolve agar flakes in three cups boiling water until clear. Cool down. Blend with the pignoli nuts into a thick creamy liquid. Mix in minced vegetables. Add Braggs. Pour into a 10" inch spring-form pan and chill until firm. Slice and serve with a salad. This is excellent.

Greek Style Seed Cheese

1   cup seed cheese
¹/₂   cup black cured olives, pitted
1   lb. spinach
1   garlic clove, minced
1   tbsp. fresh mint, chopped
         juice of 1 lemon
         Braggs to taste

Wash and chop spinach. Coat with Braggs and lemon juice. Let sit one hour. Add olives, garlic, mint, and seed cheese. Toss well and serve.

Garlic and Lemon Seed Cheese

1   cup raw tahini
¹/₂   cup lemon juice
2 ¹/₂   tbsp. agar flakes
1   stalk celery, minced
1   scallion, minced
2   cloves garlic
         dash paprika
         Braggs to taste
2   tbsp. parsley for garnish

Dissolve agar flakes in ¹/₂ cup boiling water until clear. Cool. Blend all ingredients except celery and scallion. Combine these vegetables with the mixture. Pour into springform mold and chill until set. Serve with parsley garnish.

Tahini Cream Cheese

1   cup raw tahini
6   tbsp. agar flakes
1   red pepper, finely minced
¹/₂   red onion, minced
2   tbsp. fresh dill, minced
         dash cayenne
         Braggs to taste

Dissolve agar flakes in two cups water by heating until clear. Blend tahini and agar mixture together. Mix in pepper, onion, cayenne, and Braggs. Pour into a 8" springform pan and chill. When solidified, serve on a bed of vegetables and sprouts.

Pignoli "Smoked Fish Pâté"

2	cups pignoli nuts
3/4	cup raw white sauerkraut
1/4	cup fresh dill
1/4	cup fresh parsley
	Braggs to taste

Put all ingredients into the food processor with the S blade. Blend until smooth. When this was prepared for a class at Hippocrates we all tasted it and decided that we were reminded of a smoked fish flavor. I hope you get the same results. We made a mold in the shape of a fish and served it to many amazed lunch guests.

Spinach Quiche

1	lb. spinach
1	cup flaxseed soaked in 2 cups water
1	cup almond mayonnaise
1/2	cup pignoli nuts
1/4	cup lemon juice
1	garlic clove
2	tbsp. Braggs
3	tbsp. agar flakes
1/2	bunch scallions, minced
4	tbsp. fresh dill, minced
1 1/2	cups walnuts
1	tbsp. Braggs
1	garlic clove

Heat agar flakes in one cup water until dissolved. Set aside. Wash and finely mince spinach in processor with S blade. Set aside. Process last three ingredients and press into 10" pie plate. Pour off one cup mixed flaxseed liquid and blend with pignoli nuts, lemon juice, one garlic clove and Braggs. Combine minced spinach, almond mayonnaise and above flaxseed mixture and agar mixture in a bowl. Mix well, adding scallions and dill. Pour into shell. Let chill and set before serving. Make buttermilk dressing with the one cup of leftover soaked flaxseeds.

Sunflower Peppers

4	red peppers, seeded and halved
2	cups sunflower seeds
1/2	cup cauliflower, chopped
1	carrot, chopped
1/2	red onion, sliced
1/4	cup fresh basil
	Braggs to taste
1/4	cup fresh parsley, minced

Place sunflower seeds in food processor with S blade. Process until smooth. Remove and add remaining ingredients except red peppers. Process until finely minced. Combine seeds and vegetables with Braggs. Stuff red pepper halves. Top with some basic tahini dressing for a real treat and garnish with parsley. Substitute sprouted rye for sunflower seeds for a variation.

Walnuts and Belgian Endives

1	cup walnuts, chopped
4	Belgian endives, sliced
1	bunch watercress, chopped
2	shallots, minced
	juice of 1 lemon
1/4	cup tahini dressing
	Braggs to taste

Mix all ingredients well and serve.

Stuffed Mushrooms

1	lb. large mushrooms
1/2	cup almonds
1	cup walnuts
1/2	cup pignoli nuts
1	garlic clove
1	stalk celery, minced
1/2	cup fresh parsley, minced
	Braggs to taste
1/2	cup tahini dressing
	poppy seeds
	paprika

Clean an remove stems from mushrooms. Set aside. Place nuts in processor with S blade and blend until creamy. Add remaining ingredients to processor and blend until well combined. Stuff mushrooms and garnish with paprika and poppy seeds.

Sprouted Wheat Mold

4	cups sprouted wheat, 1 day old
2	tbsp. extra virgin olive oil
1	red pepper, diced
4	shallots, chopped
2	stalks celery, minced
1	garlic clove
1	carrot, shredded
1	tbsp. curry
	Braggs to taste
4	tbsp. psyllium seed powder

Grind sprouts in processor with S blade for one minute. Set aside. Then combine shallots, garlic, curry and 1/2 cup water in processor. Put sprouts back into the processor with above mixture to combine quickly. Remove and mix well with remaining ingredients and press into mold. Chill for one hour or more and serve. Two days of sprouting is OK for this recipe.

Vegetable Loaf

2	carrots
1/2	red onion
1	sweet potato or yam
6	stalks celery
1	rutabaga
1	beet
5	tbsp. psyllium seed powder
	Braggs to taste
	parsley garnish

Peel and slice all vegetables except celery. Put all ingredients except psyllium seed powder through the Champion juicer with the blank blade. Mix in psyllium seed and Braggs. Press into a mold and chill. Unmold and garnish with parsley.

Walnut Beet Salad

1	cup walnuts, chopped
4	beets, peeled and diced
1	red onion, diced
1/4	cup fresh dill, minced
2	stalks celery, minced
1/2	tsp. coriander
1/4	tsp. cayenne
	Braggs to taste

Combine all ingredients and mix well. Serve on a bed of sprouts.

Pecan Parsnip Paradise

1	cup pecans
6	parsnips
4	stalks celery, minced
2	shallots, minced
1/2	cup pignoli nuts
	dash cayenne
	Braggs to taste

Peel and shred parsnips. Add celery and shallots. Blend pignoli nuts with cayenne and one cup water to a creamy consistency. Mix all ingredients. Substitute scallions for shallots for variation.

Sensational Sprouts

1	cup pumpkin seeds
1	cup lentil sprouts
1	cup mung bean sprouts
1/2	cup aduki bean sprouts (optional)
1	large carrot, shredded
4	scallions, minced
	tahini dressing

Combine all and coat with ample tahini dressing or any other dressing of your choice. Add Braggs if necessary. Add one tsp. poppy seeds for variation.

Confetti Rye Salad

2	cups sprouted rye
2	tbsp. extra virgin olive oil
2	ears corn, decobbed
1	red pepper, chopped
4	scallions, minced
4	stalks celery, minced
	Braggs to taste
1/2	inch piece ginger, minced and peeled

Combine all ingredients and serve on a bed of lettuce.

Sprouted Grain Salad

1	cup sprouted rye
1	cup sprouted wheat
2	carrots, shredded
1/2	head cauliflower, chopped
6	large mushrooms, chopped
2	stalks celery, minced
1	zucchini, chopped
1	tbsp. oregano
1/2	tsp. cayenne
2	cloves garlic, minced
2	tbsp. extra virgin olive oil
	Braggs to taste
	juice of 1 lemon

Combine all. Mix well and adjust seasonings. Serve on a bed of greens.

Wheaty String Bean Salad

1	cup green beans, diced
1	cup sprouted wheat
1	cucumber, peeled and diced
1/2	red onion, minced
2	carrots, shredded
1/2	cup fresh parsley, minced
1	cup pignoli sauce

Combine all ingredients and serve. You can substitute another sauce for pignoli sauce for variation. Remove seeds from cucumber for a more refined taste.

Grains and Beans

2	cups sprouted wheat
1	cup mung bean sprouts
1/2	red cabbage, shredded
1/2	cup fresh dill, chopped
4	scallions, minced
2	cloves garlic, minced
1/2	tsp. cayenne
2	tbsp. extra virgin olive oil
2	tbsp. fresh ginger juice or lemon juice
	Braggs to taste

Combine all ingredients. Adjust seasonings to your liking and serve.

Green Goddess Vegetable Mold

1/2	lb. spinach
1/2	bunch watercress
1/2	head green leaf lettuce
3/4	cup almond mayonnaise
1	garlic clove, minced
3	tbsp. agar flakes
	juice of 1 lemon
	Braggs to taste
4	tbsp. fresh dill, minced

Clean and wash vegetables. Process leafy greens with S blade until finely minced. You need to end up with three cups minced greens. Dissolve agar in one cup of water by heating gently. Mix all ingredients, adjust seasonings, and press into a springform pan. Chill until set.

Garden Salad Olive Aspic

1	cup black cured olives, pitted
1	red pepper
1	ear corn, decobbed
1/2	red onion
3	stalks celery
1	cucumber, peeled and seeded
3/4	cup almond mayonnaise
	juice of 1 lemon
3	tbsp. agar flakes
2	tbsp. Braggs
2	tbsp fresh parsley
	dash cayenne

Dissolve agar flakes in one cup of water by heating gently. Mince all the vegetables except corn. Combine all the ingredients together and pour into a springform pan. Chill until firm.

Vegetable Nut Mold

2	medium carrots, shredded
2	stalks celery, shredded
1/2	cup green peas, shelled
1/2	bunch scallions, minced
1 1/2	cups walnuts, chopped
2	ears corn, decobbed
1	small yellow squash, shredded
3	cups vegetable broth
1/2	cup almond mayonnaise
2	tbsp. Braggs
5	tbsp. agar flakes
	minced parsley garnish

Dissolve agar flakes in three cups of vegetable broth, heating gently. Set aside. Combine all remaining ingredients. Mix together with agar broth until well combined. Put into a bundt pan mold or springform. Chill until firm. Serve on bed of sprouts with a minced parsley garnish.

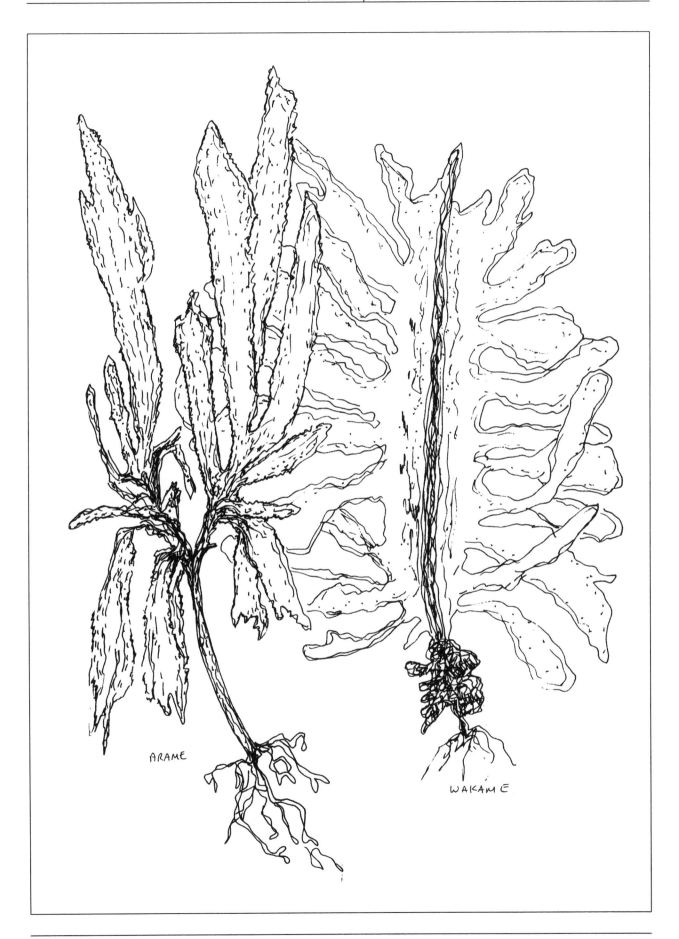

ARAME

WAKAME

CONTENTS
ANCIENT SEAPLANTS AND CONDIMENTS

Ancient Seaplants and Condiments

The seaweeds I use in this chapter are arame, hiziki, "instant" wakame, kombu, agar, dulse, and nori. I would like to explain preparation techniques here. Arame, hiziki and wakame are soaked in a bowl of water for about 15 minutes, drained and then rinsed. Minerals are lost in the soaking and rinsing process so do not overdo it. Size and thickness of each seaweed crop varies so you may have to soak some a little longer, particularly hiziki. They usually expand to three or four times their original size. Nori does not need to be soaked unless indicated; if it happens to get wet you can turn it into a delicious sauce. It is necessary to rinse the dulse thoroughly and quickly before adding to any recipe unless otherwise explained. This makes it easier to work with, less salty and easier to chew. If you wet it too much it will fall apart. Again you can make a sauce.

Be sure to store your seaweeds in a cool, dry, dark place. If they become too moist, dry them out by placing in your dehydrator for one or two hours or in your oven near the pilot light. Excess heat and humidity for a prolonged time will destroy nutrients, especially vitamins A and C, so take care of your supply. Properly stored, they will last for years.

I'd like to help familiarize you with an idea of the taste of these sea vegetables along with some of their nutritional contributions to your diet. Arame is a delicate sweet-tasting seaweed that's high in calcium and phosphorus. It also contains iron and potassium. Hiziki has a much stronger almost nutty flavor and is extremely rich in calcium. It also carries iron and phosphorus along with vitamins A, B1, B2 and C. Dulse is very salty and rich tasting with an extremely high concentration of iron. It carries potassium, magnesium, calcium, iodine, phosphorus and many trace minerals as well as vitamins A, B2, B6, C and E. Nori is high in calcium, magnesium, potassium, phosphorus and manganese. It is also rich in vitamins A, C and niacin. Agar seaweed makes a gelatin that has no color, taste or odor. It contains calcium, iodine, phosphorus and other trace minerals. Widely known throughout the world, agar is used for making aspics, preserves and all kinds of desserts as demonstrated in this book. Kombu is a large thick flavorful sea green that is sweet-tasting and used for soup stocks by the Orientals. It contains vitamins A and B as well as potassium and sodium. Also known as kelp, it is eaten around the world. Kombu contains glutamic acid, which is a natural flavor enhancer and tenderizer that imitates monosodium glutamate. The Japanese often use kombu not only for flavor but also for softening beans while they are being cooked.

If for any reason you can't find instant wakame in your local health food store, use regular wakame. Soak the wakame for about ten minutes, drain it, remove any stems, and slice into small pieces before adding to your recipes. You will have to estimate the amount necessary to replace the instant wakame. Do not oversoak because it will get too soft. If so, add to a soup. Instant wakame is superior in texture and flavor and maintains both these qualities in any recipe. It is rich in calcium, niacin, iron and sodium. It also contains vitamins A, B1, B2 and C.

There are many varieties of sea vegetables you can learn about and enjoy. Seaweeds contain glutamic and alginic acids that aid in body cleansing and functioning. They also assist in weight loss by speeding up the metabolic rate. Because seaweeds help eliminate heavy metals from the body, cigarette smokers would do well to eat them since cigarettes contain a high concentration of heavy metals.

If we become what we eat, think about the essence of seaweed. Constant movement, great flexibility, water adaptability, primitive oneness and cellular autonomy are all a part of the quality of sea vegetables. I had the pleasure of harvesting different kinds of seaweed off the coast of Massachusetts with a very interesting and intelligent man named Ken Burns. He taught me so much about sea vegetables as well as wild mushrooms and herbs. He made it clear to me that consuming seaweed greatly increases body activity. Be careful not to overeat this wondrous food. It may prevent you from falling asleep at night.

In conclusion, the condiments at the end of this chapter can be exciting additions to your meals. I have noticed that men particularly appreciate these dishes. It is a way to add some extra stimulation while leaving the main dishes simple.

Please note. The amounts of seaweed added to each recipe are measured in dried form. Remember to soak before adding unless otherwise indicated.

ANCIENT SEAPLANTS

Colorful Wakame Salad

1/4	cup instant wakame
1	zucchini
1	red pepper
1	yellow pepper
1	cup avocado dressing
2	tbsp. fresh dill, minced
1/2	red onion, minced
2	tbsp. lemon juice
	Braggs

Clean and cut zucchini and peppers into small chunks. Add remaining ingredients and Braggs to taste. Mix well and serve.

Oriental Wakame Salad

1/4	cup instant wakame
1	cup mung bean sprouts
1	cup snow peas
2	jerusalem artichokes (sunchokes)
2	scallions, minced
	dash cayenne
1	tbsp. ginger juice
2	tbsp. parsley, minced
1	cup tahini dressing

Clean snow peas by removing the stems. Peel and slice sunchokes. Combine ingredients, mix well, and serve. Fresh young snowpeas make this dish very tasty. Jerusalem artichokes are also called sunchokes.

Orange Wakame Salad

1/4	cup instant wakame
2	yellow squash
	juice of 1 orange
1/2	cup tahini dressing
	Braggs

Julienne yellow squash and coat with Braggs. Let sit 20 minutes. Add remaining ingredients and serve. If too salty, wash excess Braggs off the squash before adding to remaining ingredients.

Wakame Cucumber Salad

1/4	cup instant wakame
2	cucumbers, peeled and seeded
2	scallions
4	red cabbage leaves
1/2	cup avocado dressing
	juice of 1 lemon
	Braggs

Slice cucumbers in half lengthwise. Slice again. Mince scallions. Shred cabbage leaves. Combine all ingredients, adding Braggs to taste.

Wakame Corn Salad

1/4	cup instant wakame
2	ears corn, decobbed
1	small jicama
1	tbsp. toasted sesame seeds
2	tbsp. fresh parsley, minced
1/2	cup tahini dressing

Peel and dice jicama. If jicama is not available, add an extra ear of corn. Combine the ingredients, mix well, and serve.

Sea Green Spinach Salad

1	lb. spinach
1/4	cup wakame
1	clove garlic, minced
	juice of 1 lemon
	Braggs

Wash and chop spinach. Use a food processor with the S blade to mince the spinach. Combine all ingredients, adding Braggs to taste. Add your choice of dressing to this recipe for a richer salad instead of Braggs.

Avocado Wakame Salad

1/4	cup instant wakame
1	avocado, firm
1	cucumber, peeled
2	tbsp. fresh cilantro
2	scallions
2	tbsp. lemon juice
1/2	cup avocado dressing

Peel and slice the avocado into thin strips. Cut the cucumber into julienne pieces. Mince the cilantro and scallions. Combine the ingredients, adding Braggs if necesary. A nice addition to this would be ripe cherry tomatoes.

Marinated Wakame Salad

1	large bermuda onion
1/4	cup instant wakame
1/4	cup tahini dissolved in 1/4 cup water
	Braggs
1	tsp. oregano

Peel and slice the onion into thin rounds. Coat with Braggs by separating the circles of onions in a bowl. Let sit one hour. Drain off excess Braggs and add remaining ingredients. Mix well, coating the onions and wakame with the tahini.

Mediterranean Wakame

1/4	cup instant wakame
4	large mushrooms
1/2	cup cured black olives, pitted
2	stalks celery
6	red radishes
2	scallions
1	clove garlic
	juice of 1 lemon
2	tbsp. extra virgin olive oil
	dash cayenne
	Braggs

Slice the mushrooms. Mince the celery, radishes, garlic, and scallion. Combine all ingredients. Add Braggs to taste and serve with sprouts. If the olives are salty, you may not need Braggs.

Sweet and Sour Wakame

1/4	cup instant wakame
1/2	red onion
1	red pepper
1	carrot
1	inch piece ginger
3	dates
	juice of 1 lemon
2	tbsp. tahini
	Braggs

Mince onion and pepper. Shred the carrot. Peel and mince the ginger. Pit the dates and blend with remaining ingredients, adding 1/2 cup water to make a sauce. Pour over vegetables and wakame. Let sit 1/2 hour before serving. This recipe is not properly combined with the addition of dates.

Marinated Arame Delight

1/4	cup arame
1/2	white cabbage
1/2	red onion
1	parsnip
1/2	cup tahini dressing
1/4	tsp. fennel seeds
2	tbsp. parsley, minced
	Braggs

Clean and shred the cabbage, onion, and parsnip. Marinate in Braggs for 1/2 hour. Drain. Combine all the ingredients, mix well, and serve. Rinse vegetables to remove excess Braggs for a less salty taste.

Arame Vegetable Salad

1/4	cup arame
1	zucchini
3	stalks celery
1	red pepper
	juice of 1 lemon
2	tbsp. dried onion flakes
1/2	tsp. caraway seeds
1	cup tahini dressing

Mince vegetables and combine all ingredients. Mix well and serve.

Arame and Broccoli

$1/4$	cup arame
1	cup broccoli florets, chopped
1	cup mung bean sprouts
1	carrot, shredded
1	clove garlic, minced
1	tbsp. fresh ginger juice
1	cup almond mayonnaise
	Braggs

Combine the ingredients, adjust flavors and serve. Be advised that almond mayonnaise is rich in fats.

Arame Sprouted Lentil Salad

$1/4$	cup arame
$1 1/2$	cups sprouted lentils
$1/4$	cup toasted sesame seeds
2	tbsp. parsley, minced
1	carrot, shredded
1	cup red pepper dressing

Combine ingredients, mix well, and serve. You can use basic tahini dressing for a variation.

Hiziki Salad

$1/4$	cup hiziki
1	cup string beans, sliced
1	large carrot, julienned
$1/4$	cup sunflower seeds
1	shallot, minced
1	tsp. dried orange peel
$1/2$	cup pignoli sauce
1	tbsp. lemon juice

Combine ingredients, mix well, and serve. Add more pignoli sauce for a richer taste.

Hiziki and Sprouts

$1/4$	cup hiziki
1	cup sprouted peas
1	carrot, shredded
1	jicama, peeled and shredded
2	scallions, minced
1	tsp. dried lemon peel
1	cup pesto sauce

Combine ingredients and serve. You can use fresh peas instead of sprouted peas, if available.

Italian Hiziki Salad

$1/4$	cup hiziki
2	carrots
$1/2$	red onion
1	cup cauliflower, chopped
1	tsp. dried basil
$1/2$	cup fresh parsley, chopped
$1/2$	cup Italian dressing
2	tbsp. toasted sesame seeds

Combine ingredients. Adjust flavors. Add Braggs if necesary and serve.

Hiziki and Sprouted Chickpeas

$1/4$	cup hiziki
1	cup sprouted garbanzos
	juice of 1 lemon
1	carrot , shredded
2	ears corn, decobbed
1	cup tahini dressing
	dash cayenne

Combine ingredients, mix well, and serve. Chickpeas are also called garbanzos.

Please note:
Sometimes a crop of dulse may have tiny sea shells, debris or other small pieces of seaweed intermingled. Remove the above before rinsing.

Vegetables and Dulse

1	cup dulse
2	red onions
1	parsnip
1	head fennel
2	tbsp. fresh basil, minced
	Braggs

Clean and shred onions, parsnip, and fennel. Marinate in Braggs for $1/2$ hour. Rinse to remove Braggs. Wet and chop dulse. Add dulse and basil. Mix well and serve.

Patty Pan Seaweed Salad

2	patty pan squash
$1/2$	cup dulse
1	clove garlic, minced
1	carrot, shredded
$1/2$	cup fresh parsley, chopped
1	shallot, minced
2	tbsp. lemon juice

Clean and thinly slice patty pan squash. Wet and chop dulse. Combine all ingredients. Mix together and serve. Substitute zucchini or yellow squash for patty pan for a variation.

Dulse Italiano

1	cup dulse
2	large mushrooms, sliced
1	clove garlic, minced
$1/2$	head escarole
$1/2$	head radicchio (optional)
1	tsp. dried oregano
1	tbsp. extra virgin olive oil
	juice of 1 lemon

Wet and chop dulse. Clean and cut escarole and radicchio into thin strips. Add remaining ingredients. Mix well and serve.

Dulse Salad

1	cup dulse, chopped
1	cucumber, peeled and diced
2	ears corn, decobbed
2	scallions, minced
$1/2$	cup parsley, minced
1	tbsp. dried orange peel

Combine and mix well before serving. Remember to wet dulse before adding.

Seaweed Sprout Salad

2	cups mung bean sprouts
1	cup dulse
2	carrots, shredded
$1/2$	cup parsley, chopped
1	tbsp. fresh ginger juice
2	scallions, minced
	dash cayenne

Wet and chop dulse. Combine all and mix well before serving. Substitute aduki beans sprouts for mung bean sprouts for a variation.

Dulse and Pumpkin Seeds

1	cup dulse
$1/4$	cup pumpkin seeds
$1/2$	head red cabbage
$1/2$	cup fresh dill, chopped
1	cucumber, peeled
	juice of 1 lemon
	dash cayenne

Wet and chop dulse. Shred cabbage and cucumber. Combine all ingredients and serve.

Nori Vegetable Rolls

2	carrots
4	scallions
1	zucchini
1	cucumber
	alfalfa sprouts
	Braggs and lemon juice
	nori sheets

Clean and slice vegetables into long thin strips. Marinate in Braggs and lemon juice for one hour. Drain and dry vegetables with a paper towel. Arrange an assortment on your sheet of nori. Top with lots of sprouts and roll up. Eat whole.

Nori Sprout Salad

2	sheets nori, slivered
$1/2$	cup lentil sprouts
$1/2$	cup mung bean sprouts
1	cup napa cabbage, shredded
1	carrot, shredded
1	tbsp. ginger, minced
1	cup tahini dressing
1	tsp. 5-spice powder (optional)

Combine all. Mix well and serve.

Nori Scallions Salad

4	sheets nori, slivered
1	bunch scallions
2	stalks celery
2	inch piece daikon
1	cucumber
1	tbsp. lemon juice
1	cup avocado dressing

Cut scallions into one inch pieces. Mince the celery. Peel daikon and cucumber and cut into julienne strips and serve immediately.

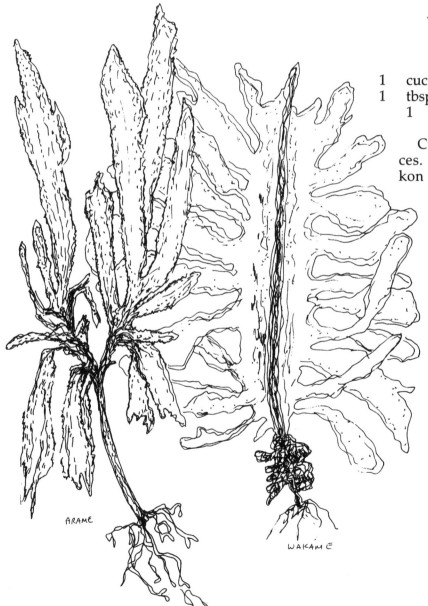

ARAME

WAKAME

CONDIMENTS

Dulse Condiment

1	cup dulse
$1/4$	cup dried onion flakes
$1/2$	cup toasted sesame seeds

Clean any debris from dulse. Dehydrate overnight. It should break up into crispy little pieces. Add onion flakes and sesame seeds. Use as a flavoring for your salads. Put dulse in a processor with S blade to break it up or use a suribachi.

Dulse Sauce

$1/2$	cup dulse
2	red peppers
1	clove garlic
$1/2$	tsp. dried oregano
1	tbsp. fresh basil
2	tbsp. extra virgin olive oil
$3/4$	cup water

Wet and chop dulse. Combine all ingredients. Blend into a sauce.

Nori Lemon Sauce

2	sheets nori
1	cup water
	juice of 1 lemon
	dash cayenne
1	tbsp. dried onion flakes
	Braggs to taste

Soak nori in one cup water until it falls apart. Add remaining ingredients. Adjust seasonings, mix well and serve.

Nori Condiments

Variation I:

2	sheets nori, slivered
$1/4$	cup sesame seeds, toasted
1	tbsp. dried orange peel
1	tsp. cayenne
1	tbsp. dried jalapeño peppers

Variation II:

2	sheets nori, slivered
$1/2$	cup pumpkin seeds, toasted
$1/4$	cup dried garlic flakes

Variation III:

2	sheets nori, slivered
$1/4$	cup poppy seeds, toasted
$1/2$	tsp. dry mustard
$1/2$	cup almonds, toasted and finely ground
1	tsp. dried lemon peel
1	tbsp. dried onion flakes

Combine these variations together to create a special taste enhancer that can be sprinkled over your salads. Be creative and make up your own combinations. Toast the nuts and seeds lightly or dehydrate overnight..

Dried Fruit Relish

$1/2$	cup dried apricots
1	cup dried peaches
1	cup dried pears
1	whole orange, peeled
2	tbsp. lemon juice
$1/2$	tsp. allspice or pumpkin pie spice

Soak dried fruit for about six hours. Drain and mince into very fine pieces by hand. Process remaining ingredients with $1/2$ cup of the minced fruit. Mix this purée with remaining minced fruit. Refrigerate. For variation, include orange rind.

Cucumber Relish

3	cucumbers, peeled and minced
1	red pepper, seeded and chopped
1	leek (white part only) or 2 shallots, sliced
	juice of 2 lemons
1/2	cup fresh cilantro or parsley, chopped
2	medjool dates, pitted (optional)
1	stalk celery, chopped
2	tbsp. Braggs
	dash cayenne

Process all ingredients except cucumbers until well combined. Mix in cucumbers and let sit one hour before serving. Do not over process the vegetables. You should end up with finely minced relish ingredients.

Triple Onion Relish

1	small red onion
1	small bermuda onion
1	bunch scallions
	juice of 1 lemon
1	tsp. dried orange peel
1	tsp. pizza seasoning
	dash cayenne
1	tsp. herbamare
2	tbsp. extra virgin olive oil
1/4	cup fresh parsley, minced

Peel and mince onions. Mince scallions. Combine all ingredients together and let sit for at least two hours before serving. Store in refrigerator.

Onion Chutney

1	large apple
1	large bermuda onion
1	jalapeño pepper, minced
	juice of 1 lemon
2	tbsp. maple syrup
2	tbsp. Braggs

Peel, core and mince apple. Peel and process onion with S blade until minced. Add remaining ingredients and process for a few more seconds until well combined. Let sit for two days before serving.

Carrot Relish

2	carrots
4	shallots
2	medjool dates, pitted
1	orange, seeded
1/4	cup fresh parsley
1/2	inch piece fresh ginger, peeled
1	tsp. Braggs

Process all with the S blade until well combined. Let sit for one hour before serving. Refrigerate. Remove orange peel for variation.

Cranberry Walnut Relish

1	cup cranberries
1/2	cup walnuts
1	orange, peeled
4	stalks celery, chopped
1/2	cup dates, pitted
1	tsp. pumpkin pie spice
1	tsp. Braggs

Put all ingredients in food processor with S blade and blend together into a coarsely chopped mixture. Chill and serve. This is delicious!

Mint Relish

1	cup fresh mint
1	yellow onion, sliced
1/2	cup fresh parsley
2	medjool dates, pitted
	juice of 1 lemon
1	tbsp. Braggs

Process all ingredients with S blade until well combined. Let sit for one hour before serving. Refrigerate.

PLEASE NOTE:
The recipes on this page take liberties with the laws of food combining.

Apple Raisin Cranberry Relish

2	apples, peeled and cored
1	cup raisins, soaked and drained
1	cup cranberries
	juice of 1 lemon
1	tsp. pumpkin pie spice

Process apples and cranberries with S blade until coarsely chopped. Combine all ingredients and let sit overnight in the refrigerator before eating.

Red Pepper Salsa

6	red peppers, chopped
3	cloves garlic, minced
2	jalapeño peppers, seeded
1	red onion, chopped
	juice of 1 lemon
$1/2$	cup fresh cilantro, chopped
1	tsp. ground cumin
1	yellow squash, chopped
$1/2$	ripe avocado, peeled and mashed
	Braggs

Process all ingredients together until they are finely minced, but not puréed. Add Braggs to taste and chill. For hotter salsa, add another jalapeño pepper.

Tomato Salsa

4	ripe tomatoes, chopped
1	onion, chopped
	juice of 1 lemon
	juice of 1 lime
1	tsp. cayenne
	Braggs
$1/2$	cup fresh cilantro

Process all ingredients with S blade until combined but still chunky. Add hot dried chili pepper flakes instead of the cayenne for a twist. If you do not have vine-ripened juicy tomatoes, you will need to add some tomato juice to help create a sauce.

Curried Salad Dip

1	red pepper, seeded and chopped
1	cucumber, peeled and sliced
1	stalk celery, chopped
1	clove garlic, minced
2	scallions, minced
1	tsp. curry
2	tbsp. fresh parsley, minced
1	tsp. Braggs
1	cup almond mayonnaise

Process first three ingredients with S blade until finely minced. Mix into mayonnaise. Add remaining ingredients and mix well. Serve with raw vegetable sticks.

Avocado Dip

2	ripe avocados, mashed
$1^1/2$	cups red pepper salsa
	Braggs

Combine avocados and salsa. Add Braggs to taste. Serve with an array of raw vegetable sticks for dipping. Substitute tomato salsa for red pepper salsa as a variation.

Pickled Cucumbers

$1^1/2$	lb. pickling cucumbers
1	large yellow onion
	Braggs
1	tsp. mustard seeds
1	cinnamon stick
$1/4$	tsp. celery seed
$1/2$	tsp. whole cloves

Clean and slice cucumbers and onions and marinate in Braggs for one hour. Drain and set aside. Boil cinnamon, celery seed, mustard, and cloves for 15 minutes in one cup water to release flavors. Strain and add liquid to vegetables. Let sit in a covered jar in the refrigerator for one day before serving. Add sweetener to achieve a sweet pickle for a variation. Add a dash of cayenne for a hot, sweet pickle.

Dilled Horseradish Dip

1   tsp. fresh horseradish, grated
1   clove garlic
1/4   cup fresh dill, chopped
1   stalk celery, chopped
1   cup almond mayonnaise
1   tsp. Braggs

Process all ingredients except mayonnaise until combined. Mix into mayonnaise. Serve chilled. For a milder taste, cut back on the horseradish or use a commercially prepared product.

Corn Relish

4   ears corn, decobbed
1   cup cabbage
1   red pepper
2   stalks celery
2   scallions
1   tsp. pumpkin pie spice
      Braggs

Mince pepper, celery, cabbage and scallions. Combine all ingredients, adding Braggs to taste. Substitute five-spice powder for pumpkin pie spice. Add a little olive oil for extra flavor.

Tomato Chutney

4   large ripe tomatoes
1   apple, peeled and cored
1   onion, minced
1   pear (ripe), seeded
1/4   cup lemon juice
2   tsp. Braggs
2   tbsp. pickling spices

If you drop the tomatoes in boiling water for just a few seconds, the skins will crack and peel off easily. Process the apple and pear with S blade, leaving a chunky consistency. Process the tomatoes separately. Combine all ingredients and mix well. Let sit several hours before serving.

Homemade Curry Powder

2   tbsp. coriander
1   tbsp. cardamon
1   tbsp. tumeric
1   tbsp. cumin
2   tsp. cayenne
1   tsp. cinnamon
1   tsp. cloves

Mix all finely ground spices together. Store in refrigerator.

Refreshing Cucumber Dip

2   cucumbers, peeled and diced
1/2   tsp. dried peppermint or 1 tbsp. fresh mint
1   clove garlic, minced
1   cup almond mayonnaise
1   tbsp. lime juice
1   tsp. herbamare
1/4   tsp. cayenne

Mix all ingredients together and serve with your favorite vegetables. Substitute dill for mint as a variation.

Spicy Rainbow Relish

1   red pepper
2   stalks celery
1/2   head red cabbage
1   head fennel
1   jicama
1   small yellow onion
1/4   tsp. ground ginger
1   tsp. cinnamon
1   tsp. curry
1/8   tsp. cloves
      Braggs

Clean and chop each vegetable. Process separately with S blade until finely minced. Combine all ingredients and add Braggs to taste. Let the relish sit overnight in the refrigerator to combine flavors.

CONTENTS
TASTY DEHYDRATES

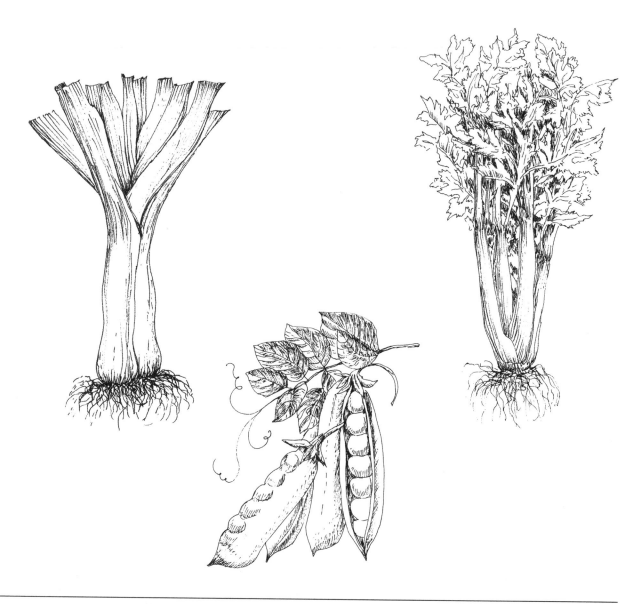

Tasty Dehydrates

Dehydrating provides us with a connection between the worlds of cooked and raw foods. It is a method of preservation that helps retain food enzymes and nutrients. This process removes enough water to prevent growth of bacteria, yeast, and mold. The ph factor of the food determines how much moisture must be removed. High-acid fruits unlike low-acid vegetables can retain 15-20% water. They will be softer, more pliable and wonderfully chewy. Vegetables should be brittle and have no more than a 5% moisture content but pay attention to the process. Be careful not to overdry your foods. The longer the drying time, the more nutrients, flavor, texture and color are lost.

In order for fruits to dehydrate properly, you must perforate the skin to allow the moisture to escape. This is accomplished by slicing, halving, pitting, or dipping the fruit in boiling water long enough to open the skins. It's a good idea to dry your own fruits because many commercial growers use chemicals such as lye for perforating skins to prepare the fruit for drying. Other commercial methods used to preserve fruits include coating them with sulfur dioxide, sodium bisulfite and/or refined sugar. Needless to say, these additives retard spoilage, do not enhance your health. If you purchase dried fruits in the health food store, be sure to read the labels carefully.

When processing your own fruits it is necessary to wash them well, throw away any bruised or rotten pieces and remove the skin if you prefer a more tender product. Fill your dehydrator with similarly cut pieces and keep an eye on their progress. Once the dehydrator is filled, do not add more fresh fruit at a later time because the added moisture will slow down the process for the first batch. When dehydrating fruits or fruit leathers with a high water content use parchment paper to cover the trays. Do not use tin foil, wax paper or saran wrap. Remember to dehydrate at or below 105° to help preserve enzymes and nutrients. Fruits not recommended for dehydration are avocados, acid fruits, melons and seeded berries unless these berries are used with other fruits. Once your fruit is dried, be sure to cool it completely before packaging. If you are using home-grown organic fruits and want to prevent spoilage from insect contamination, you have the option to freeze your fruit for two days before storing. Keep these foods in airtight glass or plastic containers in the coolest, darkest, driest place you can find. For maximum long-term safekeeping, vacuum sealing is the best procedure with a storage temperature of 60° or below. Dried fruit is adversely affected by light, air, and moisture as are all dehydrated foods. Properly stored, they have a shelf life of 6 to 12 months depending on the quality of preparation and product. Once you understand a few simple rules, dehydration is a rewarding way to preserve bumper crops.

When rehydrating fruits, be prepared to use them in the very near future because they will eventually start to spoil. Keep them refrigerated because reabsorption of moisture can lead to mold and mildew.

Now let's talk about vegetables and how they are best dehydrated. The quality of your fresh vegetable will determine the taste and texture of the finished product. Be sure to wash them well and remove any inedible parts. Cut the vegetables uniformly and fill the dehydrator. Do not disturb the drying process by adding more vegetables at a later time. Interestingly enough, dried vegetables deteriorate at a much faster rate than dried fruits because their increased

zucchini and summer squash paper thin and then marinating in Braggs creates a crisp chip that is guaranteed to please.

Dehydrated vegetables are going to have a tougher texture than fresh or frozen produce. If the fresh vegetable is tender to begin with, the final product will taste better. Drying time and temperature greatly affect the texture. To maintain enzyme activity, dehydrate vegetables at or below 105°. When they are hard and brittle they are ready to remove. The danger of food poisoning from dried vegetables is nil. As I mentioned before, more water needs to be removed from vegetables than fruits. If not properly dried, mold will form on your produce letting you know it is inedible. Completely cool your dried produce before packaging. Freeze two days if you fear insect contamination. For maximum shelf life, store in vacuum-sealed plastic bags. Once you open a sealed bag, use all the contents directly. When exposed to light, air and moisture, the vegetables deteriorate rapidly. Make sure to follow the same storage procedures as for fruits.

Rehydrating vegetables takes longer than fruits because they have lost more moisture. It is better to rehydrate in cool water before adding to hot foods to prevent a tougher texture. Do not allow vegetables to rehydrate unrefrigerated for more than one or two hours. Leave them in the refrigerator until you are ready.

Herbs and spices are fun to dehydrate also. Their concentrated flavors add so much to our recipes. It only takes a few hours. Be sure to dry separately from fruits and vegetables. Increased drying time will dissipate valuable essential oils. It is best to store dried herbs and spices in opaque jars. Protection from heat, light, air and moisture prolongs shelf-life. They will keep up to one year if properly stored. When using dried herbs or spices in place of fresh, a good rule of thumb is to cut back the amount by two thirds.

Now let's discuss dehydrating nuts and seeds. Once harvested they must reach a low moisture content for storage. If they are left in the shell, they can be dried and stored at room temperature for months. If they are both shelled and dried, they should be refrigerated. Most of us do not dry our own harvested nuts and seeds. If you have the opportunity to do so, minor preparation is necessary. Place unshelled nuts and seeds in a tub of water. Throw away the ones that float. Place on trays and dehydrate at 100° for about 12 hours. If they

enzyme activity is not buffered by the higher concentration of sugar and acid found in dried fruits. Therefore, the longer dried vegetables are stored, the less flavor, color, texture and nutrient content remain. You can increase shelf life and retard spoilage by blanching or steaming the vegetables before dehydrating. You will kill enzymes, but this is not the goal. It is best to try and use your supply of dehydrated vegetables within a six month period.

Common sense tells you not to dehydrate vegetables and fruits in the same dehydrator. For example, garlic or onions would not work well with bananas or apples. Vegetables not recommended for dehydrating are artichokes, Brussels sprouts, cucumbers, eggplant, lettuces, potatoes and hard squashes. Dark green leafy vegetables like collard greens, kale, mustard greens, spinach, turnip greens and Swiss chard can be very successfully dehydrated. Remove all of the stems, wash and cut into small pieces, coat with Braggs liquid aminos, and fill the dehydrator. The tastes are unique and these crisp dried vegetables are best eaten immediately upon removal from the dehydrator. If it is humid, they will soak up moisture and lose their crispiness. If you dehydrate for too long, the leaves will crumble, but do not be too concerned. They are great added to soups and salads. Potatoes will turn black if not partially cooked before dehydrating. Even then they have a short shelf life. Add Braggs to broccoli, cauliflower, asparagus, yellow summer squash, and zucchini to improve their flavor and texture when drying. You can let them marinate for an hour or two before dehydrating. Slicing

are shelled, reduce drying time by several hours. The same storage techniques apply here with special attention given to temperature. Because of their high fat content they are more likely to become rancid if left in an inappropriate storage place. They must be kept very cool. Also be sure to package your shelled nuts and seeds separately because they can absorb flavors from other foods. The maximum shelf life of shelled nuts is two months if kept at room temperature.

Look in the source section to find out where you can purchase a dehydrator. Excalibur is a company that carries special kitchen parchment paper as well as reusable dehydrator sheets to cover your dehydrator shelves.

Please remember to soak your nuts and seeds for the following recipes

TASTY DEHYDRATES

Pumpkin Seed Patties

2	cups pumpkin seeds
1/2	cup tahini or pignoli nuts
1/2	red pepper, finely chopped
2	tbsp. dried onion flakes
1	zucchini, shredded
	Braggs
1	tsp. oregano

Process seeds and tahini to a chunky paste using the S blade and adding a little water if necessary. Add remaining ingredients and form into patties to dehydrate. Turn over after 12 hours, if using parchment sheets. Dehydrate one or two days depending on size and thickness.

Sunburgers

2	cups sunflower seeds
1/2	cup carrots
1/2	cup celery
1/2	bunch scallions, sliced
1	red pepper, sliced
1/4	cup fresh basil
1/4	cup fresh parsley
	Braggs

Process all ingredients with S blade. Make patties and dehydrate for two days until dry. Turn them over after one day when dehydrating on a sheet. Don't press the patties down when placing for the first time on an uncovered sheet. They are easier to remove when dried.

Flat Bread

1	cup sprouted rye
1	cup sprouted lentils
1/4	tsp. caraway seeds
1	tsp. dried onion flakes
1	tbsp. Braggs
1/4	cup tahini

Put rye and lentils through Champion with blank blade. Mix in remaining ingredients. Press into patties and dehydrate for one to two days until crisp.

Savory Sprouted Crackers

1/2	cup sprouted rye
1 1/2	cups sprouted wheat
1/2	tsp. fennel seeds
4	scallions, minced
1	tbsp. dried vegetable bouillon.

Put rye and wheat through the champion juicer with the blank blade. Add remaining ingredients. Mix well. Press into thin patties and dehydrate for one to two days until crisp.

Almond Patties

2   cups almonds
1/2   cup tahini
1   cup carrot, shredded
1/4   cup parsley, minced
3   scallions, minced
1   clove garlic
         Braggs

Process almonds with tahini using the S blade. Blend to a paste, adding Braggs, garlic, parsley, and a little water if necessary. Scoop out and mix with carrots and scallions. Form patties and dehydrate. Substitute walnuts for almonds. Turn over after 12 hours if you are using parchment sheets to cover the shelves. Dehydrate one or two days depending on thickness. Nut and/or seed patties usually take two days. I like them very dry and crispy.

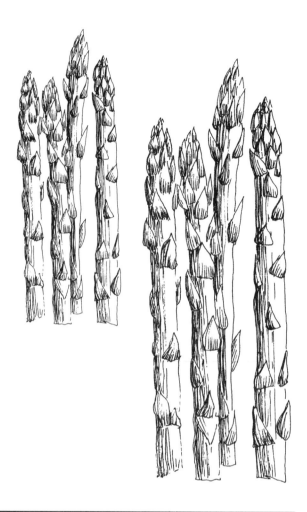

Pizzazz Rye Crisps

3   cups sprouted rye,
2   tbsp. Braggs
1   clove garlic
1/2   tsp. caraway seeds
         mushrooms
         red onions
         red peppers
         zucchini
         fresh or dried oregano and basil

Blend first four ingredients together with enough water to create a thick creamy, pancake-like batter. Pour onto dehydrator screens covered with parchment paper. Try to spread batter evenly. Take thinly sliced vegetables and place on top of the batter like creating a pizza. Sprinkle with oregano and basil and dehydrate at 105° for one day. If batter is very thick, it may take two days to dehydrate. When pouring batter on sheet, don't overpour or it will run off the paper and make a sticky mess in your dehydrator. This is exceptional with pignoli sunflower topping. Spread the purée over the top of the pizza and dehydrate another four to six hours.

Pignoli-Sunflower Topping

1   cup pignoli nuts
1   cup sunflower seeds
1   clove garlic
         Braggs

Blend all ingredients with enough water to make a very thick pourable purée. Pour some over rye crisps and dehydrate about four to six hours before serving.

Variations for toppings:

Cauliflower or broccoli slices
finely minced scallions
thinly sliced yellow squash or peppers
dried thyme or pizza seasoning
poppy seeds or sesame seeds
dried garlic or onion flakes
shredded fennel or sunchokes

Sprouted Chickpea Patties

1 1/2	cups sprouted chickpeas
1	cup sprouted rye
1	clove garlic
3/4	tsp. curry
2	tbsp. fresh dill
	Braggs
	tahini

Process all ingreditents with S blade until well combined and sticky. Add tahini if necessary to help hold patties together. Make patties and dehydrate until crisp. Use leftover hummus to make dehydrated patties as well. It takes about two days.

Vegetable Patties

2	cups sprouted wheat
1/2	yellow squash
2	stalks celery
1/2	small red onion
1/2	carrot
2	tbsp. fresh basil
	Braggs
	tahini

Clean and chop the vegetables. Process all ingredients with S blade until sticky. Add tahini to help mixture stick together. Form into patties and dehydrate for one to two days until crisp.

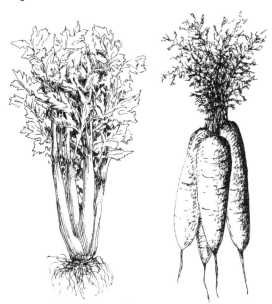

Rehydrated Vegetable Salad

2	red peppers
1	bermuda onion
1	zucchini
1	yellow squash
1/2	tsp. Italian seasoning
1	tbsp. extra virgin olive oil
1	cup mung bean sprouts
	juice of 1 lemon
	Braggs to taste

Clean and slice vegetables. Dehydrate peppers, onion, zucchini, and yellow squash until crisp. (Whenever I have extra vegetables in the refrigerator or if I know I'm going away for a few days, I'll dehydrate for future use.) Later on soak the dried vegetables for 30 minutes until soft and then drain. Add remaining ingredients and serve. Add more fresh vegetables to this salad for a variation.

Vegetable Kebabs

4	mushrooms
1	zucchini
1/2	cauliflower
1	red pepper
2	carrots
1	onion
2	inch piece fresh ginger, peeled
2	cloves garlic
1/2	cup Braggs
2	cups water
1/2	tsp. cayenne
1	tsp. each dried basil and oregano

Clean and cut first six vegetables into chunks. Blend remaining ingredients and pour over vegetables in bowl. Marinate overnight in refrigerator. Put onto wooden skewers and dehydrate for 24 hours.

CONTENTS
UNIQUE DESSERTS

Unique Desserts

Wonderfully healthy desserts are created in this chapter by using the main ingredients of nuts, seeds and fruits. Fresh fruits and their juices along with dried fruits are united to create different flavors and textures. If you purchase organic fruits try to include the skin of the fruit when appropriate because of its nutrient content. Some recipes call for dried fruits to be soaked in order to create a softer consistency and others require a chewy dried texture. I will indicate when they should be rehydrated.

All nuts and seeds should be soaked for the proper amount of time so the enzyme inhibitors are fully dissipated. Moreover, this procedure improves compatibility with fruits.

For concentrated sweeteners, I often use a particular variety of dates called medjool dates because of their moistness and taste. It is not necessary to soak them. If you use other varieties you may have to rehydrate. I recommend the use of 100% pure maple syrup because it is one of the most natural and least harmful sweeteners. Try stevia extract, a natural herbal sweetener to see if you find the flavor exceptable.

For me, cookies have taken on a whole new meaning now that I am using a dehydrator to dry different combinations of fruits, nuts and seeds. These cookies are quick, easy and a lot more healthful than traditional ones. Refined flours and sweeteners along with refined fats and oils lead to ill-combined, mucous-forming, enzymeless, hard-to-digest desserts. We want to avoid this. Try the dehydrator method. Your taste buds and your tummy will appreciate it.

To say a few words about coconut, it is best to use it fresh and not dried. Because of the high oil content, commercially dried coconut is often rancid due to improper long term storage. Substitute dried coconut only when fresh is not available. You can also dry your own. Coconut meal is a party food and is not recommended for daily consumption.

Carob is a sweet tropical fruit that is ground into a powder and used as a substitute for chocolate or cocoa. (Chocolate is high in sugar, fats, cholesterol and a stimulant similar to caffeine. It is not recommended.) Carob is the seed pod of an evergreen tree. It is the pod rather than the seed that is used to actually make carob (also called St. John's bread or lo-

cust bean). The seeds of the pod are used to make locust bean gum, a food additive. Carob is an incomplete protein rich in potassium and calcium and low in fat. It is usually sold in roasted form. (It gets its other name, St. John's bread, because the Bible speaks of John the Baptist eating husks that many believe were carob pods.)

When purchasing extracts, read the labels and be sure to buy the real thing and not an imitation flavor. They are cheaper, but are harmful to your health. Rice syrup, barley malt, psyllium seed and tahini can be found at the health food store. Frontier Herbs is a company listed in the source section that carries natural extracts, wonderful spices, raw carob, citrus peels, psyllium seed powder, and many other ingredients used in this chapter.

The following recipes go from simple to gourmet. Choose your desserts with your condition of health in mind. Desserts should be eaten as a separate meal distanced by about three hours from any other main meal. A standard bundt-pan mold, a 10-inch glass pie plate, an 8-inch square glass pan and a 10-inch springform pan are useful servers to have in your kitchen to make these desserts. I often utilize the above in the following recipes.

Please note: If you are living in a very hot climate, you may want to soak you nuts and seeds in the refrigerator to prevent spoilage.

UNIQUE DESSERTS

Dehydrator Cookies

When making cookies, the goal is to end up with a sticky mixture you can pat into a cookie shape. Add a dash of Braggs to the mixture to bring out more flavor. You will see the possibilities for combinations are endless. To make a tighter cookie, there will be times when you may not want to soak the dried fruit. Some varieties must be soaked to soften in order to be able to combine with other ingredients. You can play with the amounts of each ingredient in any of these recipes or leave one ingredient out. I use a food processor with the S blade to make these cookies. First break down the nuts into a chunky texture. Add the fresh and/or dried fruit to quickly reprocess until the fruits and nuts are intermingled. Add remaining ingredients and reprocess a few more seconds. Remove and pat into shapes and dehydrate at 105° F for one or two days depending on cookie size and the type of chewiness you desire. The drier they are, the crispier they become and the longer they keep. Cool them completely before packaging. Store in sealed plastic bags in the refrigerator for quick snacks, dessert time or travel food. If your cookies seem too wet or loose you can make one big square cookie on a dehydrator tray covered with parchment paper. Score the cookie with a knife into squares. As it dehydrates it will break into somewhat even pieces. This is also a good method to use if you want to eliminate some dates or other dried fruit to cut down on the sweetness. Stevia extract is a good substitute sweetener for those on a low sugar diet. I hope you find these treats as much fun to eat as they are to make.

For those of you who do not have a dehydrator, eat these cookies in the raw or bake them at a very low temperature until crisp and dry.

Please note: All dried fruit must be pitted although it may not always be mentioned in the recipes.

CAROB COCONUT
1   cup shredded coconut
$1/2$ cup carob
$1/2$ cup dates, pitted
$1/2$ cup orange juice
1   tsp. orange peel

PECAN FIG
2   cups figs, stems removed
1   cup pecans
1   tsp. cinnamon
2   tbsp. lemon juice

DATE FILBERT
2   cups dates, pitted
2   cups filberts
1   tbsp. pumpkin pie spice

SUNFLOWER POPPY
1   cup sunflower seeds
$1/2$ cup shredded coconut
$1/2$ cup pumpkin seeds
$1/2$ cup poppy seeds
1   cup dates, pitted

PAPAYA PIGNOLI
1   cup rehydrated papaya pieces, unsweetened
1   cup pignoli nuts
$1/2$ cup shredded coconut

ALMOND FILBERT
1   cup almonds
1   cup filberts
1   cup dates, pitted
1   tbsp. orange peel
1   tbsp. vanilla extract

COCONUT FIG
2   cups shredded coconut
1   cup orange juice
$1/2$ cup dried figs, stems removed
$1/2$ tsp. cinnamon

SUNFLOWER TAHINI
2 cups sunflower seeds
$1/2$ cup tahini
$1/2$ cup dates, pitted
$1/4$ cup dried currants
1 tsp. pumpkin pie spice

CAROB WALNUT
1 cup carob
1 cup walnuts
$1/2$ cup shredded coconut
$1/2$ cup dates, pitted

PUMPKIN PEAR
2 cups pumpkin seeds
1 cup dried pears
$1/2$ cup raisins
$1/2$ tsp. cinnamon

WALNUT RAISIN
2 cups walnuts
1 cup raisins
juice of 1 orange
1 tsp. dried orange peel

BANANA PECAN
2 cups pecans
1 cup dried bananas
$1/2$ cup raisins
$1/2$ tsp. cinnamon

APPLE PRUNE
1 cup dried prunes, pitted
1 cup dried apples
1 cup brazil nuts
2 tbsp. lemon juice

APRICOT ALMOND
$1 1/2$ cups dried apricots
1 cup almonds
$1/2$ cup dates, pitted
$1/2$ tsp. cinnamon

FLAXSEED COCONUT
$1/2$ cup flaxseed
1 cup shredded coconut
$3/4$ cup dates, pitted
enough orange juice to bind

Nutola
1 cup almonds
$1/2$ cup coconut, shredded
$1/4$ cup currants
1 cup dried apples, chopped
1 tsp. cinnamon

Dehydrate soaked almonds for one day. Coarsely chop. Mix with remaining ingredients and eat in place of traditional granola. You can use other combinations of dried nuts and fruits. Keep refrigerated.

Basic Crust Recipe

$1 1/2$- 2 cups nuts and/or seeds
$1/2$ cup medjool dates, raisins, and/or figs
$1/2$- 1 tsp. cinnamon or other spice
1 tsp. Braggs (optional)
1 tsp. orange or lemon rind (optional)

You can create many different crusts in minutes. I use dates most often, but use any dried fruit you like. Nutmeg, pumpkin pie spice, allspice, five-spice powder, and cloves are interchangeable. Braggs enhances flavor and the rind adds zest. Process nuts with the S blade to a coarse meal. For this recipe you do not want to soak the dried fruit. It will make a mushy crust. Be careful not to overprocess. Combine all. Press into crust form. For another dimension, dehydrate the soaked nuts one day before adding to the recipe. You can freeze pies for future use or cut recipe in half for two people. For variation, omit dates and add $1/4$ cup maple syrup. The nuts should still stick together enough to create a crust. If not, add a little psyllium to help. As I indicated in the recipe ingredients, use seeds instead of nuts or a combination of both. Excess moisture should be fully removed from the nuts and seeds before processing into crust.

Basic Fresh Fruit Pie

3	cups fresh fruit, sliced
1	cup apple juice
3	tbsp. agar flakes
1	tbsp. kuzu powder dissolved in $1/4$ cup water
$1/2$	tsp. cinnamon
$1/4$	cup maple syrup (optional)
1	tsp. vanilla extract
1	basic crust

Pile your sliced fruit into the crust. Heat agar flakes in juice until dissolved. Add kuzu mixture to thicken for a few seconds. Add cinnamon and vanilla extract. Pour over fruit and chill until firm. Apple juice is good to have on hand when you need to put a pie together for friends or family at a moment's notice. Most health food stores also have a selection of exotic juice blends for that unusual flavor addition on a special occasion.

Variation:

4	cups fresh fruit, sliced
$1/2$	cup fruit juice
$1/2$	cup dates, pitted
4	tbsp. psyllium powder
$1/2$	tsp. cinnamon
1	basic crust

Take one cup of the fresh fruit and combine it with the remaining ingredients in a food processor with the S blade. Blend it well and mix it with the the rest of the fresh fruit. Press all into the basic crust. Garnish with additional nuts, seeds or fruit. Chill several hours and serve. Psyllium is the ingredient that soaks up the extra liquid when you think the pie filling won't hold together. When purchasing psyllium at the health food store, try to get the powdered form. It is more refined for desserts. Add more powder if you think you need to, but be careful. It can ruin the taste of the pie.

Mincemeat Pie

1	apple
1	ripe pear
$1/2$	cup raisins
$1/4$	cup currants
$1/2$	cup dried figs, stems removed
$1/2$	cup dried unsweetened papaya
1	cup fresh cranberries
$1/4$	cup fresh orange juice
2	tbsp. dried orange peel
1	tbsp. fresh lemon juice
1	tbsp. pumpkin pie spice
$1/8$	tsp. nutmeg
$1/4$	tsp. cloves
1	tbsp. Braggs
2	tbsp. psyllium powder
1	basic crust

Core the apple and pear. Chop into very small pieces. Soak the raisins, currants, papaya and figs several hours to soften. Drain. Coarsely chop the cranberries in a food processor with S blade. Do the same with the dried fruit. Combine all the ingredients together. Mix well. Add a little more psyllium to hold filling together if necessary. Press into a basic crust. Chill. Press this into a bundt mold to create a raw fruit cake as well.

Apple Pie

7-9	apples
$1/2$	cup dates, pitted
1	tbsp. fresh lemon peel
2	tsp. pumpkin pie spice
	juice of 1 lemon
1	tbsp. psyllium powder
2	cups walnuts
$1/2$	cup dates, pitted
1	tsp. cinnamon
1	tsp. Braggs

I prefer to use Granny Smith apples but any apple will do. Core the apples, peel and then slice thinly. Take one cup of the apples and process with the dates, spice, lemon and psyllium. Mix into the sliced apples. Prepare the crust with remaining ingredients and press into pie plate. Pat apples into pie shell. Garnish with walnuts lined around outside of pie plate and chill.

Guava Banana Pie

6	ripe bananas, sliced
1 1/2	cups guava juice
1/4	cup lime juice
2	tbsp. kuzu dissolved in 1/4 cup water
2	tbsp. agar flakes
1/4	cup maple syrup (optional)
2	cups almonds
1/2	tsp. cinnamon
1/2	cup dates, pitted
1	tsp. Braggs

Process last four ingredients until coarsely ground. Press into pie shell. Add bananas. Set aside. Heat guava juice with agar flakes until dissolved. Add kuzu and mix until thickened. Combine with remaining ingredients and pour over bananas. Chill until set before serving. Use more bananas if necessary to fill pie plate.

Waikiki Pineapple Pie

1	large ripe pineapple
2	tbsp. kuzu dissolved in 1/4 cup water
1/4	cup maple syrup (optional)
1	tbsp. lemon juice
1	tsp. fresh lemon grind
1	tsp. Braggs
1	cup apple juice
1 1/2	tbsp. agar flakes
2	cups brazil nuts
1/2	cup dates, pitted
1/2	tsp. each of cinnamon and orange peel dash Braggs

Process last four ingredients with S blade until coarsely chopped but well combined. Press into pie shell. Peel, core and slice pineapple. Layer into pie shell. Heat apple juice with agar flakes until dissolved. Add kuzu and thicken. Mix in remaining ingredients. Pour over pineapple. Chill until firm and serve. If the pineapple is properly ripened, it is sugar sweet and maple syrup is not necessary.

Excellent Key Lime Pie

2	cups almond cream
3	tbsp. agar flakes
2	tbsp. kuzu dissolved in 1/4 cup water
1/2	cup maple syrup
	juice of 4 large or 6 small limes
1 1/2	tbsp. psyllium powder
1	basic crust

Prepare almond cream ahead of time. Chill. Heat agar in one cup of water until dissolved. Add kuzu and mix well. Remove from heat and chill. Combine almond cream, agar mixture, maple syrup, lime juice and psyllium in food processor with S blade. Pour into pie shell and chill until firm. Almond cream recipe is on the following page.

Key Lime Mango Pie

3	cups fresh ripe mango
	juice of 3 limes (1/3 cup)
1/3	cup apple juice
4	tbsp. psyllium seed powder
1/2	tsp. cinnamon
1/4	tsp. nutmeg
1	basic crust
	kiwi fruit garnish

Peel, pit and slice mango. Mix all the ingredients together in a bowl until well combined. Press into crust and chill until set before serving. Garnish with kiwi slices surrounding the pie plate.

Strawberry Almond Pudding

1 1/2	cups almond cream
2	cups ripe strawberries, stemmed
1/4	cup maple syrup
2	tbsp. agar flakes
1	tbsp. lemon juice

Dissolve agar in 1/2 cup water by heating gently. Set aside. Mash strawberries. Mix all ingredients together and spoon into cups. Chill two hours before serving. You can whip this pudding and re-chill for a varied consistency. Almond cream recipe is on the following page.

Almond Cream

2	cups blanched almonds
3	tbsp. agar flakes
1	tsp. Braggs
1/3	cup maple syrup
1	tbsp. vanilla extract
1	tbsp. kuzu dissolved in 1/4 cup water

Heat agar in one cup water until dissolved. Add remaining ingredients except almonds and simmer one minute. Let cool. Liquefy all ingredients in a blender. Chill and blend again before serving. Serve over fresh strawberries for an excellent taste treat. Store in refrigerator.

Papaya Passion

2	cups fresh papaya purée
4	tbsp. psyllium powder
1	cup unsweetened dried papaya pieces
	kiwi slices (optional)
2	cups pecans
1/2	cup dates, pitted
1	tsp. Braggs
1/2	tsp. cinnamon

Soak papaya five hours. Combine last four ingredients and press into pie plate. Mix remaining ingredients with drained papapa pieces.

If this filling is not sweet enough, add some puréed dates. Fill pie plate and chill until firm. You can vary the recipe using two cups banana slices and one cup papaya purée. Decorate with kiwi slices surrounding the pie plate. Add a little more psyllium if necessary to hold pie together.

Apricot Pudding

2	cups almond cream
1	cup dried apricots

Rehydrate apricots four hours. Drain. Blend with almond cream to make a thick pudding. Pour into parfait cups and chill. Instead of blending together, you can layer alternately almond cream and apricot purée. Almond cream recipe is above.

Sweet Potato Pie

6	medium sweet potatoes (or yams)
1/2	cup dates, pitted
1/2	cup pignoli nuts
1	tsp. coriander
1/2	tsp. 5-spice powder
2	tbsp. psyllium powder
2	cups walnuts
1/2	cup dates, pitted
1/2	tsp. 5-spice powder
1	tsp. Braggs

Process last four ingredients with S blade. Press into pie shell. Set aside. Peel and slice sweet potatoes. Put through Champion juicer alternating with nuts and dates using blank blade. You should end up with approximately three cups potato purée. Add remaining ingredients to mixture. Mix well. Press into pie shell. Garnish with pignoli nuts around outside edge of pie and chill. The champion juicer is a necessary tool for the success of this pie.

Pignoli Cream

1	cup pignoli nuts
1	tbsp. psyllium powder
2	tbsp. maple syrup
1/4	cup water
1	tsp. vanilla extract

Blend into a cream and use as a topping for any number of desserts.

Poppyseed Strudel

1	cup poppy seeds
1/2	cup currants
1/2	cup figs, stemmed
1	tbsp. dried orange rind
1	tsp. Braggs
1	basic crust

Blend seeds and figs in food processor with S blade. Mix in currants, rind, and Braggs. Press basic crust into 8" x 8" pan. Top with poppyseed mixture. Press firmly and chill. Cut into squares.

Strawberry Pie

3	pints strawberries
1/2	ripe pineapple
1/2	cup apple juice
1/2	cup dates, pitted
1	tbsp. dried orange peel
1	tsp. cinnamon
4	tbsp. psyllium powder
1	basic crust
	pignoli cream topping (optional)

Clean and slice strawberries. Peel, core and chop pineapple. Blend one cup strawberries with juice, dates, peel, cinnamon and psyllium. Mix all ingredients. Press into crust. Chill until set. Serve with pignoli cream (recipe on page 114).

Pignoli Peach Sherbet

2	cups pignoli cream
3	large ripe peaches, peeled and pitted
1/4	cup maple syrup
2	tbsp. psyllium seed powder

Blend peaches, maple syrup and psyllium. Mix with pignoli cream (recipe on page 114) and freeze in an ice cube tray. You can try almond cream or substitute other ripe sweet fruits. Put the frozen mixture through the Champion juicer with blank blade for a delicious treat.

Spiced Pignoli Topping

1	cup pignoli nuts
3	tbsp. maple syrup or 2 pitted dates
1/2	tsp. pumpkin pie spice
1/2	tsp. Braggs
1	tsp. dried orange rind
1	tbsp. vanilla extract
1/4	cup orange juice

Combine all ingredients in a processor with the S blade. Blend until creamy. For a thinner cream or a sauce, add more fresh orange juice to desired consistency. Serve over a fresh fruit salad.

Blueberry Pie

3	pints fresh blueberries
1/2	cup orange juice
1/2-3/4	cup dates, pitted
4	tbsp. psyllium powder
1/2	cup coconut, shredded
1	tbsp. lemon juice
1	tsp. cinnamon
1	cups pecans
1/2	cup almonds
1/2	cup dates, pitted
1/2	tsp. pumpkin pie spice
1	tsp. Braggs

Clean blueberries. Set aside. Process last five ingredients with S blade to a coarse meal. Press into pie plate. Take one cup blueberries and combine with remaining ingredients in a processor using the S blade. Mix together with remaining blueberries. It may be necessary to use more dates if berries are sour. Press into crust and chill. Garnish with whole pecans lined around the outside of the pie plate.

Banana Coconut Cream Pie

6	ripe bananas (large)
3/4	cup dates, pitted
2	cups coconut, shredded
1/4	cup water
1/4	cup orange juice
1	tbsp. dried orange peel
1/2	tsp. Braggs
1	cup almond cream
1 1/2	cups pecans
1/2	cup dates, pitted
1	tsp. psyllium powder
1/2	tsp. cinnamon

Process last four ingredients with S blade and press into pie plate. Process coconut with dates, water, juice, peel and psyllium to make a creamy paste. Layer three whole sliced bananas into crust. Then add half the coconut cream. Spread over top. Follow with 1/2 cup almond cream (recipe on page 114). Then three more whole sliced bananas. Smooth over the rest of the coconut mixture. Top with the remaining almond cream. Chill and serve. Cut small pieces. It's rich. If using dried coconut, cut back to 1 1/2 cups and increase water to one cup.

Tahini Cream Cheese Cake

1 1/2	cups raw tahini
1/2	cup maple syrup
4	tbsp. agar flakes
2	cups ripe fruit, sliced
1	cup apple juice
1	tbsp. agar flakes
1	tsp. kuzu dissolved in 2 tbsp. water

Dissolve four tablespoons agar in one cup boiling water until clear. Blend with tahini and syrup. Spread tahini over the bottom of a springform pan. Chill until firm. Top with sliced ripe fruit. Dissolve one tablespoon of agar in apple juice. Mix in kuzu. Pour over fruit and chill again until firm.

Pignoli Cheese Cake

3	cups pignoli nuts
1	tsp. orange rind
1	cup coconut, shredded
1/2	cups dates, pitted
4	tbsp. agar flakes
2	cups apple juice
1/4	cup maple syrup

Process coconut, orange rind and dates with S blade until combined and press into a springform pan. Heat agar in apple juice until agar is completely dissolved. Blend the nuts, agar mixture and syrup together. Pour over crust in springform and chill until firm.

Date Pecan Rolls

2	cups pecans
1	cup dates, pitted
1	tsp. lemon rind
1	tbsp. orange rind
1	tsp. Braggs
1	cup coconut, shredded(optional)

Put pecans into a processor with the S blade and chop. Add dates, rinds and Braggs. Blend until combined but not mushy. Form into log shapes and roll in coconut. Store in refrigerator as a sweet treat. Substitute carob for coconut.

Walnut Poppyseed Cake

1	cup poppy seeds
2	cups walnuts
1	cup dates, pitted
2	cups carrot purée
2	tbsp. dried orange peel
1	tbsp. Braggs
2	tbsp. psyllium seed powder

Put enough carrots to make two cups of purée through the Champion juicer with blank blade . Chop walnuts into a fine consistency in the food processor with the S blade. Set aside. Combine carrot purée and remaining ingredients in processor until well blended. Mix all ingredients together. Add a little more psyllium if necessary to hold cake together. Press into bundt pan and chill to set.

Pineapple Pignoli Cake

3	cups pignoli nuts
1/2	cup maple syrup
1/4	tsp. orange extract
1/2	tsp. pumpkin pie spice (optional)
1/2	tsp. Braggs
1	tbsp. orange rind, grated
3	tbsp. psyllium seed powder
2	cups ripe pineapple, sliced
2	cups apple juice
3	tbsp. agar flakes

Combine nuts, syrup, extract, spice, Braggs, rind and psyllium powder in a food processor with the S blade until creamy. Press into a 10 inch springform pan and chill. Heat agar in one cup apple juice until clear. Mix in remaining juice and pineapple. Chill until it starts to gel and add to springform. Smooth over pignoli mixture and refrigerate until firm.

Apple Pear Torte

.3	cups apples
3	cups pears
3	tbsp. psyllium seed powder
1	tbsp. fresh lemon peel, grated
1	tbsp. vanilla extract
	juice of 2 lemons
1	tbsp. pumpkin pie spice
1/2	cup dates, pitted
1	cup pignoli nuts

Process fruit with S blade until chunky but not puréed. Place in bowl. Process dates, lemon juice and nuts into fine paste. Mix all ingredients together. Press into bundt pan mold and chill two hours until set.

Fruity Pecan Ring

2	cups apple juice
2	tbsp. agar flakes
1/2	cup chopped pecans
2	ripe bananas
1	ripe papaya
1	tbsp. fresh ginger juice (optional)

Dissolve agar flakes in one cup apple juice heating gently until dissolved. Add remaining apple juice and ginger juice to agar mixture. Peel and slice bananas. Peel, seed and slice papaya. Layer pecans, bananas and papaya in bundt mold. Pour agar mixture over fruit and chill until firm.

Pineapple Perfection

4	cups fresh ripe sweet pineapple
1	12 oz. bag cranberries
4	large apples, cored
6	tbsp. psyllium powder
1	tsp. Braggs
1	tbsp. pumpkin pie spice
2	tbsp. agar flakes
1/2	cup orange juice

Heat agar in orange juice until dissolved. Process cranberries with S blade until coarsely chopped. Do the same with the pineapple and apples. Combine all, mix well and pour into bundt pan mold. Chill until set and serve.

Spicy Fruit Mold

2	cups apple juice
2	tbsp. agar flakes
5	ripe pears, peeled
1/2	cup walnuts, chopped
1/2	cup raisins
1/2	tsp. pumpkin pie spice
1	tsp. lemon juice
1	tsp. Braggs

Dissolve agar in two cups apple juice by heating gently until dissolved. Cool slightly. Seed and chop pears. Combine all ingredients together and chill in bundt pan mold until set.

Carrot Cake I

5	cups carrots, puréed
2	cups walnuts, finely ground
1	cup dates, pitted
1	tbsp. pumpkin pie spice
3	heaping tbsp. psyllium seed powder
1	tbsp. orange peel, grated

Put carrots and dates through Champion juicer (with blank blade). Mix all ingredients together and press into round mold. Chill two hours before serving. Mixture should be very tight before pressing into mold. Add more psyllium if necessary.

Carrot Coconut Cake

5	cups carrots, puréed
1	cup pignoli nuts
1/4	cup raisins
1/2	cup dates, pitted
1 1/2	cups coconut, shredded
2	tsp. pumpkin pie spice
	grated peel of 1 lemon
3	tbsp. psyllium seed powder

Process carrots with S blade to a fine purée. Set aside. Process pignoli nuts, raisins and dates into a creamy consistency adding a little water to help the blending process. Mix carrots with nut mixture. Add coconut, spice, lemon rind and psyllium. Mix all together and press into mold. Chill two hours or until set.

Cranberry Cake

2	(12 oz.) bags fresh cranberries
4	cups walnuts
2	apples, peeled
2	oranges, seeded
1	cup dates, pitted
1	tbsp. lemon juice
1	tbsp. pumpkin pie spice
4	tbsp. psyllium seed powder

Process cranberries with S blade until coarsely chopped. Set aside. Core apples and process until chopped. Set aside. Peel oranges and section. Put walnuts, oranges and remaining ingredients into processor with S blade. Blend for several seconds. Mix together all ingredients and press into bundt pan mold. Chill for two hours and serve. You can use frozen cranberries if fresh are not available.

Avocado Fruit Mold

4	tbsp. agar flakes
3	cups juice, either apple, orange, or both
1	ripe but firm avocado
1	ripe pear and mango
1	tbsp. lemon juice

Heat one cup juice with agar flakes until they are dissolved. Set aside. Peel and slice avocado and mango. Discard pits. Peel, core and slice pear. Layer fruits in a bundt mold. Add remaining juices to the agar mixture. Pour over fruits. Chill and serve with a decoration of orange slices.

Rainbow Fruit Salad

1	ripe pineapple
1	pint strawberries
4	ripe kiwi fruit
1	ripe mango
1	pint blueberries

Wash fruits well. Peel, core and dice pineapple. Stem strawberries and cut in half. Peel and slice kiwi and mango. Combine all and enjoy a beautiful combination of flavors, colors and textures. For a twist, add an avocado.

Kiwi Orange Aspic

4	ripe kiwi fruit
2	cups fresh orange juice
2	tbsp. agar flakes
1	cup ripe pineapple, sliced
1	navel orange, peeled and sectioned

Dissolve agar flakes in one cup orange juice by heating for several minutes. Set aside. Peel and slice kiwis. Layer pineapple, orange and kiwi in an 8" X 8" serving dish. Add remaining juice to agar mixture and pour over fruit. Chill until set and serve.

French Fruit Torte

2	kiwi, peeled and sliced
1	cup fresh strawberries, sliced
1	cup fresh blueberries
1	cup fresh ripe pineapple, cubed
1 1/2	cups apple juice
2	tbsp. agar flakes
1/2	tsp. cinnamon
1	tbsp. kuzu dissolved in 1/2 cup juice
1	basic crust

Press basic crust recipe into a springform pan. Pile four sections of fruits into each quarter of the pan. Heat agar flakes in apple juice to dissolve. Add remaining ingredients and pour over fruits. Chill until set.

Melon Salad

1	muskmelon
1	cantaloupe
1	honeydew melon
1	santa claus melon
1	persian melon
1	casaba melon
	cinnamon

Take your choice of these melons and combine to your heart's content. Make sure they are truly ripe. Add a dash of cinnamon after you have peeled, seeded and sliced the melons. Combining different melons turns this simple idea into a gourmet meal. Make melon balls for a touch of elegance.

Gingered Fruit Salad

2	apples
1	ripe pear
2	ripe plums
1	tsp. fresh ginger juice
1	orange, peeled and seeded
1	tbsp. maple syrup (optional)
1/2	tsp. fresh orange rind, grated

Put last four ingredients in a blender and liquify. Peel, core and chop fruit. Combine with sauce and let chill before serving.

Mango Peach Jam

1	ripe mango
3	ripe peaches
1/2	tsp. cinnamon
1/4	tsp. nutmeg
	juice on 1 orange
1-2	tbsp. psyllium powder

Peel, remove pits and slice fruits. Process all ingredients with S blade until combined. Don't over process! The more you blend, the less fruit chunks you'll have. Use a whole, peeled orange for a tarter taste.

Orange Coconut Cream

	white meat of 1 fresh coconut
2	cups water
1/4	cup tahini
	juice of 2 oranges
1/2	cup raisins soaked in 3/4 cup water
1/4	tsp. cardamon
1	tsp. Braggs

Blend all ingredients together except the raisin mixture to produce a thick cream. Blend the raisins and 3/4 cup water separately. Chill all ingredients. Swirl the raisin purée into the coconut mixture in a soup bowl and serve. For variation, omit raisins and use as a coconut cream sauce.

Cranberry Conserve

1	lb. cranberries
2	navel oranges or valencias, seeded
8	medjool dates, pitted

Process cranberries with S blade until coarsely chopped and set aside. Process oranges until finely minced. Add dates and blend. Combine all and mix well. Add more dates to increase sweetness. Chill. Try to buy organic oranges since this recipe calls for the use of the orange skin. Omit the skin if you prefer.

Spicy Apple Butter

2	lbs. apples
1	tsp. dried orange rind
1/4	cup fresh orange juice
1	tbsp. psyllium powder
1/2	tsp. pumpkin pie spice

Peel, core and chop apples. Place in food processor with remaining ingredients. Use the S blade to process into a fine cream. Chill and serve. Try substituting ripe pears for the apples. It's even tastier.

Lemon Tahini Custard Parfait

2	cups apple juice
3	tbsp. tahini
	juice on 2 large lemons
1	tbsp. dried orange rind
1	tsp. Braggs
3	tbsp. maple syrup
3	tbsp. agar flakes
1	tbsp. kuzu dissolved in 1/4 cup water

Dissolve agar flakes in one cup apple juice by heating. Add kuzu mixture and let thicken a minute. Combine all ingredients and liquify in blender. Chill and whip again. Pour into parfait cups and chill two hours before serving. Garnish with fresh mint leaves. For a gourmet touch, layer with fresh fruit.

Mint Jelly

2	cups apple juice
2	tbsp. agar flakes
1/2	cup fresh mint leaves
1	tsp kuzu dissolved in 2 tbsp water

Heat the agar flakes in one cup apple juice until dissolved. Add kuzu and stir until clear in color. Add remaining ingredients and blend until smooth. Chill to form a thick jelly.

Sweet Cherry Delight

1	lb. bing cherries
1/2	lb. seedless grapes
2	ripe pears
1/2	tsp. orange extract
1/4	tsp. cinnamon

Wash fruits well. Remove grapes from stems. Pit cherries. Peel, core and slice pear. Liquify all ingredients in blender. Chill before serving in parfait cups.

Carob Pudding

1/2	cup carob powder
1/4	cup medjool dates, pitted
3	large ripe bananas, partially frozen
1	cup pignoli nuts, chilled

Process with S blade into a smooth creamy pudding adding just enough water to reach a thick consistency. Be careful. Don't add too much water. Pour in parfait cups and serve.

Dessert Sauce

1/2	fresh ripe pineapple, peeled and chopped
1	orange, peeled and seeded
1/4	cup fresh cranberries
4	medjool dates, pitted
1	tbsp. psyllium powder

Process all ingredients with S blade until creamy.

Walnut Carob Truffles

2	cups walnuts
2	tbsp. tahini
1/2	cup carob powder
1/3	cup maple syrup
1	tbsp. vanilla extract
1/2	tsp. 5-spice powder
1	tsp. Braggs

Dehydrate soaked walnuts for one day if you can. Process with S blade into a fine meal. Add remaining ingredients and process until mixture sticks together. Add more tahini if necessary. Form into balls and roll in carob.

Almond Coconut Fudge

1/2	cup dates, pitted
2	cups almonds, blanched
1	cup carob powder
1 1/2	cups coconut, shredded
2	tbsp. vanilla extract

Alternately put the almonds and dates through the Champion juicer with the blank blade. Add remaining ingredients. Press into an 8" x 8" glass dish and chill. Cut into squares before serving.

Sweet Seed Balls

1	cup sunflower seeds
2	cups dates, pitted
1/4	cup tahini
1	tbsp. Braggs
1	tbsp. dried orange peel
1	tsp. ginger juice
1	tsp. cinnamon or pumpkin pie spice

If you are able, dehydrate seeds overnight for a roasted flavor. Process all with S blade until well blended. Shape into balls and chill. Add more tahini if mixture is not sticky enough to hold together.

Marzipan

2	cups almonds, blanched
2	cups rice syrup
2	tsp. almond extract
2	tbsp. arrowroot
	shredded coconut

Process all ingredients with S blade to a claylike mixture adding just enough coconut to make a stiff dough. Make balls. Store in covered container in refrigerator. You can use carrot or beet juice to dye the marzipan different colors.

Almond Carob Bars

1 1/2	cups almonds
1/4	cup tahini
1/2	cup barley malt
1	tsp. vanilla
2	tbsp. carob powder
1	tsp. cinnamon
1	tbsp. Braggs

If you can, dehydrate almonds one day to get a roasted flavor. Process almonds with S blade to a fine meal. Add remaining ingredients and process until well combined. Add enough carob to hold together. Shape into bars. Roll in carob powder and chill. Substitute rice syrup for barley malt for variation.

Carob Malted

1/4	cup flax seed
1	cup water
1/2	cup pignoli nuts
2	tbsp. carob
2	tbsp. maple syrup or 4 dates, pitted
1	tsp. vanilla extract

Soak the flax seed in one cup water for 24 hours. Soak and drain pignoli nuts. Add remaining ingredients to this flaxseed mixture and liquify. Chill before serving. You better double this recipe. It's delicious.

Carob Sauce

1/2	cup carob powder
1/4	cup dates, pitted
1	tsp. cinnamon
1	tbsp. vanilla extract
	cold water

Combine all ingredients in a blender and add enough water to make a thick sauce. Add more or fewer dates to reach desired sweetness. Serve over banana ice cream. Substitute apple juice for water.

Strawberry Apple Orange Sauce

1	navel orange, peeled and seeded
1	pint strawberries, stemmed
3	apples, peeled and cored

Starting with strawberries, then orange, then apples, blend on high speed to create a fruit sauce.

Banana Smoothie

1	ripe banana, chilled
1/4	cup sunflower seeds
1	cup fresh papaya, chilled
	dash cinnamon

Blend seeds with one cup cold water. Strain out pulp. Combine liquid with fruits and cinnamon and blend together.

Almond Milk

| 1 | cups almonds |
| 2 | cups ice water |

Liquify and strain through sprout bag for a delicious drink.

Carob Shake

1 1/2   cups almond milk
3   tbsp. carob powder
1   tbsp. maple syrup

Liquify and serve chilled.

Color Decorations for Desserts

orange - add carrot juice
green - add spinach juice
red - add beet juice

This is a great way to color foods for a special party attraction.

Homemade Soda

seltzer
fruit juice of your choice

Pour a glass of seltzer and add some fruit juice to sweeten and flavor it for a healthy alternative to commercial sodas.

Banana Ice Cream

Peel ripe bananas and freeze. Put through Champion juicer with blank blade. To keep ice cream from melting quickly, put all the parts of the juicer in the freezer to chill before preparing banana cream. If you don't have a Champion juicer, use bananas to make frozen smoothies. Add other frozen fruits. Frozen cantaloupe and watermelon with pits and skin removed make delicious sorbets. Make sure the cantaloupe and watermelon are sweet before freezing to insure a tasty treat.

Sweet Seed Milk

1   cup sunflower seeds
1   tbsp. vanilla
   dash cinnamon
2   cups cold water

Blend all ingredients to make a milk. Strain out the pulp. Blend in dates and/or carob powder for sweetness and flavor.

Piña Colada

1/2   cup pignoli nuts
1/4   fresh ripe pineapple, peeled and chopped
1   orange, peeled and seeded
1/4   cup coconut, shredded
1   cup ice water

Put all ingredients in blender with water to make a thick creamy drink. Chill well. Add maple syrup if it is not sweet enough.

Pineapple Punch

1   whole ripe pineapple
   juice of 1 lemon
1   tsp. fresh ginger juice (optional)
1   apple
1   orange, peeled

Chill the fruits. Wash and juice pineapple with the skin as well. Also juice the apple and orange. Mix all ingredients and serve.

Carob Cream Delight

1 1/2   cups piping hot herbal tea
1   tbsp. maple syrup
2   tbsp. carob
2   tbsp. tahini
1/2   tsp. kuzu dissolved in 1/4 cup water

Brew your favorite herbal tea. Thicken with kuzu mixture. Blend together all ingredients and serve hot or cold.

COOKING WITH THE BUFF

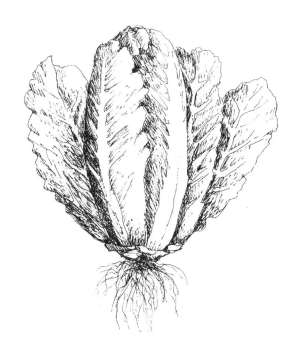

As the pendulum swings from an American-inspired diet high in meats, fats, refined carbohydrates and processed fast foods, to one reliant on whole grains, beans, fresh vegetables, sprouts, seaweeds and fruits, we are beginning to see a resurgence of vegetarian cooking among affluent societies. Over one-third of the world's population is starving and at least half of the people on the planet go to bed hungry. The industry of raising livestock to generate "second-hand nutrition" uses up tremendous amounts of plant sources to nourish the growth of just one carcass. Due to a host of reasons more and more people are turning toward new eating patterns. Aside from religious or philosophical concerns, ecologically, nutritionally and socially, vegetarianism makes sense. No matter what your beliefs are, protecting your health and the health of your loved ones should be the bottom line.

My goal in this section is to present exciting cooked-food alternatives to the typical American diet by choosing wholesome ingredients and demonstrating better cooking techniques. Why eat cooked plant foods? There are several reasons; they satisfy taste desires, help regulate internal energies, provide certain nutritutional benefits and are beneficial for the sake of social interaction. Cooking also removes metabolic inhibitors that hinder digestion, which we know can also be achieved by sprouting.

For those who listen to their bodies, the excess consumption of animal foods, fats and refined carbohydrates will eventually lead to the desire for more nutritious choices. If one engages in an overall cleansing process, which can take years, ample amounts of live sprouts and raw produce together with cooked plant foods comprise a health-enhancing diet. The proportions are up to you and your personal needs. A 50/50 ratio is considered well balanced.

The majority of plant foods have an underlying sweet taste. According to Oriental philosophy, 80% of the meal should allow the natural sweetness of fruits, vegetables, grains and legumes to dominate. The other 20% should share the tastes of bitter, salty, sour and pungent in the side dishes. It sounds complicated, but is really quite simple. Here is an example. The use of salty Braggs or seaweed, raw sauerkraut or pickles, pungent ginger, daikon or garlic together with bitter greens like watercress, dandelion, or arugula will easily round out your meal whether it is cooked or raw. Providing this varied flavor at mealtime is very satisfying.

When planning a dinner I always try to include one leafy vegetable that grows above the ground, one round vegetable that grows on the ground and one root vegetable for balance. Using different cutting and cooking methods for the sake of diversity is important. Slicing, chopping, mincing and the many other ways to cut your vegetables along with blanching, steaming, stir-frying, pressure cooking, baking, pickling and dehydrating all produce different effects and create an overall variety of style.

Try to use quality cookware like heavy stainless steel, cast iron or enamel. Well made pots and pans are expensive but they are worth the investment. European cookers are well designed and constructed and I recommend pots made in Italy. Please note that aluminum cookware is considered highly toxic because the aluminum leaches into your foods. For the serious vegetarian chef, the proper vegetable cutting knife is also important. My favorite is a stainless steel knife with a carbon edge. Carbon holds a better edge while the stainless steel does not rust.

A pressure cooker is not an absolute necessity, but it sure makes working in the kitchen a pleasure. I have several different sizes. A metal plate or flame tamer is also a useful purchase. It is placed between the pot and the stove to help prevent you from burning the food. You must first bring the pot up to pressure before counting cooking minutes. As soon as the pot is pressurized, the heat must be turned down to a low temperature and then the timing process begins. Novices tend to not pay close attention and allow the pot to run on high pressure causing the food to burn. This is where the flame tamer is a valuable tool. It will save many pots of food. Often people are afraid to use these pressurized pots. The latest European models have safety features that make it easy and safe. Any recipe with an asterisk indicates a request for the use of a pressure cooker.

There are a number of salt sources used in the cooked food section. I use Braggs amino acids, tamari, herbamare, umeboshi, miso and plain seasalt. Use them separately or in combination. For example, add a little seasalt first and then some flavorful miso at the end of preparation. The Orientals believe that it is beneficial to add salt sometime during the cooking process, which allows it to be absorbed into the fibers of the plant food. It helps break down the tough walls of cellulose fiber so that nutrients are more easily released and the salt itself is more easily assimilated. In addition, the food will taste better. Moreover, try not to add any extra salt at the dinner table. Salt is an

aid when it is properly used and consumed in moderation.

A beneficial way to add salt along with various flavors to your soups and sauces as well as vegetable, legume and grain dishes is with a product called miso. I have had the pleasure of studying vegetarian cuisine and the uses of miso with Aveline Kushi, Cornelia Aihara, Lima Oshawa, Wendy Esko and Tonia Gagne as well as many other visiting chefs at the Kushi Institute. Miso is a fermented food that is said to contain healthful lactobacillus and enzymes much like raw sauerkraut. It aids digestion and helps build the immune system. Unpasteurized miso is the preferred choice. It is a paste made from various combinations of beans, grains and sea salt and is found in the refrigerated section of the health food store. Soybeans are most often used but there are many other kinds to choose from. Articles have been written about miso having the ability to help eliminate radioactive elements from body tissues. Studies were conducted in Japan after WWII demonstrating the beneficial qualities of hatcho and mugi miso.

Along with miso, the use of garlic and all forms of onions are also prevalent in my cooking. Garlic has a very interesting background history. Both the Greeks and Egyptians thought garlic had supernatural powers. Reputed to scare away vampires, it has been used in generous amounts through the centuries to cure many different ailments. Considered a diuretic, stimulant, expectorant, disinfectant and natural antibiotic, it contains a volatile

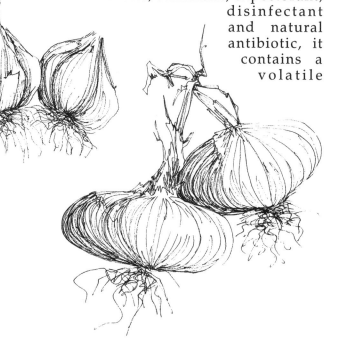

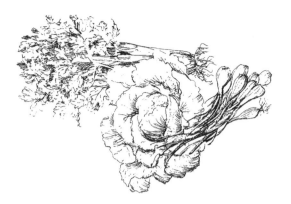

oil rich in sulfur. It promotes perspiration, cleanses the stomach and aids digestion. During the seventeenth century it was credited with saving many from the plague. During WWI it was used in hospitals to bandage wounds. Its antiseptic value for preventing infection was well known among the gypsies of Europe. Its list of uses for different diseases is too numerous to mention. The most outstanding value is twofold: it can reduce blood pressure by opening up the blood vessels and also attacks disease-producing bacteria without destroying normal body flora the way prescribed antibiotics do. Aside from its wonderful therapeutic value it adds incredible flavor to either raw or cooked cuisine.

Onions, like garlic, are considered a natural medicine as well. Both members of the allium family, they contain some similar chemical compounds that help suppress the clumping of platelets and can decrease the possibility of heart thrombosis. Overall, both onions and garlic are good for the circulation. In the 1970's studies revealed that routine consumption of onions helped reduce cholesterol levels by aiding the body in maintaining healthy blood-fat levels. Interestingly enough, research has also indicated that heating onions does not destroy their therapeutic value. Onions have even more to offer. Recent studies have also shown that eating raw onions helps regulate blood sugar levels. Diabetics may be interested in this addition to their diets. In the last decade experimental biologists have reported that onions contain an inhibitor that slows down the growth of cancer. And again, heating or boiling does not destroy the therapeutic value. This all sounds incredible, yet doctors, biologists, and scientists have documented studies demonstrating the versatile therapeutic qualities of the onion. An old wife's tale we've all heard champions the use of chicken soup to clear up colds and check congestion. According to scientific research, it is not the main ingredient of chicken that relieves congestion, but the therapeutic value of eating a hot broth prepared with plenty of onions!

I know you will find this section filled with stimulating recipe ideas that are easy to prepare. Be sure to read each chapter introduction. There is more useful information about recipe ingredients you may not be familiar with and also some ideas for alternative cooking techniques.

In conclusion, cook your foods with happy, peaceful thoughts in mind and learn to trust your creative intuition. The quality of the meal will surely be enhanced. It's a great idea to cook with a hungry eye. If you refrain from sampling often and stay empty, you'll prepare tastier meals and enjoy them more at the dinner table. Quality organic produce and dried goods, as well as the use of food combining and suitable cooking techniques will help maintain a properly nourished, healthy body. Always remember you become what you eat. Your biological destiny depends upon your daily food choices.

*Note: Recipes with an asterisk indicate the recommended use of a pressure cooker.

CONTENTS
SUPERB COOKED SOUPS

Superb Cooked Soups

Geographical location, the different seasons of the year, and even daily climate will help you decide what kind of soup you would like to prepare. For instance, a raw chilled soup for a blazing summer day could turn into a light hot vegetable broth (with a few vegetables to adorn it) on a chilly autumn evening, or be transformed into a heartier, stew-type soup to warm your body on a cold winter's night.

Once you decide what kind of a soup you want to make, the next decision is how you will do it. I often use pressure cookers to create special flavor combinations and to vary textures. Let the vegetables work for you to create soup stocks and vegetable sauces easily. For example, high water content vegetables cooked together make delicious soup bases in a minimal amount of time. Place the vegetables in the pot with little or no water and a salt source of your choice. The pot is brought to pressure and allowed to cook for about ten minutes. It is removed from the stove and the pressure is released. Add water along with seasoning and a garnish to complement the final mixture. The amount of water will control the concentration of flavors as well as the consistency of your soup. Eliminate the addition of water and you will have a delicious sauce.

Be careful about how many vegetables you combine in any one recipe. Your creation can go from dynamic to chaotic. Never eat vegetables that have gone sour. This may be acceptable for grains, but not for vegetables. It is important to thoroughly wash your ingredients to remove small debris, insect larvae, dirt, etc.

The use of salt is particularly important to the preparation of these soups and sauces. Because of its contracting effect, its addition to a pot of vegetables from the start forces the vegetables to release their juices. The pressure cooker is the perfect tool for this technique.

When preparing bean soups in a pressure cooker, soaking and sprouting will change cooking time. For example, sprouted chickpeas pressure cook in 15 minutes, soaked chickpeas in one hour and dry chickpeas take two hours. Since I have become a raw and living foods enthusiast, I want to cut my cooking time to an extreme minimum for the sake of ease and optimum health. It is interesting to note that

sprouting decreases the time necessary to prepare cooked beans.

Pressure cooking should not always be your choice of method. In very hot weather I do not use the pressure cooker as often. However, no matter what type of soup you prepare, you always want to start with a flavorful broth. Serve it with a few vegetables for a light soup or go in another direction by adding cooked grains and/or beans. You have many interesting recipes to choose from in this chapter. Pressure cookers are wonderfully useful for making heartier-style soups and stews with leftovers. First make your soup base and then add yesterday's cooked ingredients. If the beans or grains are dry or hard, add more water and bring the pot back up to pressure for five to ten minutes to soften the mixture. Finish with the seasoning and a garnish.

Adding fresh herbs and minced or shredded raw vegetables for a garnish to plain broths and soups as well as stews adds a final touch of flavor and texture. It is also advantageous because it helps to balance and lighten these cooked meals.

Overall, cooked soups are a pleasing addition to any menu and usually set the whole pace for dining. They relax you and help prepare your digestive juices for the rest of the meal. When planning a dinner, it is customary to choose lighter soups with heavier entrees or serve more substantial soups with salad main courses. My soup recipes travel from America to the Mediterranean to the Orient. A variety of ethnic cuisine helps to keep your family's interest in eating at home.

SUPERB COOKED SOUPS

Autumn Harvest Soup *

1	large onion
2	cloves garlic
1	leek
1	cup Brussels sprouts
2	stalks celery,chopped
1/2	cup cauliflower florets
1/2	small red cabbage
1/2	butternut squash,peeled
	several stalks of kale
1/2	bunch parsley,minced
	barley miso
	herbamare

Clean and wash all vegetables. Chop first three ingredients. Layer onion, garlic and leek in bottom of a pressure cooker. Add some herbamare. Pressure cook for 15 minutes. Cut Brussels sprouts in half. Remove stems from kale and slice into small pieces. Dice cabbage and squash. Add remaining vegetables to the pot and cover with water. Bring to a boil and then simmer about 15 minutes. Vegetables should be tender. Add miso to taste. Garnish with fresh parsley.

Sweet Chickpea Soup

1	cup chickpeas
1	cup fresh corn, decobbed
3	inch piece kombu, chopped
1	large bermuda onion, minced
1/2	buttercup or butternut squash
	white miso

Peel and chop squash in small pieces. Layer kombu, squash and chickpeas in a pot with enough water to cover. Cook until beans are tender. Add water as needed. Remove from heat and add minced onions and corn kernels. Add miso to taste. Mix well and cover pot. Let sit for several minutes before serving. For an additional flavor, add two tsp. fresh ginger juice.

Cream of Carrot Soup *

6	large California-style carrots
2	bermuda onions
1	jicama optional
	white miso
2	tbsp. minced parsley
1/2	tsp. herbamare

Peel and slice onions and jicama. Place in pressure cooker with 1/2 tsp. herbamare and cook for 15 minutes. The soup will take on a different flavor if you cook the onions first before adding the carrots. Clean and chop carrots. Add them to the pot with enough water to cover. Pressure cook another ten minutes until tender. Liquify the mixture after it has cooled and add miso to taste. Add more water as needed. Garnish with parsley. If you don't have a pressure cooker, cook the onions and carrots together with water to cover until tender. For a different twist, peel and shred jicama. Add it at the end instead of the beginning. Substitute hard squashes for the carrots in this recipe for variation.

Black Bean Soup

1	cup black beans
1	clove garlic
1	carrot
1	onion
2	stalks celery,minced
3	inch strip kombu,chopped
1	bay leaf
	tamari to taste
1	red pepper,minced
	dash cayenne
	dash cumin

Clean and chop onion, garlic and carrot. Cook beans with onion, garlic, carrot, kombu, bay leaf, spices and enough water to cover until beans are tender. Remove bay leaf. Add more water as needed. Season with tamari. Add minced celery and red pepper and serve. Celery and red pepper will wilt from the heat of the soup.

Cream of Broccoli Soup *

1	bunch broccoli
2	shallots
1	clove garlic
1	small onion
3	stalks celery
1	large carrot
1	cup almonds
	dash cayenne
	herbamare
2	tbsp. minced fresh basil

Clean and mince shallots, garlic, onion and celery. Combine and place in a pressure cooker with some herbamare. Cook for about 15 minutes without water. Meanwhile, blanche and remove skins from soaked almonds. Blend them with three cups water. Strain out pulp. Clean and chop broccoli and carrot into very small pieces. Blanche separately in boiling water until tender. Mix the vegetables and almond milk with the onion mixture. Simmer gently with added herbs, herbamare and cayenne to taste just for a minute or two for the flavors to combine before serving.

Cabbage Soup *

1/2	head cabbage
1	large onion
3	stalks celery
1	tbsp. umeboshi paste
1/2	tsp. caraway seeds optional
4	oz. tempeh
	herbamare
	minced parsley

Wash all vegetables well. Peel and slice onion in half moons. Shred cabbage and mince celery. Cut tempeh into small pieces. Layer onions, cabbage, celery and tempeh in a pressure cooker with a sprinkle of herbamare. Bring to pressure and cook 30 minutes without water. Open pot and add umeboshi paste along with enough water to create desired soup thickness. Garnish with parsley. Liquify the soup for a different twist. Add caraway seeds. If you don't have umeboshi paste, add corn or barley miso.

Cream of Mushroom Soup *

1/2	lb. mushrooms
1	clove garlic
1	large onion
1	tbsp. extra virgin olive oil
1	tbsp. whole wheat flour
1	cup soy milk
	dash cayenne
	dash nutmeg
	minced parsley
	herbamare

Clean and slice vegetables. Layer onions, garlic and mushrooms in a pressure cooker. Cook 15 minutes with a sprinkle of herbamare. In another pot, mix olive oil and flour together using a whisk. Over a low heat, gradually whisk in soy milk to produce a thick sauce stirring constantly. Add cooked mushroom mixture to the sauce. Add cayenne, nutmeg and minced parsley. Add more water as needed to achieve desired consistency. Adjust seasonings and serve. Substitute vegetables like cauliflower, celery or asparagus instead of mushrooms for variation.

Carrot Plantain Soup

3	carrots
2	ripe plantains
3	shallots
	chickpea miso
1/2	tsp. five spice powder
1	cup soy milk
2	tbsp. minced parsley

Clean and slice carrots and plantains. Plantains look like large bananas and must be very ripe and sweet for this recipe to work. Their skins should be turning black and soft to the touch before peeling. Cover carrots and plantains with water and cook until soft. Add miso, soy milk, spice and enough water to process into a creamy soup. Garnish with parsley before serving. This combination is not the best.

Cream of Yellow Squash Soup *

3	medium yellow squash
1	large bermuda onion
2	cups soy milk
1	tsp. curry
	dash cayenne
2	tbsp green scallion tops
1/2	tsp. herbamare
	sweet white miso

Clean and slice squash and onion. Layer onion slices and squash in pressure cooker with herbamare. Bring to pressure and cook 10 minutes without water. Open pot , cool and move vegetables to a blender or food processor. Add soy milk, miso to taste, and more water to create desired soup consistency. Mix in curry, cayenne and scallions. Reheat gently before serving. Try substituting fresh pumpkin for the squash when in season. "Vitasoy" plain soy-milk works well with this recipe.

Dandelion Greens Soup

2	cups dandelion greens
1	carrot, juliénned
2	cloves garlic, minced
2	scallions, minced
1/2	inch piece ginger
1	cup sugar snap peas
4	mushrooms, sliced
	sweet white miso

Use very young tender dandelion leaves in this recipe for best results. Dandelion is reputed to be a great cleanser especially beneficial for the liver. Put first five ingredients in a pot and cover with water. Bring to a boil and simmer until greens are cooked. Add snow peas, mushrooms and miso to taste. Let the pot sit a few minutes. Add scallions for a nice garnish as a variation.

Cream of Vegetable Soup

1	lb. green beans
3	stalks celery
1	onion
2	yellow squash
1/2	bunch fresh parsley
	dash cayenne optional
1/2	cup dulse

Clean and chop vegetables and parsley. Green beans should be young and tender. Cover with water and cook until soft. Cool and liquify, adding enough water to create a creamy soup. Blend in dulse. Substitute herbamare for the dulse or omit salt entirely. This soup is very satisfying for people on a controlled fast. I use it for that purpose.

Creamed Corn Soup

4	ears corn
	herbamare to taste
1	cup soy milk
1	tbsp. kuzu dissolved in 1/2 cup water
2	tbsp. minced chives

When corn is in season and it is sweet, this soup is a winner. Boil corn in water to cover for several minutes. Cool and remove from cobs. Use some corn broth to liquify the corn. Add the soy milk. Return to pot and add kuzu to thicken the soup. Serve with chive garnish. Substitute asparagus for corn and add one tsp. dry mustard for a whole new recipe.

Kombu Broth With Chinese Greens

6	inch piece kombu
1	cup bok choy
1	cup Chinese napa cabbage chopped
1	tbsp. fresh dill, minced
	umeboshi paste

Boil kombu in three cups water for 20 minutes. Clean and chop bok choy and cabbage. Add greens to kombu broth and simmer five minutes. Add umeboshi paste to taste. Garnish with fresh dill before serving.

French Onion Soup *

2	large bermuda onions,sliced
1	tsp. herbamare
2	fresh shitake mushrooms
	tamari to taste
2	tbsp.parsley,minced

This recipe only works well with a pressure cooker. Peel and slice onions and put into pot. Sprinkle with herbamare. Do not add water. Bring to pressure and immediately turn to low heat. Cook for 30 minutes. Open pot and add several cups of water to create desired consistency. Clean, remove stems and slice shitake mushrooms or use any choice of mushrooms. Add mushrooms with tamari to taste. Garnish with parsley.

Fennel Celery Leek Soup

2	large leeks
6	stalks celery
1	bulb fennel
1	bay leaf
	dash cayenne
2	tbsp. extra virgin olive oil
2	tbsp. kuzu
	mellow white miso
2	tbsp.parsley, minced

Clean and chop leeks, celery and fennel in very small pieces. Cover with water, add bay leaf and cook until tender. Add miso to taste. Turn off heat. Dissolve kuzu in 1/2 cup water and add to thicken the soup. Add oil, cayenne. and parsley. For added smooth texture, liquify some of the soup and vegetables and return to the pot.

Creamy Lentil Soup With Dulse

1	cup sprouted lentils
1	clove garlic
1	carrot
1	onion
2	stalks celery
1	bay leaf
1/2	tsp. thyme
	dash cayenne
1/2	cup tahini
1/2	cup dulse

Clean and chop vegetables. Layer onion, celery, carrot, garlic, lentils and bay leaf into a pot. Cover with water. Bring to boil and simmer until lentils are soft. This soup cooks in less than 15 minutes. Remove bay leaf. Blend tahini, dulse, cayenne, thyme and one cup water together. Mix into the lentils and vegetables. Add more water if necessary. For a variation, add one cup cooked grain to this recipe.

Green Leafy Vegetable Soup *

4	cups collard greens or escarole or kale
	tamari to taste
2	cloves garlic, minced
2	tbsp. extra virgin olive oil

Remove stems, wash and chop your leafy vegetables in small pieces. Use one or more with leaves that are similiar in thickness in any combination. Pressure cook with one cup water for three to five minutes. The thickness of the leaves will decide length of cooking time. I usually turn off the heat when the pot comes up to pressure. I count several minutes and then open the pot. Add more water and tamari to taste. Add the garlic and oil. Instead of garlic, substitute 1/2 cup minced red onions. The heat of the greens will wilt the onion. Young tender greens will always make a better soup. The addition of pasta or noodles makes this dish especially delicious. Add cooked beans for another variation.

Japanese-Style Miso Soup

1/4   lb. tofu, cubed
1   tbsp. bonita flakes
3   inch strip kombu, chopped
3   cups water
    sweet white miso
2   scallions, minced
1   mushroom, thinly sliced

Boil fish flakes in three cups water about ten minutes. Strain and discard flakes. Add kombu to fish broth and cook 15 minutes. Add tofu, mushroom slices, scallion and miso to taste. Let sit several minutes before serving. You can find these fish flakes in health food stores.

Watercress Soup

1   bunch watercress
1/2   bunch scallions
1/2   cup fresh peas
2   stalks celery
2   mushrooms, sliced
4   thin slices lemon
    white miso

Bring four cups water to boil. Clean and chop scallions, watercress and celery. Add scallions, peas, mushrooms and celery to the boiling water. Cook five minutes. Turn off heat. Add watercress, lemon slices and miso to taste. Let sit several minutes before serving.

Daikon Wakame Miso Soup

1/2   lb. daikon, juliénned
2   tbsp. instant wakame
1   onion, sliced
4   oz. tofu, cubed
    barley miso
2   tbsp. green scallions, minced
1   shitake mushroom, sliced

Put all ingredients except miso and scallions into a pot with four cups water. Bring to a boil and simmer for ten minutes. Add miso to taste. Serve with a minced scallion garnish. If fresh shitake isn't available, you can use dried shitake mushrooms.

Kidney Bean Soup

1   cup kidney beans
1   small rutabaga
1   carrot
1   large onion
3   inch strip kombu, chopped
1   bay leaf
1   tsp. ginger juice
    brown rice miso
    minced parsley

Peel and chop rutabaga and carrot. Layer kombu, onion, carrot and rutabaga in a pot with bay leaf. Add beans and approximately four cups water. Cook until beans are tender. Remove bay leaf. Add thyme, ginger juice and miso to taste. Add more water to adjust consistency. Garnish with some fresh minced parsley before serving.

Wild Rice Vegetable Soup

1   cup wild rice
1   yellow squash
1   red onion
1/2   head cauliflower
2   kohlrabi
    Braggs aminos
2   tbsp. extra virgin olive oil
1/4   tsp. herbamare
    minced parsley

Boil wild rice in three cups water with herbamare for about 45 minutes or until rice is soft. Clean, peel and chop vegetables. Add to the cooked rice with more water to cover. Cook about ten minutes until vegetables are tender. Remove from heat. Add olive oil, Braggs to taste, and garnish with some minced parsley.

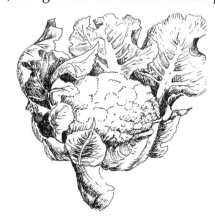

Lima Bean Squash Soup

1	butternut squash
1	cup fresh lima beans
3	inch strip kombu, chopped
6	scallions, minced
1	ear corn, decobbed
	dash cayenne pepper
	sweet white miso

Peel, seed and chop squash into small pieces. Layer kombu, squash and beans in a pot. Cover with water. Pressure cook 15 minutes or simmer for 30 minutes with pot cover on. When beans and squash are tender, remove pot from heat source. Add corn, scallions, cayenne and miso to taste. Add more water if necessary to create a creamy delicious soup.

Minestrone Soup Extraordinaire

2	carrots
1	large onion
2	cloves garlic
1	cup string beans
2	ear corn decobbed
1	tbsp. instant wakame flakes
2	stalks celery
1	small yellow squash
1/4	head cabbage
1	cup cooked kidney beans
1/2	cup whole wheat macaroni
	umeboshi paste to taste
3	tbsp. extra virgin olive oil
	herbamare to taste
3	tbsp. minced basil

Clean and chop all the vegetables. Place in a pot with wakame. Cover with water. Cook until soft. Meanwhile, cook pasta and drain. Add kidney beans, pasta, oil and umeboshi paste to taste with more water as needed. Garnish with fresh basil. If so inclined, add one tbsp of tomato paste for a more traditional flavor.

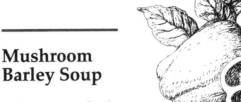

Mushroom Barley Soup

1	cup barley
1/2	lb. mushrooms
1	clove garlic
1/4	cabbage sliced
1	onion
1	carrot
2	stalks celery
2	tbsp. olive oil
	tamari to taste
1	tsp. dried oregano
2	tbsp. fresh parsley, minced
	herbamare

Clean and chop vegetables. Layer onion, cabbage, garlic, mushrooms, celery, carrot and barley in a pot. Cover with six cups water and cook until barley is tender. Add more water if needed. Remove from the heat and add tamari to taste, oil, oregano and fresh parsley. Let sit 15 minutes before serving. Use any variety of mushrooms. For a variation, cubed seitan adds more interest to the soup as well as flavor and texture.

Mushroom Soup

1/2	lb. white button mushrooms
4	scallions
2	tbsp. lemon juice
1	tbsp. kuzu dissolved in 1 cup water
1	sheet mori seaweed
	white miso
2	tbsp. parsley, minced

Clean and slice mushrooms and scallions. Shred nori with a scissor. Bring three cups water to a boil. Add lemon juice, mushrooms and scallions to the boiling water and simmer for five minutes. Remove from heat. Add kuzu to thicken with white miso to taste. Garnish with minced parsley and nori slices.

Pinto Bean Soup

1   cup pinto beans
3   inch strip kombu, chopped
2   parsnips
1   carrot
1   onion
1   inch piece ginger, peeled
       onazaki miso
       1 tbsp. fresh oregano

Clean and chop parsnips, carrot and onion. Put all ingredients in a pot except miso. Cover with water. Cook until beans are tender. Add more water as needed. Remove from heat and discard piece of ginger. Add onazaki miso to taste. Garnish with fresh minced oregano. Add 1/2 tsp. dried oregano with two tbsp. minced scallions if fresh oregano is not available.

Soba Noodle Soup

6   inch piece kombu, chopped
3   cups water
2   tbsp. tamari
1   tbsp. mirin
1   tsp. dark sesame oil
1   tsp. fresh ginger juice
       dash cayenne
4   oz. tofu cubed
2   cups cooked soba noodles
2   tbsp. green scallions, minced
       shredded nori

Boil soaked kombu in water for 20 minutes. Add tamari, mirin, ginger juice, cayenne and tofu. Simmer five minutes. Remove from heat and add oil. Arrange some noodles, shredded nori and scallions in a deep soup bowl for each person. Ladle soup into bowls to cover noodles and serve immediately. Use udon noodles or any kind of pasta instead of soba noodles.

Split Pea Soup

1   cup split peas
3   inch strip kombu, chopped
1   onion
2   carrots
2   stalks celery
1   bay leaf
1/4   tsp. thyme
       dash cayenne
       mellow white miso
       minced parsley

Clean and dice onion, carrots and celery. Layer kombu, vegetables and peas in a pot. Cover with water. Add bay leaf, thyme and cayenne and bring to boil. Simmer until peas are soft adding water if necessary. Remove from heat and discard bay leaf. Add miso to taste. Blend soup to make it creamy and smooth for a variation. Serve with minced parsley as a garnish.

Sweet Spicy Lentil Soup

1   cup lentils
1   sweet red pepper
1   parsnip
1   large bermuda onion
1   carrot
1/2   tsp. cumin
1/2   tsp. chili powder
1   jalapeno pepper, minced
2   tbsp. fresh cilantro, minced
       Braggs amino

Clean and chop parsnip, onion and carrot in small pieces. Mince the red pepper and set aside. Layer onion, carrot, parsnip, lentils, jalapeno pepper and spices in a pot. Add five cups water. Bring to boil and then simmer until lentils are tender. Add Braggs to taste. Garnish with cilantro and minced red peppers. Add more water to soup as needed.

Vegetable Borscht

3	beets
2	carrots
1	large onion
2	stalks celery, minced
1	small parsnip
2	tbsp. dill
2	tbsp. scallions
	red miso

Clean, peel and slice beets, parsnip and onion. Mince dill and scallions and set aside. Put the vegetables in a pot and cover with water. Boil until soft or you can pressure cook 15 minutes. Purée ingredients. Add red miso to taste and more water as needed. Mix in dill and scallions. For an extra taste treat, top with tofu sour cream before serving. Serve this soup hot or cold. For variation, leave some chunks of beet in the finished soup.

White Bean Kale Soup

1	cup white beans
3	inch kombu, chopped
1	red onion, minced
1	clove garlic
1/2	lb. young kale
2	tbsp. parsley
	onozaki miso
2	tbsp. extra virgin olive oil

Cook beans in four cups water with kombu and garlic for about 50 minutes until beans are tender. Add water as needed. Remove from heat and add miso to taste. Wash, remove stems and chop kale in small pieces. Quickly blanche in boiling water for one minute or until tender. Drain and mix into the soup. Add oil and red onion. Serve with a minced parsley garnish. Interchange beans and greens to make different combinations.

Basic Vegetable Stock

1	leek
2	parsnips
2	white turnips
4	stalks celery
2	large carrots

Clean and chop vegetables. Put in a pot, cover with water and boil 20 minutes with a pot cover. Add nothing else. Let the vegetables cool for 30 minutes. Strain out broth. This broth is soothing, alkalizing and cleansing to the system. Purée the vegetables separately with added water, herbamare and a little olive oil. Use as a sauce over noodles or grain.

Variation:

2	carrots
2	parsnips
1/2	head white cabbage
1	large bermuda onion

Follow above procedure. This broth is sweet and is beneficially soothing to those suffering from blood sugar problems.

CONTENTS
WHOLE BEANS, TEMPEH AND TOFU

Whole Beans, Tempeh and Tofu

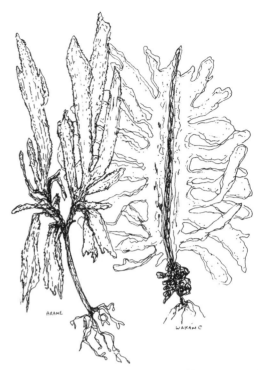

ARAME   WAKAME

Along with a resurgence of interest in whole grains is also a new look at the use of legumes, which includes beans, lentils, peas and pulses. They are nutritious, inexpensive and easy to store. Legumes have been cultivated since early recorded history, but their popularity has fluctuated. Once considered a poor man's food, there has been a modern revival of interest with the trend toward presenting bean products as meat substitutes. For example, tempeh and tofu are my answer to high-protein fast foods.

Tempeh is a fermented food made from soybeans. It contains beneficial bacteria the Orientals believe aids elimination of radioactivity. It originated in Indonesia, was introduced to the U. S. in the 60's, and has grown in popularity over the last decade. Cooked whole legumes, like tempeh, are high in dietary fiber and can help lower cholesterol as effectively as bran. There are many kinds of tempeh available. They are made with soybeans and different combinations of grains, vegetables and/or seaweed. The taste of the tempeh varies from company to company. Experiment and discover your favorites.

Like tempeh, tofu is also made from soybeans; both are already pre-cooked and can be prepared quickly. Tofu is made from the milk of the soybean and curdled into a "cheese". It is cholesterol free. Rich in protein, tofu is incredibly versatile and can be used in a variety of dishes from soups to desserts. Chinese and Japanese-style tofu each have a distinctive taste and texture. There are also different flavored varieties of tofu and several consistencies labelled soft to firm. Become familiar with the products available to you at your local health food store. If you have an Oriental market in your area, you can purchase deliciously fresh tofu.

Different varieties of whole dried beans are readily available at your supermarket and they are easy to prepare. It is highly recommended that you soak dried beans to help prevent gas formation, increase digestibility and significantly decrease cooking time. Discard the soaking water. Once the beans are drained, add two cups of water for every one cup of beans. This is an approximate rule of thumb. For dried beans, the ratio is usually three to one. The amount of water and time you use to cook the beans will make a big difference in the final texture. In addition, dried to soaked to sprouted conditions change the final taste. One can see the possibilities are endless. You can prepare the same bean in different ways to create varied taste and texture. Remember that when it comes to the use of salt, it is added after the beans are cooked. Salt tends to contract the bean instead of allowing it to cook properly. When preparing soups or stews, kombu seaweed is used instead to help tenderize the bean while it cooks. Moreover, it is better to cook beans separately and then mix them together. They cook better and are easier to digest.

Most sprouted beans can be cooked in five to fifteen minutes and are a whole new sensation of taste and texture. They are easy to work with and save time in the kitchen. For example, sprouted lentils cook in minutes and can be added to soups, salads or served as a main course. I hope to encourage you to take the time to germinate before cooking. It is a new arena of creative possibilities.

The tempeh and tofu recipes in this chapter are more "gourmet" in nature. Additional oils, spices, rice wines, and sweeteners have been used in these recipes to enhance flavor and texture. All the cuisines of the world use sweeteners and salts in some form to release the characteristic qualities of foods. We can also utilize the natural juices of cooked vegetables to enhance the taste of our foods. For example, the natural oils and concentrated sweet essence of cooked onions provide a great starting place for many recipes. Celery has a high content of natural sodium, which makes it a great zesty addition. These two vegetables are a necessary staple in my kitchen along with sweet California carrots and pungent garlic. I always try to keep a stock of vegetables that are sweet tasting when cooked like parsnips and cabbage as well as a varied assortment of green leafy vegetables.

I often demonstrate the use of cooked vegetables to produce wonderful aromatic flavors in order to keep salts, sweeteners and oils to a minimum. I practice combining substantial amounts of raw vegetables with cooked food dishes to lighten the meal. Tempeh, tofu and whole beans are a pleasure to eat when combined with a variety of vegetables and their characteristic, elegant juices.

WHOLE BEANS

Aduki Bean Casserole

1   cup aduki beans
1   small rutabaga
1   carrot
1   cup string beans
1   onion
3   inch strip kombu, chopped
     tamari

Clean and dice string beans and set aside. Peel and chop onion, carrot and rutabaga. Layer kombu, onion, carrot, rutabaga and beans in a pot. Add three cups water and cook until beans are tender, about 45 minutes. Sprouted aduki casserole cooks in 20 minutes. When beans are cooked, add diced string beans and tamari to taste. Mix well and let sit five minutes before serving.

Chestnut Aduki Stew *

1   cup aduki beans
1/2 cup dried chestnuts
1   large carrot sliced
1   onion, sliced
1   tbsp. dried orange rind
     Braggs

Soak chestnuts for about six hours and drain. Remove any brown shells on the chestnuts. Layer onion, orange rind, carrots, beans and chestnuts in a pressure cooker. Add three cups water and cook for 45 minutes. Open pot and add Braggs to taste. Add some fresh orange zest, if available, as a garnish.

Aduki Bean Salad

2   cups sprouted aduki beans
1/2 head cauliflower
1/2 head broccoli
1   large carrot, diced
1/2 bunch green scallions, minced
1/4 cup parsley
1   tbsp. each tahini, umeboshi paste, maple syrup

Steam sprouted beans until tender. Set aside. Break cauliflower and broccoli into tiny florets. Steam the florets and carrots until tender but crisp. Mix beans and cooked vegetables together. Combine last four ingredients with 1/2 cup water in a suribachi or use a blender. Mix into beans and vegetables along with minced scallions. The maple syrup is optional.

Aduki Beans and Sweet Squash

2   cups sprouted aduki beans
1   butternut or buttercup squash
1   large onion, chopped
     tamari

Peel, seed, and chop squash into pieces. Layer onion, squash and sprouted beans in a pot with one cup water. Cover and simmer for about 20 minutes or until soft. Season with tamari to taste and mix well. Use this recipe with sprouted chickpeas or try adding a parsnip for variation.

Chickpea Hummus I

2	cups chickpeas
2	inch piece kombu
1	tbsp. umeboshi paste
4	scallions chopped
1/4	cup fresh oregano or basil
1/4	cup tahini
	juice of 1 lemon
1/4	tsp. cayenne
1/2	tsp. cumin
	tamari

Cook soaked chickpeas with kombu and four cups water until tender, about 45 minutes. Drain. Save liquid. Put all ingredients in food processor with S blade. Blend until creamy. Add tamari to taste and chickpea juice to desired consistency.

Chickpea Hummus II

2	cups chickpeas
1/2	red onion, chopped
2	inch piece kombu
1	tsp. umeboshi paste
1/2	cup tahini
	juice of 2 lemons
1/2	cup fresh dill

Follow same instructions as above.

Chickpea Hummus III

2	cups chickpeas
1/2	butternut squash
2	inch piece kombu
1	tbsp. natto miso
2	tbsp. tahini
2	scallions, chopped
1/4	cup fresh parsley
1	stalk celery, minced
1	carrot, minced
	Braggs

Peel, seed and chop squash. Cook kombu, squash and chickpeas in four cups water until tender. Drain. Save the liquid. Put all ingredients except celery and carrots into a processor. Blend until creamy. Mix in the celery and carrots. Add Braggs to taste. Try substituting sweet potato for the squash.

Chickpea Hummus IV

2	cups sprouted chickpeas
1/2	cup toasted sesame seeds
1	stalk celery, chopped
2	cloves garlic, minced
	juice of 2 lemons
1/4	tsp. cayenne
1/2	tsp. paprika
1/4	cup tahini
	Braggs

Boil chickpeas with enough water to cover until soft, about 25 minutes. Drain. Save liquid. Process all ingredients with S blade until creamy. Add Braggs to taste and chickpea juice as needed.

Italian Rice and Beans

2	cups cooked kidney beans
4	cups cooked long-grain brown rice
1	large onion
2	cloves garlic
2	large carrots
1	red pepper
2	stalks celery
3	tbsp. extra-virgin olive oil
1/2	bunch fresh parsley
1	tsp. dried oregano
1	tbsp. fresh basil
	herbamare
	dash cayenne

Clean all the vegetables. Dice the carrots, red pepper, celery and onion. Mince the garlic, parsley and basil. Sauté onions, garlic, and pepper in water with some herbamare until wilted. Add carrots, and celery. Cover pan and cook five minutes with 1/4 cup water added. Remove from heat and add herbs, olive oil and cayenne. Toss in beans and rice. Season with more herbamare and serve. The traditional recipe calls for the addition of four ripe chopped tomatoes at the end.

Lentil Corn Salad

2	cups sprouted lentils
2	ears corn, decobbed
1	carrot, shredded
1	red onion, minced
1	tbsp. umeboshi paste
2	tbsp. tahini
	juice of 1 lemon
1/4	cup fresh parsley, minced

Steam sprouted lentils and corn together until tender, about five minutes. Add carrots and red onion. Blend last four ingredients with 1/2 cup water. Pour over lentil mixture. Mix well and serve.

Chickpea Patties *

2	cups sprouted chickpeas
1/2	cup millet
1 1/2	cups water
2	tsp. curry
2	scallions, finely minced
1	tsp. cumin
1/2	tsp. caraway seeds
1/2	tsp. dried oregano
1/2	tsp. dried basil
2	tbsp. extra virgin olive oil
	tamari

Pressure cook chickpeas for 15 minutes in enough water to cover. They should be tender. Drain and process with S blade until smooth. Pressure cook millet for 15 minutes in 1 1/2 cups water. Mix with chickpeas and remaining ingredients. Add tamari to taste. Press into patties and serve. Bake at 350° on oiled sheet until golden brown for variation.

Cucumber Sauce
2	cups plain soybean yogurt
1	large cucumber
1	tsp. fresh mint
1	tbsp. fresh cilantro
2	cloves garlic, pressed
1/2	tsp. herbamare
	dash cayenne

Peel, seed and shred cucumber. Mince mint and cilantro. Mix all ingredients in a bowl and let sit one hour before serving with patties.

Lima Bean Potage

2	cups fresh lima beans
1	large onion, minced
1	clove garlic, minced
1	jalapeño pepper, chopped
2	tbsp. extra virgin olive oil
1	tsp.grated lemon rind
	dash cayenne
	dash of pumpkin pie spice
3	tbsp. fresh cilantro, minced
	herbamare

Sauté onion, garlic, and jalapeño in a little water with some herbamare until wilted. Add beans and water to cover. Use pot cover and simmer until beans are tender. Add oil, lemon rind, cayenne, spice and cilantro. Adjust seasonings. Add more water if necessary and more herbamare to taste.

Simply Sweet Lentil Stew

4	cups sprouted lentils
1	clove garlic, minced
1	large onion, sliced
1	parsnip, diced
2	carrots, chopped
3	stalks celery, minced
$1/2$	tsp. thyme
$1/2$	tsp. sage
	Braggs

Layer onion, garlic, celery, carrots, parsnip, herbs and lentils in a pot. Add one cup water and bring to boil. Turn down heat to a simmer and cover. Cook about ten minutes until vegetables are tender. Add Braggs to taste.

Savory Lentils and Rice I

2	cups sprouted lentils
2	onions,sliced
1	clove garlic, minced
1	stalk celery, minced
1	tsp. curry
$1/2$	tsp. cumin
$1/2$	tsp. chili powder
$1/4$	tsp. tumeric
$1/4$	cup extra virgin olive oil
1	cup basmati rice
	tamari
	minced red pepper

Cook basmati rice in two cups of water with a pinch of salt until tender, about 35 minutes. Keep pot covered. Layer onions, garlic and celery in pressure cooker. Add one cup water, spices and some tamari. Bring to pressure and cook ten minutes. Open pot and add lentils. Cook another five minutes. Remove from heat. Add oil and more tamari to taste. Serve lentils over rice or use any other grain. Garnish with minced red pepper.

Kidney Beans, Greens, and Barley

$1/2$	cup kidney beans
1	inch piece kombu
1	cup cooked barley
1	onion, chopped
4	mushrooms, sliced
1	bunch young kale
2	tbsp. lemon juice
$1/4$	tsp. rosemary
2	tbsp. olive oil
	Braggs

Cook kidney beans and kombu with one cup water until soft, about 45 minutes. Add lemon juice, olive oil and rosemary. Wash, remove stems, and chop kale into small pieces. Steam the kale, onions and mushrooms until tender. Mix all above ingredients together, adding Braggs to taste.

Savory Lentils and Rice II

Follow the same recipe procedure above and substitute the following ingredients. Eliminate the curry, cumin, chili powder and tumeric. Instead add one stick cinnamon, $1/2$ inch piece minced ginger root, $1/2$ tsp. cayenne and a bay leaf. Before serving the lentils remove the bay leaf and cinnamon stick. Add the juice and grated rind of one fresh lemon for a special flavorful garnish.

Sprouted Chickpea Stew I *

2	cups sprouted chickpeas
1	large onion, sliced
1	stalk celery, sliced
2	kohlrabi, peeled and diced
1/4	cup fresh dill, minced
2	tbsp. extra virgin olive oil
	Braggs

Layer onion, celery, chickpeas and kohlrabi in a pressure cooker. Add one cup water and cook for 15 minutes. Open pot and add dill, olive oil and Braggs to taste.

Sprouted Chickpea Stew II *

2	cups sprouted chickpeas
1	red pepper, diced
2	stalks celery, minced
1	red onion, sliced
1/4	head cabbage. shredded
2	tbsp. olive oil
	Braggs

Layer red onion, cabbage, celery, red pepper and chickpeas in pressure cooker. Add one cup water and cook 15 minutes. Open pot. Add oil and Braggs to taste. Mix well.

Summer Bean Salad

2	cups sprouted chickpeas
1	carrot, minced
1/2	red onion, diced
1 1/2	cups string beans, diced
1	yellow squash, shredded
1/4	cup olive oil
	juice of 1 lemon
1	tbsp. fresh parsley, minced
	Braggs

Steam the sprouted chickpeas until tender. Lightly steam the carrots and string beans. (They should be crunchy). Mix the red onion and squash together with the carrots, beans and chickpeas. The heat from the cooked vegetables will wilt the raw squash and onions. Add remaining ingredients and mix well. Let sit one hour before serving to allow the flavors to blend. Use any bean you like for this recipe.

Split Pea Squares

1	cup split peas
2	inch piece kombu
3	tbsp. agar flakes
1	carrot, sliced
2	stalks celery, chopped
1	onion, chopped
1	bay leaf
1	tbsp. dried orange peel
	tamari
	lemon slices
	fresh parsley, minced

Heat the agar flakes in boiling water until dissolved. Set aside. Layer kombu, onion, celery, carrot, peas, and bay leaf in a pot with two cups water to cover. Bring to boil and simmer until peas are fully cooked. Add agar mixture, orange peel, and tamari to taste to the pot. Remove the bay leaf and cool slightly. Carefully blend mixture in small batches until creamy. Mix well and pour into a mold of your choice to set. Cool down and then refrigerate until firm. Cut into squares. Garnish with lemon slices and parsley. Be careful when blending hot soup.

Mock Baked Beans I *

2	cups cooked pinto beans
1	clove garlic, minced
1	large bermuda onion, sliced
2	inch piece kombu, chopped
1	tsp. dry mustard
1/4	cup natto miso
1/2	inch piece ginger, minced
	tamari

Layer kombu, onion, garlic, ginger, beans and a dash of tamari in a pressure cooker. Bring to pressure with 1/2 cup water and cook for 30 minutes. Open pot and add natto miso, mustard, and tamari to taste. Use more natto miso and less tamari to get a different taste. Mix well and serve.

Mock Baked Beans II *

2	cups cooked pinto beans
2	inch piece kombu, chopped
2	cloves garlic, minced
1	large bermuda onion, sliced
1	large carrot, minced
1	tsp. dry mustard
1/4	cup barley malt
1	tbsp. barley miso
1/2	inch piece ginger, minced
	tamari

Layer kombu, onion, garlic, carrot, beans, ginger and a dash of tamari in a pressure cooker. Cook with 1/2 cup water for 30 minutes. Add miso, barley malt, mustard and tamari to taste. Mix well.

TEMPEH

Tempeh and Carrots *

8	oz. pkg. tempeh, cubed
3	large carrots, sliced
1	large bermuda onion
3	stalks celery
1	inch piece ginger root, grated
2	tbsp. extra virgin olive oil
1/4	cup parsley, minced
	tamari

Clean and slice onion and celery. Layer the onion, celery and tempeh in a pressure cooker. Add some tamari and cook for 15 minutes without water. Steam carrots separately until sweet and tender. Combine carrots, ginger, olive oil and parsley. Combine all ingredients and add more tamari to taste. Mix well and serve.

Coconut Curry Tempeh

2	packages soy tempeh, cubed
1	cup fresh coconut, shredded
2	cups plain soy milk
2	tsp. ginger, minced
2	cloves garlic,.minced
1	tbsp. curry powder
2	tbsp. maple syrup (optional)
1	large bermuda onion, chopped
2	Celestial Seasonings lemon zinger tea bags
	herbamare
	cayenne

Steam the tempeh for about ten minutes and set aside. Liquify the coconut with the soy milk until smooth and creamy. Set aside. Brew two cups of tea with the lemon tea bags. Pour the tea into a saucepan and add the remaining ingredients. Simmer ten minutes. Add coconut mixture and simmer another five minutes. Add herbamare and cayenne to taste. Pour the completed sauce over the tempeh. Mix well. Adjust seasonings before serving.

Tempeh and Sauerkraut *

8	oz. pkg. tempeh, cubed
1	cup sauerkraut
1/4	white cabbage, shredded
1	onion, sliced
1/4	tsp. caraway seeds

I use commercial sauerkraut from the health food store for this recipe. Layer the onion, cabbage, kraut, caraway and tempeh in a pressure cooker. Cook for 15 minutes. The vegetables will create a wonderful sauce for the tempeh.

Spicy Tempeh

8	oz. pkg. tempeh
1	tsp. maple syrup
1	tbsp. umeboshi paste
1	tbsp. dijon mustard
1/2	tsp. dried sage
1	tsp. fresh ginger juice
1	cup water
1	tbsp. kuzu dissolved in 1/2 cup water

Cut tempeh into four pieces. Set aside. Combine all ingredients except kuzu and bring to a boil. Simmer ten minutes. Add tempeh and marinate one hour. Reheat, adding kuzu mixture to thicken sauce before serving.

Tempeh Chips Dijon

1	pkg. tempeh
1	tbsp. scallions, minced
1/2	cup dijon mustard
1	tbsp. maple syrup
	canola oil

Slice the tempeh into thin strips, brush with canola oil and broil on both sides until crispy brown. Set aside. Dilute mustard with about four tablespoons of water. Add syrup and scallions. Serve tempeh chips with mustard sauce or any sauce you like. People love tempeh when it is presented in this fashion. Add some almond mayo to the dijon mustard to heighten the taste.

Tempeh Lo Mein

1	lb. tempeh, cubed
1	onion, sliced
1	carrot, sliced
1	cup bok choy
6	mushrooms
1	cup bean sprouts
1	cup snow peas, stemmed
2	cloves garlic, minced
1	inch piece ginger, slicd
1	tbsp. kuzu dissolved in 1 cup water
1/4	cup mirin
2	tbsp. dark sesame oil
	choice of noodles
	tamari

Stir fry onion, garlic and mushrooms in sesame oil with some tamari. Add mirin, ginger, carrot and tempeh. Cook for about five minutes. Add snow peas, bok choy and bean sprouts. Cook another three minutes. Add kuzu mixture to thicken the sauce, and more tamari to taste if desired. Serve over noodles. By adding one tsp. of chili paste you can convert this recipe into a Szechuan dish. Tofu can be substituted for tempeh in this recipe.

Tempeh Party Spread

8	oz. pkg. tempeh
1/2	cup pitted, sliced black olives
2	tbsp. extra virgin olive oil
1/2	red pepper, minced
1	tbsp. tamari
1	tbsp. dried onion flakes
1/2	tsp. fennel seeds
1/8	tsp. cayenne
1/4	tsp. paprika
1/4	tsp. tumeric
1	tbsp. maple syrup (optional)

Process all ingredients with S blade except the olives and fresh red pepper until very well blended. Mix in olives and minced pepper. Let sit several hours for a richer flavor before serving.

Tempeh Piccata

8	oz. pkg. soy tempeh
1/2	cup plain bread crumbs
1	tsp. Italian seasoning
1/2	cup sake (optional)
	juice of 1 lemon
	extra virgin olive oil
2	tsp. minced shallots
2	tbsp. arrowroot dissolved in 1/2 cup water
1	sheet nori, shredded
	Braggs

Mix bread crumbs with Italian seasoning. Cut tempeh in half and then cut in half again. Dip tempeh in dissolved arrowroot and then in flavored bread crumbs. Bake tempeh on oiled sheet for 15 minutes at 375° until golden. Place baked tempeh in a sauté pan and finish recipe. Add shallots, lemon juice and sake to tempeh. Cook five minutes. Add olive oil. Remove from heat and cover. Let sit a few more minutes and then garnish with nori strips. Substitute minced parsley for the nori strips for variation. Season with Braggs to taste. Mix all ingredients well and serve.

Tempeh Bourgignon

1	lb. soy tempeh, cubed
1/2	cup peas
1	large carrot, sliced
6	mushrooms, sliced
1	large onion, sliced
1	clove garlic, minced
1/2	cup mirin
1	tbsp. kuzu dissolved in 1 cup water
2	tbsp. extra virgin olive oil
1/4	tsp. cayenne
2	tbsp. fresh parsley
1	tsp. dried basil
	tamari

Fully coat cubed tempeh with tamari. Let sit for 20 minutes. Sauté onion, garlic, and mushrooms in water until wilted. Add carrot slices and cook until tender. Add tempeh, mirin, basil and cayenne to the pot and cook another tenminutes. Add kuzu mixture to thicken the sauce. Mix in the olive oil and peas. Garnish with parsley. Substitute tofu or seitan for tempeh in this recipe for variation.

Tempeh Patties

8	oz. pkg. tempeh
2	cups cooked short-grain brown rice
1	small carrot, shredded
1	small onion, shredded
1	tbsp. tamari
2	tbsp. fresh parsley, minced
1/4	tsp. thyme
1/2	tsp. dried garlic flakes
2	tbsp. extra virgin olive oil

Process tempeh with S blade until finely minced. Add rice and process another minute to combine. Add remaining ingredients. Mix well. Shape into patties. Bake on oiled sheet at 350° for 20 minutes or until nicely browned. Make sure the rice is well cooked.

Tempeh-Stuffed Cabbage

1	large white cabbage
8	oz. pkg. tempeh, mashed
1	onion, chopped
1	clove garlic, minced
1	tbsp. tamari
1	tbsp. white miso
2	tbsp. olive oil
1/4	cup mirin (optional)
1/4	tsp. cayenne
1	tbsp. lemon juice
1	cup cooked grain
1	cup sauerkraut

Steam the cabbage, separate the leaves and cut out stems. Set aside. Sauté onion and garlic in a little water until wilted. Dissolve miso in mirin or 1/4 cup water. Combine onions, garlic, miso broth and remaining ingredients except sauerkraut. Fill flattened leaves with tempeh mixture. Gently roll the cabbage around the filling. Place rolls into the bottom of a stew pot. Cover with sauerkraut and one cup water or vegetable broth. Cook covered until cabbage is soft and easy to slice. For variation, use seitan instead of tempeh. I use commercial sauerkraut for this recipe.

Tempeh Tettrazini

1	lb. tempeh, cubed
2	tbsp. extra virgin olive oil
1	onion, sliced
1	clove garlic, minced
1	tbsp. white miso
2	tbsp. tahini
1	tsp. dried tarragon
1/2	tsp. each dried marjoram and basil
1/4	tsp. each cayenne and paprika
1 1/2	tbsp. kuzu dissolved in 1 cup water
1/2	cup peas
1	carrot, sliced
3	mushrooms, sliced
2	tbsp. fresh parsley, minced
	tamari

Dissolve miso in one cup water. Sauté onion and garlic with miso broth until wilted. Add tempeh, dried herbs, mushrooms, cayenne, paprika and sliced carrot. Cook for ten minutes. Add tahini and peas. Mix ingredients until well combined. Cook five minutes. Remove from heat and thicken with kuzu mixture. Add oil. Top with fresh minced parsley and tamari to taste. For variation, substitute fresh or frozen tofu for tempeh. Freeze the tofu first. Thaw it out and shred into pieces. Freezing gives the tofu a tough, meaty consistency.

Tempeh Stew

8	oz. pkg. tempeh, cubed
3	inch strip kombu, sliced
1	leek
1/2	head cabbage
1	tsp. poultry seasoning
3	inch piece daikon root
2	tbsp. extra virgin olive oil
	tamari
1	tbsp. kuzu dissolved in 1/2 cup water

Clean leek well and slice into thin pieces. Shred cabbage. Clean and julienne daikon root. Layer kombu, leek, daikon, and tempeh in a stew pot. Add 1/2 cup water, poultry seasoning and some tamari. Cover and simmer until vegetables are soft. Remove from heat. Mix in kuzu to thicken the sauce. Add olive oil and more tamari to taste. Mix well and serve. Omit tempeh and use seitan for variation.

Tempeh Salad

8	oz. pkg. tempeh, cubed
1/4	cup tofu mayonnaise
1	red pepper, minced
2	stalks celery, minced
2	scallions, minced
1	tsp. lemon juice
1	tbsp. white miso
2	tbsp. parsley, minced

Steam tempeh for ten minutes. Mash with fork. Add remaining ingredients. Mix well and chill before serving.

Tempeh with Nori Sauce

8	oz. pkg. tempeh, sliced
2	sheets nori, shredded
2	tbsp. white miso
1	clove garlic, minced
2	scallions, minced
1/2	cup sake (optional)
3	tbsp. extra virgin olive oil
	juice of 1 lemon
	scallion garnish

Dissolve the white miso in one cup water. Simmer garlic, scallions and tempeh in miso broth with sake for ten minutes. Add nori and lemon juice. Cook another five minutes. Mix in oil and garnish with more minced scallions.

Tempeh Teriyaki

8	oz. pkg. tempeh
1/4	cup tamari
1/4	cup sake
1	tbsp. maple syrup
2	tsp. grated ginger root
2	cloves garlic, minced
1	tbsp. sesame oil
1/2	tsp. dry mustard

Cut tempeh into six pieces. Combine remaining ingredients to make the teriyaki sauce. Marinate tempeh for several hours. Broil on both sides until nicely browned. This is a good all-purpose marinade. For variety, try using tofu or seitan instead of tempeh. Broil tofu until speckled and brown.

TOFU

Tofu Scampi

1	lb. tofu
5	cloves garlic, minced
2	tbsp. fresh basil, minced
	juice of 1 lemon
1	cup small broccoli florets
	extra virgin olive oil
1/2	cup arrowroot
6	mushrooms, sliced
	cayenne
	herbamare
1/2	cup sake

Cut tofu into strips. Roll in olive oil and arrowroot and bake in a pan until crisp and brown at 400°. Water sauté broccoli, mushrooms and garlic until broccoli is tender. Add sake, basil and lemon juice with cayenne and herbamare to taste. Add tofu last. Cook several minutes until flavors mingle. Mix well and serve.

Baked Tofu and Vegetables

6	cakes baked tofu
2	stalks celery, chopped
1	onion, sliced
1/2	cup snow peas
2	ears corn, decobbed
1	tbsp. white miso dissolved in 1 cup water
1	tsp. kuzu dissolved in 1/4 cup water

Soak baked tofu in hot water for ten minutes and drain well. Cut into thin strips. Layer onions, celery, and tofu in a pressure cooker. Add miso broth. Pressure cook for 10 minutes. Open pot and add snow peas with corn kernels. Cook three minutes. Remove from heat and add kuzu to thicken sauce. Baked tofu is a ready to eat product sold in health food stores. Its chewy texture is very appealing.

Tofu Cheese and Crackers

1/2	lb. firm tofu
	sweet white miso
	crackers of your choice
	sliced cucumber
	sliced green scallion tops
	sliced red peppers

Slice tofu into small thin pieces. Coat both sides with miso and let sit all day to marinate. Wash off miso just before serving. Use any miso you prefer for variation. Layer cracker, tofu, cucumber slice, red pepper and scallions. Make up your own hors d'oeuvre ideas as well. This is always a winner.

Barbecue Tofu

2	packages plain baked tofu
2	large onions, minced
6	cloves garlic, minced
1/4	cup extra virgin olive oil
	juice of 2 lemons
1	cup barley malt
1	tsp. each cumin and chili powder
2	tbsp. whole grain mustard
1/2	cup ketchup (optional)
1	bulb fennel, shredded
1	large carrot, shredded

Steam fennel, onion, garlic and carrot until very soft. Set aside. Combine remaining ingredients except oil and tofu. Cook about five minutes stirring well. Do not add any additional salt because baked tofu is already salty. The ketchup is not a necessary addition but adds a lot of extra flavor and makes a more traditional barbecue sauce. Mix the steamed vegetables into the sauce and cook together another five minutes. Add oil. Add more or less of any ingredient to create your own taste. Grill the slices of baked tofu on your barbecue or inside grill until well browned and crisp. Coat the hot tofu slices with enough sauce to please the palate and reserve the rest for future use.

Tofu Mushroom Pâté

1	lb. tofu
2	large onions
2	carrots
1/2	lb. mushrooms
3	tbsp. tahini
1	large clove garlic
2	tbsp. tamari
	herbamare

Clean and chop onions, carrots, garlic and mushrooms. Toss all with some herbamare to help the vegetables release their juices. Bake at 350° for approximately one hour until soft and dry. Blend the vegetables with tofu, tahini, and tamari to taste.

Corn Cheese Casserole

4	ears corn, decobbed
1	bermuda onion, minced
1	lb. tofu
1 1/2	tsp. flint corn miso
1 1/2	tsp. umeboshi paste

Put all ingredients into a food processor with the S blade. Blend well and spoon into an oiled baking dish. Bake at 375° for about 20 minutes or until top is bubbly and golden. For variation, water sauté the onions and mix with a little olive oil. Then add to remaining ingredients before baking.

Tofu Sprout Salad

1/2	lb. tofu, cubed
2	cups mung bean sprouts, chopped
2	ears corn, decobbed
2	scallions, minced
1	carrot, shredded
1/2	cup dulse, rinsed and chopped
1/2	cup tofu mayo
	herbamare

Mix all ingredients together until well blended. Add herbamare to taste and serve. Add more tofu mayo for a richer flavor.

Tofu Hiziki Quiche *

2	lbs. soft tofu
1	tbsp. tahini
2	tbsp. kuzu dissolved in 1/4 cup water
1/2	cup hiziki
1	large onion, chopped
1	tsp. each olive oil and tamari
1	medium-sized butternut squash
1	tbsp. tamari
1/2	cup water
1	cup seitan, chopped (optional)
	chickpea crust

Soak hiziki for 30 minutes. Drain, rinse and set aside. Peel, seed, and chop squash. Pressure cook ten minutes with water to cover and then drain well. Process squash with the S blade until creamy. Add tofu, tahini and kuzu mixture to processor. Blend together. Sauté onion in olive oil with tamari until wilted. Mix all the above together. Add seitan if desired. Spoon into oiled pie plate lined with chickpea crust. Bake at 350° for 30 minutes or until set.

Chickpea Crust

2	cups cooked chickpeas
1/2	tsp. herbamare
2	tbsp. tahini
1	tsp. psyllium seed powder
1	tbsp. arrowroot
1	tbsp. lemon juice

Make sure chickpeas are well cooked and well drained. Mash with a fork. Add remaining ingredients and combine well. Press into oiled 10-inch pie plate. This crust is a suggestion. Use what you would prefer.

Spaghetti Squash with Tofu Alfredo

1	lb. tofu
1	large spaghetti squash
2	tbsp. sweet white miso
2	cloves garlic
1/4	cup tahini
1/4	cup sake (optional)
1	tsp. ginger juice
2	tbsp. tamari
	dash cayenne
	parsley garnish

Punch holes in the spaghetti squash with a fork. Cover with water and bring to boil. Cook until soft. Open, remove seeds and pull out squash strands from skin. Discard the skin. Set aside. This is an interesting vegetable. When you remove the pulp from the shell using a fork as if it were a miniature rake, it looks like spaghetti. Process remaining ingredients with S blade until smooth and creamy. Add more water for a thinner sauce or more tamari to taste. Don't be afraid to adjust or delete ingredients to obtain the taste you prefer. Serve over the squash. Garnish with minced parsley. Make a delicious dressing or sauce just with the tofu, tahini, tamari, and garlic recipe ingredients. This sauce is versatile and can be used on cooked or raw foods.

Scrambled Tofu

1/2	lb. tofu, crumbled
1	stalk celery, minced
3	scallions, minced
1	small carrot, shredded
1/4	cup sake (optional)
1	tsp. tamari
1/2	tsp. dry mustard
2	tbsp. extra virgin olive oil

Sauté celery, scallions, carrots and tofu for five minutes in sake (or water) and tamari. Add remaining ingredients and mix well. This is my version of a Sunday brunch entreé instead of scrambled eggs. Try tempeh as a substitute for tofu.

Pecan Tofu Cutlets

1	lb tofu
1	cup pecans
1/2	cup canola oil
1/2	tsp. curry
1	large clove garlic
1/2	cup mirin
2	tbsp. tamari
1/2	tsp. dried thyme
1/4	tsp. cayenne
1/2	tsp. coriander
1/4	tsp. nutmeg
1/2	cup arrowroot

Slice tofu into eight pieces. Set aside. Process well dried pecans with S blade until finely ground. If the pecans are wet you will end up with a paste. Dry them in the dehydrator or oven if necessary. Combine remaining ingredients except arrowroot. Put tofu into a glass loaf pan with the resulting marinade. Let sit six hours. Remove tofu and coat with arrowroot and then finely ground pecans. It may be a bit difficult to get the pecans to stick, but be patient. This is a delicious dish. Carefully put the rectangles onto a baking sheet and bake at 350° until golden brown. Watch them carefully. The pecans should not burn. This is delicious dish served with a chutney on the side.

Tofu Meatballs

1	lb. tofu, mashed
1	tbsp. kuzu dissolved in 1/4 cup water
1/2	cup bread crumbs
2	scallions, finely minced
1/4	cup carrots, shredded
2	tbsp. white miso
1	clove garlic, minced
	dash cayenne
1/2	tsp. each dried oregano and basil
2	tbsp. fresh parsley

Combine all ingredients. Work together with your hands. Keep working the tofu mixture for about five minutes to improve the consistency of the final product. Make into balls or patties. Bake on oiled sheet at 350° for 15 minutes or until golden brown.

Tofu Pizza

1	pkg. whole wheat pita bread
1	lb. tofu, mashed
1	large onion, sliced
1	clove garlic, minced
1	tbsp. each tamari and umeboshi paste
1	tsp. oregano
$1/2$	tsp. basil
4	mushrooms, sliced
1	red pepper, minced
1	tsp. extra virgin olive oil
	alfredo sauce

Sauté onion and garlic in a little water until wilted. Add tamari, herbs, umeboshi paste, and mashed tofu. Mix well. Put a layer of alfredo sauce and then the mashed tofu mixture on pita bread. Top with minced red peppers, sliced mushrooms and a drizzle of olive oil. Bake at 450° until lightly brown and bubbly. For variation, use soya kaas mozzarella cheese instead of tofu mixture. Layer alfredo sauce, mozzarella, dried oregano, sliced vegetables, and a drizzle of olive oil. Then bake.

Tofu Ricotta

$1/2$	lb. soft tofu
$1/2$	cup pignoli nuts
$1/2$	tsp. herbamare
2	tbsp. sweet white miso
$1/4$	tsp. nutmeg
	dash cayenne
$3/4$	cup water

Blend soaked pignolis in $3/4$ cup water until creamy. Add miso, nutmeg, herbamare and cayenne. Blend. Mash tofu and combine with pignoli mixture. Adjust flavors to your liking. Substitute two tbsp. umeboshi paste for the miso for a different flavor. Also try substituting one tbsp. fresh minced parsley for the nutmeg. Add more white miso for an even richer taste. Toss ricotta with steamed vegetables and serve as an entreé. Eliminate the pignoli nuts and double the amount of tofu for another variation. Serve this mixture over pasta.

Tofu Mayonnaise

$1/2$	lb. tofu
	juice of 1 lemon
$1/4$	cup olive oil
$1/2$	tsp. herbamare
$1/2$	tsp. dry mustard
1	clove garlic or 2 tbsp. minced onion

Process all ingredients with the S blade for about five minutes until very smooth and creamy. I prefer the taste of olive oil, but use other oils for variation.

Tofu Salad I

1	lb. tofu, mashed
1	tsp. white miso
1	tsp. umeboshi paste
1	tsp. dry mustard
$1/2$	tsp. tumeric
$1/4$	tsp. caraway seeds (optional)
1	tsp. fresh parsley
1	stalk celery, minced
$1/4$	cup minced chives or scallions
$1/2$	cup tofu mayonnaise
	dash cayenne

Combine all the ingredients until well blended. This makes a great sandwich filling with alfalfa sprouts. Add a minced dill pickle to this recipe for a delicious variation.

Tofu Salad II

1	lb. tofu, frozen and thawed
2	stalks celery, diced
2	scallions, minced
1	carrot, shredded
1/2	cup peas
1/2	tsp. curry
	herbamare and dash cayenne
3/4	cup tofu mayonnaise
1	tbsp. fresh dill, minced

Press any excess water out of the tofu. Break the tofu into small pieces. Add remaining ingredients. Use the herbamare and cayenne to taste. Mix well and serve. Frozen tofu gives this salad an unusual texture, but use fresh tofu if you prefer. Try using almond mayonnaise as a variation.

Tofu Sticks

1	lb. firm tofu
1	cup corn meal
2	tbsp umeboshi paste
2	tbsp. tamari
3/4	cup water
	canola oil

Slice tofu into sticks about 1/2 inch thick and two inches long. You can make them thicker if you like. Coat first with oil, then corn meal and then bake in the oven at 350° until golden. Combine umeboshi paste, tamari and water to make a sauce. Put sauce into a sauté pan and add tofu sticks. Coat sticks well by turning gently. Simmer several minutes and serve. Adjust the amount of tamari, umeboshi paste and water to your liking.

Tofu With Scallions

1/2	lb. firm tofu, cubed
1	bunch scallions, minced
6	large mushrooms, sliced
2	tbsp. toasted sesame oil
2	tbsp. water
	tamari

Sauté scallions and mushrooms in a little water and tamari. Cook several minutes. Add cubed tofu and more tamari to taste. Simmer several minutes more and add oil. This combination has an appealing flavor. Serve over grain or noodles. Use any type of mushroom for variation.

Crustless Tofu Broccoli Quiche

1	lb. soft tofu
2	tbsp. tahini
1	tbsp. tamari
1/2	tsp. herbamare
1	tbsp. arrowroot
1 1/2	cups small broccoli florets
1/2	tsp. dry mustard
4	large mushrooms, sliced
1	large onion, sliced
1	tbsp. extra virgin olive oil

Sauté mushrooms and onions in a little water with 1/2 tsp. herbamare until wilted. Add oil, mix well and set aside. Steam broccoli florets until tender. Set aside. Process the tofu, tahini, tamari, arrowroot and mustard with S blade until smooth. Mix with broccoli. Layer onions and mushrooms into oiled 10-inch pie plate. Top with tofu broccoli mixture. Smooth it over the plate. Bake at 350° for 30 to 40 minutes or until set.

CONTENTS
LAND AND SEA VEGETABLES

Land and Sea Vegetables

As we all know, purchasing quality produce involves many variables. Crop availability, where we live, what season we're in, and weather conditions affecting local crops, the age of the produce when picked and when received, and proper commercial storage all affect the final outcome of any of the recipes in this book. The bunch or pound of broccoli or spinach, for example, could be quite different where you live. Bigger, tougher stems need to be cut away, some of the leaves are yellow or bug-eaten, or part of the vegetable is spoiled shifting the amounts of ingredients in any given recipe. My point is this. Use these recipes for building blocks, creative ideas, and guidelines in the kitchen. Realize that adjustments in your vegetable creations are a regular occurrence due to quality and variance of the produce.

In this chapter, I explain various cooking techniques and include some ideas about the order in which you add ingredients to your recipes. I practice the method of adding oil last instead of first to retain its full-bodied flavor and beneficial quality. It is important to know that heating oil at high temperatures destroys its nutritional value, mutates its molecular structure, and makes it hard to digest. Unsaturated oils become saturated and deleterious. Moreover, excess fats stored in the cells diminish the body's ability to retain oxygen and make way for degeneration and disease. Eat unsaturated oils in moderation for optimum health.

It is also beneficial to keep cooking time to a minimum to retain as many nutrients as possible. I blanche or steam my vegetables in minutes. The simple process of adding water to your sauté pan while cooking the vegetables is an advantageous technique. The term used for this method is "water sauté". Some exciting new equipment has been developed and is now on the market. Non-toxic, non-stick pans as well as heavy stainless steel or cast iron enamel can be easily used to prepare meals without adding oils until you're ready.

If you understand the value of using pot covers, you will quickly learn to cook vegetables with a little water in a matter of minutes. Bring the pot almost to a boil and then turn off the heat. Quickly cover. Even though the vegetables are uncooked, they will finish cooking in their own juices without direct high heat as long as the cover is kept on the pot. As a matter of fact, they will overcook if you don't keep a watchful eye. Remove the cover when you are ready to stop the steaming process.

Moreover, there's logic behind my suggestion that you layer your vegetables in the pot in recipes throughout the cooked section. The high water content vegetables should be placed at the bottom of the pot because they break down with the help of heat and a little salt to create a liquid in which the other ingredients of greater density will stew. Take the time to do this whenever indicated.

I recommend adding fresh herbs at the end of preparation. After removing foods from the stove, there is still plenty of heat for the flavors of your seasonings to intermingle. If you add plants like dill, parsley or basil at the beginning, their flavors tend to get lost in the dish. Fresh herbs beautifully lighten any cooked meal and can better retain their own distinct flavors as well as medicinal value if not cooked with the dish.

Consuming green leafy vegetables every day is a healthy and important habit. I find the best way to prepare cooked greens is to blanche or dip them quickly a few leaves at a time in a large pot of boiling water with a pinch of salt. The larger and thicker the leaves are, the longer they need to be cooked. For example, watercress cooks in seconds while collards or kale

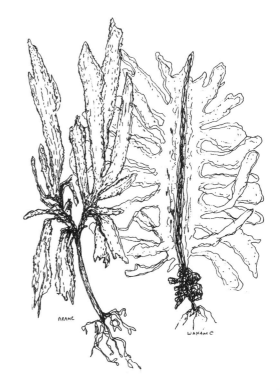

ARAME   WAKAME

might take a minute or two. When you blanche them in salted boiling water and then rinse in cold water, they become sweeter to the taste buds. In addition, the cold water drives the heat to the center and cooks the vegetable more completely throughout while retaining color, flavor, and texture. Taste test the larger leaves as they cook to get an idea of the time needed to reach desired tenderness for the rest of the batch. I find this method works well with just about all greens and most people enjoy eating them this way.

In conclusion, some of the beautiful greens, fruits and vegetables we purchase at the market could be doing us more harm than good. It is necessary to be aware of the following information. Minimum testing is done to measure the amount of chemicals used to protect fruits and vegetables from destructive bugs and disease. Recently the U.S. Department of Agriculture has decreased to an even greater degree the restrictions on control of pesticide

and fungicide spraying. The produce most affected includes broccoli, cauliflower, all cabbage varieties, kale, celery, cucumbers, string beans, potatoes, beets, bananas and apples.

Some concerned farmers use natural methods to control the problem whereas most commercial growers spray freely without concern for the health of consumers. Small commercial organic farmers normally expect to lose up to $1/3$ of the crop at each harvest to bugs and small hungry animals. In addition, they have more respect for replenishing the soil. If it is healthy and rich, the plants are usually healthy and less prone to suffer from diseases. There is less of a need for chemical combat. Furthermore, the use of a solution of garlic and water sprayed on crops has been used successfully by some organic farmers to help eliminate bug problems naturally. Overall, it would be to your benefit to try and purchase produce from reputable organic sources locally or wherever possible.

LAND VEGETABLES

Broccoli Stem and Avocado Pâté

2	cups broccoli stems
1	ripe avocado, peeled and seeded
	juice of 1 lemon
1	ripe tomato, diced
1	clove garlic, minced
1	jalapeño pepper, minced
$1/2$	red onion, minced
$1/2$	tsp. cumin
	Braggs

Boil the broccoli stems until very soft. Be sure to remove any inedible parts of the stem. This recipe is a good way to use broccoli stems and save on fat calories. Put stems in food processor with S blade. Process until smooth. Add avocado, lemon juice, garlic, jalapeño and cumin. Process until well combined. Mix in red onion and tomato. Add Braggs to taste and more lemon juice if desired. For variation, serve paté on a bed of lettuce garnished with onions and tomatoes.

Bean and Pepper Salad

$1/2$	lb. green beans
2	cloves garlic, minced
2	large red peppers
1	small head radicchio
2	tbsp. fresh parsley, minced
$1/2$	tsp. dried basil
2	tbsp. fresh lemon juice
$1/4$	cup extra virgin olive oil
	Braggs

Clean, remove stems and cut green beans french style, which means slicing them down the middle lengthwise. Steam until tender. Clean and slice red peppers in very thin strips. Shred the radicchio. Combine all vegetables with garlic and parsley. Blend together remaining ingredients and pour over vegetables. Add Braggs to taste and serve. Use minced elephant garlic instead of regular garlic for a twist.

Dandelion Dish *

1	bunch dandelions
1/2	head white cabbage
1	red onion
	juice of 1 lemon
2	tbsp. olive oil
	Braggs
	lemon zest garnish

Try to buy young tender dandelion greens. Clean and chop into small pieces. Clean and shred white cabbage. Cut onion into thin slices. Pressure cook dandelions and cabbage with a little water for several minutes until tender. Remove from heat. Add sliced onions, oil and Braggs to taste. Garnish with the lemon zest, which is another word for lemon peel.

Green Leafy Vegetable Sushi Rolls

1	lb. mustard greens or collard greens or. Swiss chard sushi mat
1	large carrot, julienned
1/4	cup toasted sesame seeds red radish garnish umeboshi paste

Wash and remove tough stems from your greens. Bring large pot of water to boil. Add a pinch of salt. Dip one or two leaves at a time into the water. They cook very quickly this way. Have a pot of cold water available to rinse leaves. This stops the cooking process and cools down the vegetables quickly. The greens are so beautiful when cooked like this. They should be bright green and full of sweet flavor yet still tender. Cook the carrots last for one minute in a strainer placed in the boiling water. They should be crisp. Layer the green leaves back to back across the whole sushi mat. Layer a strip of carrots. Take a fingerful of umeboshi paste and run it across the carrots. Top with sesame seeds. Roll tightly. Squeeze out any excess liquid. Remove the mat. Slice and arrange on a platter. This is a nice way to serve greens at a dinner party. Garnish plate with some whole red radishes for color.

Leafy Greens and Garlic *

1	lb. broccoli-rabe or kale or Swiss chard or dandelion greens or chicory or beet tops or collards or mustard greens Braggs
2	tbsp. olive oil
2	large cloves garlic

Clean and chop greens and remove tough stems. Aside from blanching or steaming, you can pressure cook the greens in less than five minutes and tenderize them at the same time. I use this method often. Since there is usually quite a bit of water clinging to the washed leaves, bring to pressure without added water. Turn off heat and wait three minutes to release pressure and remove from pot. You must pay attention or you will ruin your greens. Add extra virgin olive oil and minced or marinated garlic. Add Braggs to taste. Mix well and serve. Substitute minced scallions, chives, red onion or shallots for the garlic. The heat of the greens will wilt the raw onions so add them immediately to the hot greens. Expand this recipe by adding any other additional vegetables in small amounts to complement the greens. Convert this into a main course by adding steamed crumbled tofu and/or pasta.

String Bean Pâté

1	lb. string beans
2	stalks celery, finely minced
1	large onion, minced
1	cup walnuts
2	tbsp. extra virgin olive oil Braggs

Clean, remove stems and cook string beans until soft. Put into food processor with S blade and chop. Be careful not to end up with purée. Set aside. Process walnuts until they are a creamy paste. Sauté the onion and celery in some Braggs until wilted. Blend them in the processor with the walnuts for a few seconds. Add olive oil. Process string beans and walnut mixture together to create a pâté. Add more Braggs to taste. Use vegetable slices instead of crackers to serve with the pâté.

Broccoli Yam Sauté

1	cup broccoli florets
1	cup yams, julienned
4	scallions, minced
1	clove garlic, minced
1	red pepper, slivered
2	tbsp. dark sesame oil
1/2	tsp. dried orange rind
	dash cayenne
1	tsp. kuzu dissolved in 1/2 cup water
	tamari

Heat oil in a skillet. Add garlic and yams. Stir fry about five minutes. Add broccoli and red peppers. Cook a few minutes more. Add scallions, orange rind, cayenne and kuzu. Toss well to coat. Add tamari to taste and serve.

Parsnips with Horseradish

1/2	lb. parsnips
1/4	cup tofu mayonnaise
1	tsp. horseradish
	dash cayenne
1	tbsp. fresh parsley, minced

Clean, peel and julienne parsnips. Steam until tender. Combine remaining ingredients and coat parsnips. I don't usually have fresh horseradish in my refrigerator, so I use commercially prepared horseradish. Try to find one without additives. Increase the amount of horseradish for a stronger taste.

Carrots and Tops *

3	carrots
1	bunch carrot tops
1	tsp. toasted sesame seeds
	barley miso
1	tsp. fresh ginger juice

You must use a pressure cooker for this recipe because this process tenderizes the carrot tops. Wash and chop tops into small pieces. Clean and slice the carrots. Layer the greens with the carrots on the top. Pressure cook for several minutes. Add seeds, ginger juice and about one tsp. miso or to taste. If tops are not tender, cook a few minutes more.

Cauliflower in Chickpeaso Sauce

1	head cauliflower
1	tbsp. chickpeaso miso
1	tsp. dry mustard
1/4	cup orange juice

Steam the whole head of cauliflower until tender. Combine remaining ingredients in mortar and pestle. You can use one tbsp. prepared mustard instead of the dry mustard. Coat sauce over the steaming hot cauliflower head and let it sit a few minutes before serving.

Sweet Stuffed Cabbage

1	head cabbage
2	large sweet potatoes
1	large carrot
1	large onion, chopped
2	cups vegetable broth
1	tbsp. kuzu dissolved in 1/4 cup water
2	tbsp. extra virgin olive oil
	fresh parsley garnish
	Braggs

Steam cabbage until soft and cut away ribs. Put leaves aside for stuffing. Sauté onion with some water and Braggs for five minutes. Peel and shred sweet potatoes and carrot. Add them to the onions and continue cooking until soft. Add oil. Stuff cabbage leaves with the vegetables and roll tight. Fill oiled glass dish and top with broth. Bake at 350° for one hour or stew in a covered pot for the same amount of time. Add kuzu at the end to create a sauce. Add more Braggs to taste. Garnish with minced parsley.

Daikon and Corn

3	ears corn, decobbed
1	small daikon
1	scallion, minced
i	tsp. white miso

Cut daikon into small pieces. Sauté with a little water for about ten minutes. Add corn, scallions and miso. Cover and let sit five minutes before serving. Add more miso for a richer taste..

Daikon, Carrots and Cabbage

1	5 inch piece of daikon
1	large carrot
1/4	head cabbage
1/2	cup walnuts
	tamari

Clean and shred the vegetables. Steam until tender. Grind soaked nuts until smooth with a mortar and pestle adding one or two tablespoons tamari to taste. Add to steamed vegetables. Mix well and serve. Daikon and cabbage become sweet when cooked making this is a sweet dish.

Oven Roasted Whole Vegetables

3	whole carrots
5	whole onions
3	white turnips
6	brussels sprouts
2	parsnips
2	tbsp. extra virgin olive oil
2	large garlic cloves
1	tsp. each dried sage and rosemary
	Braggs

Pick out the smallest whole vegetables you can find. Clean vegetables and remove any inedible parts. Put vegetables in a baking pan and coat with herbs, oil and Braggs. Add one cup water to the pan. Roast at 450° for about one hour or until soft. When vegetables are cooked whole, they are so sweet.

Corn Combination

3	ears corn, decobbed
2	kohlrabi
5	scallions cut into 1 inch pieces
1/4	cup almonds, chopped
1	small jicama (optional)
1	tbsp. kuzu dissolved in 1/2 cup water
	Braggs

Peel and slice kohlrabi and jicama into small pieces. Put them in a pot with 1/2 cup of water and sprinkle with Braggs. Cover and bring to boil. Turn down heat and simmer until kohlrabi is tender. Add kuzu to thicken. Season with more Braggs and top with almonds.

Stewed Sweet Vegetables

1/2	hokkaido or butternut squash
1	large onion
1	3 inch strip kombu, soaked
1	tbsp. kuzu dissolved in 1/2 cup water
1	ear corn cut into 1 inch chunks
1	carrot
1	parsnip
	herbamare

Peel, seed, and cut the squash into large chunks. Peel and quarter onion. Clean and cut carrot and parsnip into large chunks. Layer kombu, onion, squash, parsnip and carrot in a stew pot with 1/2 cup water. Sprinkle with herbamare. Cover and bring to boil. Immediately turn down heat and simmer until vegetables are tender but firm, about 15 minutes. Mix in kuzu to create a sauce. Add more herbamare to taste. Gently toss the vegetables and serve.

Whole Cauliflower Entrée *

1	whole cauliflower
3	scallions, minced
1	tbsp. umeboshi paste
1	tbsp. lemon juice
2	tbsp. extra virgin olive oil
1/2	cup water

Pressure cook whole head of cauliflower with a little water for approximately three to five minutes until soft. Blend remaining ingredients. Pour over head of cauliflower to coat. Serve on a bed of lettuce or sprouts with a garnish of your favorite nuts or seeds.

Sweet and Sour Turnips

1	lb. white turnips
2	tbsp. white miso
1	tbsp barley malt
1	tsp. ginger juice
1/4	cup water
2	tsp. lemon juice
1	scallion, minced

Clean, slice and steam turnips until soft. Combine remaining ingredients to make a sauce and mix with turnips.

Wilted Greens

1	bunch watercress
1/2	lb. spinach
1	bunch arugula
3	red peppers
1	red onion, minced
2	tbsp. olive oil
	Braggs

Clean and chop greens. Remove stems from spinach if they are tough. Bring large pot of water to a boil. Put greens in large bowl. Pour boiling water over greens, mix and leave for one minute. Drain and return to bowl. Add red onions, olive oil and Braggs. Set aside. Broil red peppers until their skins turn black watching carefully and turning on all sides to cook evenly. Put peppers in a bowl and cover. Let sit 15 minutes. They release a lot of liquid that lifts the skin right off the pepper. Peel off the skin and remove seeds with stem. Rinse in cold water. Slice peppers and add to the greens. This is delicious over small cooked pasta. For variation, add sliced red peppers without broiling first.

Collard Greens in Shiso Leaves

1	bunch young collard greens
1/4	head white cabbage
	shiso condiment
1	bunch red radishes

Wash and remove stems from collards and cabbage. Slice into very thin strips. Clean the radishes and slice into thin pieces. Bring a large pot of water to a rolling boil with a pinch of salt. Drop small portions of greens into the pot. Boil two or three minutes, remove with a slotted spoon and dip in cold water to stop cooking process. Do this until all are blanched; blanche radishes last. Combine the vegetables and add shiso to taste. This condiment is found in health food stores and is the finely ground shiso leaf used in the process of making umeboshi plums. It is salty, so use sparingly. These leaves are reputed to help dissolve body fats. Shiso leaves have a unique flavor and add variety to your vegetarian dishes.

Boiled Salad

1	small head cabbage
1	carrot
1	stalk celery
1	cup red radishes
1/2	bunch scallions
1/2	cup fresh dill, minced
1/2	cup basic tahini dressing

Clean and cut cabbage, celery and scallions into small pieces. Clean and slice radishes and carrot. Bring a large pot of water to a boil. Blanche each vegetable separately until they are all tender, but firm. Drain and rinse them under cold water to stop the cooking process. Add the fresh dill and tahini dressing. Add more dressing for a richer taste. You can boil all vegetables together to save time. The taste will be different. Serve this salad warm or chilled.

For a dressing variation try...

1	tbsp. umeboshi paste
2	tbsp. lemon juice
4	tbsp. extra virgin olive oil
2	scallions, minced
1/4	cup fresh dill, minced

Blend first four ingredients. Add fresh dill. Combine with the salad.

Vegetables with Sauerkraut Sauce

1/2	bunch broccoli
2	large carrots
1	cup Brussels sprouts
1/2	cup sauerkraut juice
1	tbsp. white miso
1/4	cup toasted sesame seeds
1/4	cup sauerkraut, chopped
1	head lettuce

Clean and separate lettuce leaves and set aside. Clean vegetables. Peel old leaves off Brussels sprouts. Break broccoli into small florets. Cut carrots into small chunks. Blanche each vegetable until tender, but crisp. Combine remaining ingredients with a suribachi. Toss this sauce together with the vegetables and serve over a bed of lettuce. I used commercial sauerkraut for this recipe.

Broccoli and Almonds

1	bunch broccoli
2	cloves garlic, minced
1	tbsp. ginger root, minced
1	tbsp. toasted sesame oil
1/4	cup mirin
1	tbsp. tamari
1	tbsp. kuzu dissolved in 1/2 cup water
	dash cayenne
1/2	cup chopped almonds

Clean and chop broccoli into small florets. Sauté garlic and ginger in oil. Add mirin, tamari, cayenne and broccoli. Cook until broccoli is crisp. Remove from heat. Add kuzu mixture to make a sauce. Add chopped almonds. Toss all ingredients well and serve.

Fried Okra

1	lb. okra
1	shallot, minced
1/4	cup arrowroot
1/3	cup vegetable stock
1	cup cornmeal
	extra virgin olive oil
1/2	tsp. each dried oregano
	herbamare

Clean okra and remove stems. Mix arrowroot with vegetable stock and minced shallots. Mix oregano and herbamare into cornmeal. Roll okra in arrowroot mixture. Then roll in cornmeal. Lightly fry in a skillet with olive oil turning occasionally. Remove and place on sheets of paper towels to remove any excess oil.

Elephant Garlic Salad

6	cloves elephant garlic
1/2	head chicory
1	large red pepper
1	yellow pepper (optional)
1	cup tahini dressing
1/2	cup sunflower seeds

Peel and slice garlic. Steam until soft. Clean, seed and slice peppers into very thin strips. Steam until crisp. Clean and chop chicory. Arrange on a plate. Place garlic and peppers on chicory. Top with sunflower seeds. Serve with tahini dressing.

Asparagus with Sesame Sauce

1	lb. asparagus
1/4	cup toasted sesame seeds
1	tbsp. whole grain mustard
1/2	red onion, minced
2	tsp. fresh ginger juice
1	tbsp. maple syrup (optional)
1	tsp. dried orange peel
1/4	cup water
1	tbsp. Braggs
	dash cayenne

Clean, trim and steam asparagus until crisp. While still hot, mix in minced red onion. Set aside. Put all remaining ingredients in a suribachi and grind into a fine sauce. Mix sauce with asparagus tossing lightly. For variation, serve asparagus with other sauces like a raw pesto sauce.

Sweet and Sour Red Cabbage

1/2	red cabbage
2	tbsp. mirin
2	tbsp. barley malt
1	large onion
1	tbsp. umeboshi vinegar
1	tbsp. lemon juice

Clean and shred the cabbage. Peel the onion, cut in half and slice in half moon shapes. Combine all ingredients except lemon juice in a pot. Cover and steam on low heat until cabbage is soft. Mix well with lemon juice so all flavors blend.

Stuffed Artichokes

4	artichokes
1	cup plain bread crumbs
2	cloves garlic, minced
2	tbsp. fresh parsley, minced
1	tsp. dried oregano
1/4	cup extra virgin olive oil
1	cup water
	Braggs

Sauté garlic in one tbsp. oil. Remove from heat. Add oregano, remaining oil, parsley, and Braggs. Add bread crumbs and coat them by mixing well. Clean and cut about 1/2 inch off top of artichoke. Open the choke (pulling leaves apart with your hands) wide enough to stuff with bread-crumb mixture. It's a little difficult, but worth the trouble. Put stuffed chokes into a pressure cooker, add one cup water and cook 20 to 40 minutes depending on size. Check for tenderness. You should be able to put a fork through the choke when done. Add more Braggs to the artichoke sauce if desired. Serve hot or cold. For variation, omit the stuffing and follow the same procedure. Serve with mustard-flavored tofu or almond mayonnaise.

Sugar Snap Peas and Spring Onions

2	cups sugar snaps, stems removed
2	bunches spring onions, sliced
6	tbsp. lemon juice
1	tbsp. tamari
1	tbsp. whole grain mustard
2	tbsp. almond butter

Blanche sugar snaps and onions. Set aside. These vegetables cook in two minutes. Blend last four ingredients together until creamy. Pour over vegetables. Toss well. It is easy to use a suribachi to blend this sauce. Substitute scallions for onions if you prefer.

Fresh Corn Pancakes

4	large ears fresh corn, decobbed
2	tbsp. kuzu
1	tbsp. Braggs
1	tbsp. minced scallion
	canola oil or olive oil

Put corn kernels in food processor with S blade and purée them. Grind kuzu with a mortar and pestle. Mix kuzu into corn purée with remaining ingredients. Ladle the mixture onto an oiled cast-iron skillet. Cook for five minutes, and then flip over to lightly brown the other side.

Fennel Italian Style

2	large bulbs fennel
2	cloves garlic, minced
1	large mushroom
1	red pepper
1	tbsp. fresh basil, minced
	dash cayenne
	Braggs
3	tbsp. extra virgin olive oil

Clean all inedible parts from fennel bulbs and slice thinly. Clean and slice mushroom and red pepper into thin strips. Water sauté garlic, fennel, mushroom and pepper with a little Braggs. Cook until tender, but still crunchy. Add re-maining ingredients. Toss well and serve.

Onion Butter

3	large bermuda onions
	herbamare

Peel and thinly slice onions. Put into large cast iron pan with some herbamare to draw out the water from the onions. This is a long slow process. You will keep cooking and stirring these onions for hours on a very low flame until you end up with the most delicious sweet onion spread for crackers, bread or whatever. A cast-iron pan is a must for this recipe.

Green Beans in Walnut Dill Sauce

1	lb. green beans
4	scallions, chopped
	juice of 1 lemon
1/2	cup fresh dill
1/4	cup fresh parsley
11/4	cup walnuts
1	tbsp. olive oil
1	tbsp. miso
1/2	cup red radishes, shredded
2	cups sprouts

Clean, stem and cut string beans into one inch pieces. Steam until crisp. Blend remaining ingredients except radishes and sprouts. Mix sauce with the beans. Place sprouts on a platter. Top with string beans. Garnish with radishes.

Blanched Napa Cabbage

1	head napa cabbage
3	scallions
1	cup soft cooked brown rice
1	tsp. umeboshi paste
2	tsp. extra virgin olive oil
1	tbsp. lemon juice
1/4	cup fresh parsley, minced
1	cup vegetable broth or water

Clean and slice cabbage into one inch pieces. Blanche until crisp. This cabbage cooks very quickly so be careful. Blend remaining ingredients together except parsley to make a sauce. Combine cabbage, parsley and sauce together. Mix well and serve.

Sauce Variation:

1	onion, blanched
1	tsp. sesame oil
1	tbsp. lemon juice
1	cup soft cooked rice
1	tbsp. umeboshi paste
1	cup vegetable broth

Blend ingredients and serve over cabbage.

Chow Mein Vegetarian

2	large bermuda onions
1/2	head celery
2	cloves garlic, minced
2	cups mung bean sprouts
6	large mushrooms, sliced
2	Jerusalem artichokes
2	tbsp. toasted sesame seeds
1	tbsp. arrowroot dissolved in 1/2 cup water
	tamari
2	tbsp. toasted sesame oil

Peel and slice onions and artichokes. Clean and cut celery on the diagonal into thin strips. Stir fry onions, celery and garlic with oil in a wok or any skillet until crisp. Add mushrooms, sprouts and Jerusalem artichokes. Keep stir frying until vegetables are just cooked and still crisp. Add tamari to taste and arrowroot mixture to thicken. Add some water if necessary. Garnish with toasted sesame seeds.

Brussels Sprouts and Garlic

1	lb. Brussels sprouts
2	cloves garlic, minced
3	tbsp. extra virgin olive oil
3	mushrooms
3	tbsp. bread crumbs
	dash cayenne
	Braggs
1/2	tsp. dried oregano

Clean and remove inedible leaves from Brussels sprouts. Bring a large pot of water to boil. Drop the Brussels sprouts into the water and blanche until crisp. Remove and dip in cold water. Cut in half. Set aside. Sauté garlic in olive oil for just a few seconds. Add Brussels sprouts and stir fry so that the oil and garlic coat the vegetables well. Add mushrooms that have been thinly sliced. Stir fry one minute more. Add remaining ingredients. Mix well.

Mushrooms Mexican

1	lb. mushrooms
1	zucchini
1	red pepper
1	clove garlic, minced
2	tbsp. fresh cilantro
1	small onion
	dash cayenne
2	tbsp. extra virgin olive oil
	herbamare

Clean and slice mushrooms, zucchini, red pepper and onion. Sauté onions in a little water for a few minutes with herbamare. Add the mushrooms, zucchini, and red pepper. Sauté a few minutes more. Add garlic, cilantro, and cayenne. Take off heat, cover, and let sit five minutes. Add olive oil and more herbamare to taste. Mix well and serve.

Spicy Carrots and Cabbage

2	large carrots
1/2	head cabbage
1	bunch scallions
2	tbsp. fresh mint, minced
1/2	tsp. allspice
1/4	tsp. cayenne
2	tbsp. mirin (optional)
1	tbsp. kuzu dissolved in 1/4 cup water
	Braggs

Clean and shred carrots and cabbage. Slice scallions in short diagonals. Layer scallions, cabbage and carrots in a pot. Add some Braggs and 1/2 cup water. Cover and cook until tender, but crisp. Remone from heat. Add remaining ingredients. Mix well until kuzu thickens and serve.

SEA VEGETABLES

Roasted Wakame

	several large wakame fronds
1/2	cup toasted sesame seeds

Use regular wakame in long dried pieces for this recipe. Do not soak. Bake wakame in your oven at 350° until wakame crumbles easily. It's tricky because you don't want to burn it. Remove the fronds and break into small pieces. Grind down the seaweed with a suribachi and suricogi. Gradually add the sesame seeds and grind together. This is worth the trouble because the flavor of this combination is delicious. It's a great condiment. Add more  or fewer seeds to your own taste. Also substitute dulse for wakame as a variation. Instead of oven roasting, try dehydrating wakame until it begins to crumble and then complete recipe as indicated.

Dulse and Vidalia Onions

1/2	cup dulse
1	vidalia onion
2	tbsp. fresh parsley, minced
1	large cucumber, peeled and seeded
1	tbsp. lemon juice
2	tbsp. sunflower seeds

Peel, cut in half and slice onion thinly. Blanch for two minutes. Rinse dulse and chop it. Mince the cucumber. Combine all ingredients and mix well before serving.

Seasoned Nori

	nori sheets
1/4	cup barley malt
2	tbsp. mirin

Combine barley malt and mirin. Use a brush to baste nori sheets. Place in dehydrator until dry, or in a 250° oven for about ten minutes. Eat as is or use to make sushi.

Dulse and Lettuce Sauté

1	head iceberg lettuce, shredded
1/2	cup dulse
1	tbsp. extra virgin olive oil
1/4	cup pitted black olives (optional)

Blanch lettuce quickly. Don't overcook. Rinse and chop dulse and add to lettuce with black olives and oil. Mix well and serve. Substitute 1/2 of a large head of white cabbage for the lettuce.

Leeks and Dulse

2	large leeks
1/2	cup dulse, chopped
1	tbsp. toasted sesame seeds
1/4	head napa cabbage
1	tbsp. extra virgin olive oil (optional)

Carefully clean and chop leeks into small pieces. Cut cabbage the same size. Layer leeks and cabbage in a pan. Add a little water to cook the vegetables until tender. They cook very quickly. Add remaining ingredients. Toss well and serve. Substitute cauliflower for cabbage. Add a shredded carrot for more color.

Dulse, Pignolis, and Kale

1	bunch kale
1	clove garlic, minced
2	tbsp. extra virgin olive oil
1/2	cup pignoli nuts, chopped
1/2	cup dulse, chopped

Use young tender kale. Remove stems and chop into small pieces. Bring a large pot of water to a boil. Blanche leaves a few at a time until tender, about two minutes. Drain well. Add remaining ingredients and mix well. Substitute other greens in this recipe for variation. Use marinated garlic for a sweeter flavor.

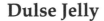

Dulse Jelly

2	cups dulse
1	cup water
1	tbsp. kuzu dissolved in 1/4 cup water

Clean and chop dulse. Put into a small pot with one cup water and simmer for about ten minutes until dulse dissolves. Combine kuzu mixture with dulse. Cook one minute more. Put into a jar, cool and refrigerate. If you like this idea, add other ingredients in tiny amounts like minced onions, lemon juice, sweetener, ginger juice, etc. to create different table condiments.

Rich Bouillon *

2	long strips kombu
6	cups water
1/4	cup umeboshi extract
1/2	cup tamari

Soak kombu with remaining ingredients for an hour in your pressure cooker. Cook for 30 minutes. Open pot and remove kombu. You can also blend kombu into the stock. For a richer taste, let the bouillon continue to cook with top removed to evaporate some of the water.

Kombu and Shitake Mushrooms *

5	strips kombu
6	dried shitake mushrooms
	tamari or Braggs
1/2	cup water

Soak kombu and mushrooms for about two hours and drain. Chop kombu into one inch pieces. Discard mushroom stems and cut caps in half. Put kombu in pressure cooker with caps on top. Add 1/2 cup water and cook 20 minutes. Open pot and add tamari or Braggs to taste. This is delicious served with wild rice or noodles. Fresh daikon cooked with the kombu and mushrooms is a nice variation.

Sweet Carrots and Kombu

2   strips kombu
2   large carrots
1   tbsp. toasted sesame seeds
        Braggs

Soak kombu and slice into small pieces. Peel and matchstick carrots. Layer kombu and carrots in a pot with one cup water. Cover and simmer for about 20 minutes. Remove cover. Add seeds and Braggs to taste. Simmer longer if you want to evaporate excess water. Mix and serve.

Tororo Kombu Condiment

$1/4$ cup tororo kombu
$1/4$ cup water
        juice of 1 lemon
1   tbsp. scallions, minced
1   tsp. fresh ginger juice
1   tbsp. rice syrup
        Braggs

Combine all and mix well. Tororo kombu is finely shredded and pressed tightly in its package. Cut it up enough so that it can be combined with the other ingredients. It is great for instant preparation and is found in most health food stores in the macrobiotic section.

Wakame and Bamboo Shoots *

$1/2$ cup "instant" wakame
1   cup cauliflower, chopped
$1/2$ cup bamboo shoots, sliced
$1/2$ cup fresh peas
2   tbsp. tahini
        tamari

Pressure cook cauliflower with $1/2$ cup water for three minutes until soft. Purée cauliflower with tahini. Add remaining ingredients with tamari to taste. Steam or blanche the peas for variation.

Land and Sea Greens

I
2   cups young kale, thinly sliced, stems removed
1   cup white cabbage, shredded
2   tbsp. pumpkin seeds
$1/4$ cup "instant" wakame
        Braggs to taste

II
2   cups bok choy, thinly sliced
1   cup red onions, minced
$1/4$ cup "instant" wakame
1   tbsp. toasted sesame seeds
1   tsp. ginger juice
        Braggs to taste

III
2   cups young collards, thinly sliced, stems removed
1   large onion, thinly sliced
$1/4$ cup "instant" wakame
2   tbsp. tahini mixed with 1 tsp. Braggs

Follow the same procedure for each recipe. Wash and remove any inedible stems from all greens. Steam or blanche all vegetables until tender but very crisp. Add seasonings and mix well. Remember to soak and drain wakame before adding to the other ingredients.

Nori Hot Sauce

3   sheets nori, slivered
1   bunch scallions, minced
$3/4$ cup water
3   tbsp. sesame oil
1   tbsp. umeboshi paste
$1/2$ tsp. cayenne

Steam the scallions. Combine scallions with the oil, umeboshi paste, water, and cayenne in a suribachi or blender. Add more cayenne if you want it to be hotter. Add nori and mix well. Add more water for a thinner consistency.

Nori Salad Spread

1	lb. tofu, crumbled
3	tbsp. white miso or to taste
1	small bermuda onion
2	stalks celery
1	clove garlic
3	sheets nori, slivered
2	tbsp. extra virgin olive oil
1/4	cup tofu mayonnaise (optional)

Clean and mince onion, celery and garlic. Steam them for about five minutes. Put tofu in food processor with S blade and add vegetables. Process until well combined. Add remaining ingredients and quickly process. Adjust seasonings and chill before serving.

Arame in Mustard Sauce

1/2	head cabbage, shredded
1/2	cup arame
2	tsp. olive oil
1	tsp. dry mustard
2	tbsp. Braggs
1	tsp. sake (optional)

Blanche cabbage until tender, but crisp. Combine with arame. Combine remaining ingredients to create a sauce. Mix all and toss well before serving.

Spicy Arame

3/4	cup arame
1	large onion, sliced thinly
1	clove garlic, minced
1	small carrot, julienned
2	tbsp. orange juice
1/2	tsp. curry
1/4	tsp. cumin
1/4	tsp. tumeric
1	tbsp. maple syrup
	dash cayenne
	Braggs to taste

Water sauté arame, onion, carrot and garlic with Braggs several minutes. Add remaining ingredients and cook for two minutes until flavors are combined. Mix well and serve.

Seaweed Salad

1/2	cup arame
1	tbsp. extra virgin olive oil
1	small carrot
2	stalks celery
1	tbsp. lemon juice
2	scallions, minced
1	tsp. toasted sesame seeds
1	tsp. maple syrup (optional)
1/2	tsp. ginger juice
	Braggs to taste

Boil arame in a pot for ten minutes. Drain and rinse. Clean and chop carrot and celery into small pieces. Blanche until crisp but tender. Combine all ingredients and adjust seasonings. Substitute hiziki instead of arame.

Seaweed Sauté

1/2	cup arame
1	large carrot, julienned
1	large onion, sliced
1	tsp. umeboshi paste
1	tbsp. mirin (optional)
2	tbsp. extra virgin olive oil

Water sauté onion until wilted. Add carrots and arame. Cook together for about five minutes. Remove from heat. Combine olive oil, mirin and paste with 1/4 cup water. Add to pot and mix well. Adjust seasonings to taste. This is a flavorful sweet dish. Substitute hiziki with arame for variation.

Hiziki and Corn *

1/2	cup hiziki
3	ears corn, decobbed
1	large onion, diced
1	tsp. olive oil
	sweet white miso

Boil hiziki for ten minutes, drain and rinse. Pressure cook onions and corn for about three minutes. Open pot and add remaining ingredients with white miso to taste. The corn and miso sweeten the hiziki.

Hiziki Vegetable Salad

$1/2$	cup hiziki
4	oz. tofu, crumbled
1	cup string beans, stems removed
1	carrot, julienned
3	tbsp. toasted sesame seeds
	Braggs to taste
2	tbsp. extra virgin olive oil

Cut string beans into small pieces. Blanche vegetables together for several minutes until tender, but crisp. Set aside. Boil hiziki for ten minutes, drain and rinse. Combine all ingredients together and adjust seasoning before serving.

Hiziki and Peppers

$1/2$	cup hiziki
1	large onion, thinly sliced
1	clove garlic, minced
1	red pepper, sliced
1	jalapeño pepper, sliced
2	tbsp. extra virgin olive oil
$1/2$	cup water
1	tbsp. umeboshi paste
$1/2$	tsp. dried oregano

Layer onions, garlic, peppers and hiziki in a pot with a little water. Cook until vegetables are tender. Add remaining ingredients and mix well. Adjust seasonings and serve. For a variation add $1/2$ tsp. cumin or basil or thyme instead of oregano.

Hiziki

Dulse

CONTENTS
GRAINS, PASTA, AND SEITAN

Grains, Pasta, and Seitan

The importance of cereal grains should not be overlooked in our diets. They are the beginning and the end, the seed and the fruit of the plant and they represent the staff of life for many populations throughout history. Grains are good sources of carbohydrates, proteins, dietary fiber, B vitamins, iron, magnesium and zinc. Unrefined grains are infinitely higher in nutrients than breads, cereals, crackers, pastas and other refined grain by-products. Please note it is estimated that over 25 nutrients are lost in the milling process. The mandatory procedure of grain enrichment in the United States, which really restores only a few nutrients, was instated around WWII by the leaders of the Armed Forces. They were afraid that our soldiers wouldn't be able to survive combat because of the lack of proper nutrition. Idealistically, eating whole grains provides us with a great source of nutrition and refined products like pasta and noodles should only be eaten occasionally.

Many societies the world over use whole grains as a main staple in their daily diet. There are numerous ways to prepare grains but let us go to the first important steps. After washing your grains to remove dirt and debris, soaking is an important and beneficial process. It shortens cooking time, improves flavor and increases digestibility. The natural sweetness of whole grains is released. The following recipes use pre-soaked grains unless otherwise indicated. For example, it is not necessary to soak cous cous and bulghur and is an option for roasted buckwheat groats. Quinoa tastes much better using this soaking process because it removes a bitter aftertaste for a better-tasting dish. Be sure to discard the quinoa soaking water.

If you allow your grain to sit for three-to-six hours after it is soaked and drained, it continues to germinate getting softer and more delicious. Each step reduces cooking time. Each step also changes the final taste and texture of the grain. It is favorable to add salt only after soaking time is over so that it does not deter the expansion of the grain. A pinch of salt added to the cooking water helps to break down the cellulose walls of the grain aiding digestion. Combinations of grains cooked together make a delicious infinite variety of possibilities. It is good to know that grains and legumes are often difficult to digest when cooked together. It is better to prepare them separately and mix together.

For many of us who have eaten large quantities of dairy foods over the years, a layer of fat in our intestines can initially prevent proper digestion of grains. Eating a fermented food like miso, raw sauerkraut or raw pickles is tremendously beneficial at mealtime to aid the proper digestion of these foods.

Sesame seeds mixed with seasalt, also called gomasio, is another condiment used by the macrobiotic community to aid the digestion of grains. I enjoy gomasio, but have frequently substituted Braggs for the seasalt when preparing this recipe. After soaking the seeds for several hours, I drain them well with a fine strainer and toast them in a heavy skillet until golden brown and fragrant. I have at hand a spray bottle with Braggs in it which I use to spray coat the seeds. Be sure all the seeds are dry when done. This takes several minutes. You constantly stir the seeds so they don't burn. If this happens, throw away and start again. They should be lightly toasted and break up easily when rubbed between two fingers. The flavor of this condiment is exquisite. I prefer the hulled sesame seeds although the unhulled are also used. The final step is to grind them in a suribachi to blend the salty flavor with the seeds. It is also commercially prepared and sold at the health food store.

Further on in this chapter I include seitan, another interesting food that is growing in

popularity in America. It is rich in protein and easily digested. The gluten in whole wheat flour is separated from the starch and bran, then flavored and cooked in a variety of ways that successfully achieve textures similar to meat. For people who eat meat it helps to reduce desire for intake of animal food. There are a number of methods for making seitan that can be found in other available cookbooks.

Using varieties of wheat, long and short preparation procedures and various vegetable stocks creates many different types. If you have not learned how to make seitan, use commercial seitan available at your health food store. Once you have been shown the technique, it is easy to make yet time consuming. The seitan recipes are more gourmet in nature and are fun to make for dinner parties.

GRAINS

Colorful Rice Salad

2	cups basmati brown rice
1	red pepper
3	scallions, minced
2	stalks celery, minced
1/2	tsp. herbamare
1/2	tsp. dry mustard
	dash cayenne
	dash paprika
1/4	cup extra virgin olive oil
2	tsp. whole grain mustard
1/4	cup eggless mayonnaise (optional)

Cook rice in a covered pot with four cups water for approximately 35 to 45 minutes until all water is absorbed. Set aside to cool. Combine all ingredients and toss well. Adjust seasonings and serve warm or chilled. Add some small cubes of tofu to the rice for a variation.

Couscous Loaf

1	cup couscous
1/2	small carrot, shredded
1/2	stalk celery, finely minced
1	scallion, minced (green part only)
	dash Braggs

Bring two cups water to a boil. Mix in remaining ingredients. Cook several minutes until water is absorbed. Press into small loaf pan. Let cool and cut into squares. Serve with your favorite sauce.

Garam Couscous

2	cups couscous
2	tbsp. canola oil
1	tsp. garam masala
1/2	carrot, shredded
1	stalk celery, minced
2	scallions, minced
	Braggs to taste

Bring two cups water to a boil with some Braggs. Add the couscous and garam masala. Stir well, cover and remove from heat. Let sit five minutes. Spoon into a bowl. Add oil and vegetables. Toss well to coat grains with the oil. Serve warm or cold. Garam masala is a spice blend found in Indian markets.

Corn Grits Casserole

1	cup yellow corn grits
1	ear corn, decobbed
1/2	tsp. herbamare
6oz.	soya kaas jalapeño cheese, sliced

Bring four cups water and herbamare to a boil. Slowly add grits constantly stirring to prevent lumps. Cook for about 15 minutes in a covered pot on a very low heat. Add corn kernels and let sit for ten minutes. Spoon half of the mixture into an 8"x8" greased pan. Layer slices of soy cheese over the hot grits. Press in remaining grits to cover. Let rest until firm and slice. Serve with the red pepper sauce in the preceding recipe. Substitute plain soy cheese if you prefer.

Polenta with Red Pepper Sauce

1	cup polenta
1	ear corn, decobbed
2	tbsp. fresh cilantro, minced
1	tbsp. Braggs
4	large red peppers
2	tbsp. lemon juice
1	jalapeño pepper, seeded
1	tsp. dried basil
2	tbsp. extra virgin olive oil
	herbamare and cayenne

Bring three cups water and Braggs to a boil. Turn down heat and slowly add polenta constantly stirring to avoid lumps. Keep mixing until all the polenta is added. Cook until all the water is absorbed. Remove from the heat and let sit ten minutes. Spoon into a 8"x8" pan greased with olive oil. Press corn kernels into the top of the loaf. Let cool and cut into squares. Roast red peppers under a broiler until well browned. Let rest in covered bowl for ten minutes. Peel skins, remove stems and seeds and rinse. Blend with remaining ingredients to create a sauce. Serve over polenta squares. Add more jalapeño for a hotter sauce.

Barley Corn Salad

1	cup barley
3	ears corn decobbed
3/4	cup plain soy milk
1	red pepper, minced
1	tbsp. sweet white miso
3	scallions, minced
1	tsp. Braggs

Cook barley in two cups water with Braggs until all the water is absorbed and barley is soft, about 40 minutes. Set aside to cool. Cook corn kernels in a small amount of water for about five minutes. Place kernels in food processor with S blade. Add soy milk and miso. Process until well blended but still chunky. Use more or less miso to satisfy your own taste. Mix all ingredients and adjust seasoning. Serve warm or cold.

Barley Risotto

1/2	cup barley
1 1/2	cups vegetable stock
1/2	cup green peas
1/2	tsp. rosemary and a bay leaf
4	scallions, minced
1	red pepper, minced
1/2	head white cabbage, chopped
2	tbsp. extra virgin olive oil
	Braggs to taste
2	tbsp. fresh parsley, minced

Roast barley in a heavy pot until lightly browned. Cook barley in vegetable stock (or water) with some Braggs and a bay leaf until water is absorbed and barley is tender, about 45 minutes. Sauté cabbage in a little water until soft. Add cabbage with remaining ingredients to hot barley. Adjust seasonings and serve. Remember to remove bay leaf.

Creamed Barley and Broccoli

1/2	cup barley
1	tsp. Braggs
1	bunch broccoli
1	tbsp. extra virgin olive oil
	dash cayenne
1	tbsp. kuzu
1	cup plain soy milk
	Braggs to taste
3	scallions, minced

Cook barley with 1 1/2 cups water and Braggs until tender, about 45 minutes. Clean and remove stems from broccoli. Chop into florets and blanche until crisp. Set aside. Mix kuzu in soymilk until dissolved and simmer in a saucepan stirring constantly until thickened. Add olive oil, cayenne, minced scallions and Braggs to taste. Combine all ingredients. Mix well and serve.

Buckwheat and Couscous

1/2	cup buckwheat
1/2	cup couscous
4	scallions, minced
1	stalk celery, minced
1/2	cup fresh peas
1/4	cup fresh parsley, minced
1	carrot, shredded
2	tbsp. extra virgin olive oil
	Braggs to taste

Do not soak buckwheat. Wash and drain it. Put buckwheat into a pot with couscous, 1 1/2 cups water and some Braggs. Cook about 15 minutes until all water is absorbed. Add peas, carrots and celery and let rest another ten minutes. Place in a large bowl and add remaining ingredients. Mix well and serve warm or cold. Substitute quinoa for couscous with the addition of another 1/2 cup water. Try adding a little curry for a different twist. Use frozen peas if fresh ones are not available.

Bulghur Tabouli

1	cup bulghur
2	tbsp. fresh mint, minced
1	large carrot, shredded
1	cucumber, diced
4	scallions, minced
4	tbsp. fresh parsley, minced
6	red radishes, minced
3	tbsp. extra virgin olive oil
	juice of 2 lemons
	Braggs to taste

Bring 1 3/4 cups water to a boil. Wash and drain bulghur and add to boiling water. Remove from heat and let sit covered about 45 minutes. For a drier bulghur, add 1 1/2 cups water. Mix all ingredients together and adjust seasonings. Substitute two teaspoons dried mint if fresh is not available. For variation, substitute kasha or quinoa for bulghur.

Millet Yam Cakes *

1/2	cup millet
1 1/2	cups water
2	small yams
1	tsp. fresh ginger juice
	Braggs

To add an interesting flavor to these cakes, drain the soaked millet well and roast it in a pan until golden brown and starts to pop. Peel and dice the yams. Hopefully they are sweet ones. Cook the millet, yams and water in a pressure cooker for 15 minutes. Open pot and add ginger juice with Braggs to taste. Mix well, cool and press into little cakes. You could use an oiled muffin tin to create a uniform shape. Eliminate the roasting step if you are not so inclined.

Bulghur Pilaf

1	cup bulghur
2	cups vegetable stock
1	leek
2	stalks celery, minced
1	carrot, shredded
1	clove garlic, minced
5	white mushrooms, sliced
2	tbsp. extra virgin olive oil
	Braggs to taste
2	tbsp. fresh parsley, minced

Wash leek thoroughly and slice thinly. Water sauté leek, garlic and mushrooms with some Braggs. Wash and drain bulghur and add to sauté pan with vegetable stock (or water). Cover and cook for about 15 minutes. Add celery, carrot, olive oil and parsley. Mix well and serve.

Millet, Teff, and Amaranth

1	cup millet
1/4	cup teff
1/4	cup amaranth
1	tsp. Braggs

Wash and soak grains together in a pot with four cups water for about six hours. Cover the pot and cook for about 30 minutes. Let sit another 30 minutes before serving; add more Braggs to taste.

Buckwheat and Sauerkraut

1	cup buckwheat
$1/2$	head white cabbage, shredded
1	cup sauerkraut, chopped
$1/2$	tsp. caraway seeds
2	tbsp. extra virgin olive oil (optional)
2	tbsp. scallions, minced

Cook buckwheat in two cups water until water is absorbed, about 15 minutes. Set aside. Water sauté cabbage until crisp. Combine all ingredients and mix well. Adjust seasonings and serve.

Chestnut Rice

2	cups short grain brown rice
$1/2$	cup dried chestnuts
$1/4$	tsp. seasalt

Wash and soak rice in a pot with four cups water. Soak chestnuts in a separate bowl of water for about five hours. Drain and wash skins off chestnuts. Add to rice pot with seasalt. Cook with a cover until all water is absorbed, about 45 minutes. This is a very sweet tasting dish and for me it's like a dessert. You can find dried chestnuts in gourmet stores and Oriental markets.

Ginger Fried Rice

1	cup long grain brown rice
2	tbsp. toasted sesame oil
1	small carrot, shredded
3	scallions, minced
1	inch piece ginger root, peeled and minced
1	sheet nori, slivered
$1/4$	cup fresh parsley, minced
1	small clove garlic, minced
	tamari to taste

Cook rice in two cups water for about 45 minutes. Sauté scallion, garlic and ginger with some tamari and sesame oil for several minutes. Add rice and stir fry until rice is well coated and lightly browned. Remove from heat. Mix in remaining ingredients. Garnish with slivered nori.

Lemony Basmati Rice Pilaf

1	cup basmati brown rice
2	cups vegetable stock
1	tbsp. extra virgin olive oil
2	shallots, minced
1	tsp. dried lemon peel
6	shitake mushrooms, sliced
2	tbsp. fresh dill, minced
1	stalk celery, finely minced
	Braggs to taste

Sauté shallots with mushrooms in a dash of Braggs and water until tender. Cook rice in vegetable stock (or water) for 45 minutes. When all water has been absorbed and rice is tender, add dill, celery, lemon peel and olive oil. Mix well and serve. You can substitute any mushroom.

Grainburgers *

$1/2$	cup sweet brown rice
1	cup millet
$1/2$	cup bulghur wheat
1	clove garlic, minced
1	small carrot, shredded
$1/2$	red onion, shredded
$1/4$	cup fresh parsley, minced
$1/2$	tsp. dried basil
$1/4$	tsp. thyme
	tamari to taste

Pressure cook millet and brown rice in 2 $1/2$ cups water with some tamari for 30 minutes. While this is cooking, bring one cup of water to a boil and pour over bulghur. Cover and let sit 30 minutes. Remove any excess water from bulghur. Mix all ingredients together, adding more tamari to taste. Press into patties and serve. For variation, eliminate bulghur and increase rice to one cup and water to three cups before cooking. You can bake patties at 350° for 15 minutes on a greased sheet if you prefer. These patties taste delicious served with an onion sauce.

Couscous Vegetable Salad

1	cup couscous
1	tsp. extra virgin olive oil
1/2	cup cabbage, shredded
1	small carrot, shredded
2	scallions, minced (green part only)
1	small red pepper, slivered
1/4	cup fresh parsley, minced
	pinch dried rosemary
1	tbsp. extra virgin olive oil
	Braggs to taste

Bring one cup water to a boil. Add one tsp. Braggs and couscous. Stir well, cover, turn off heat and let sit five minutes. Add remaining ingredients to couscous with more Braggs if desired. Toss very well and serve. Substitute curry for rosemary as a variation.

Millet Pot Pie *

1	cup millet
1	tbsp. Braggs
1/2	head cauliflower, chopped
2	ears corn, decobbed
2	cups seitan, minced
1	large bermuda onion, sliced
1	tbsp. extra virgin olive oil

Pressure cook millet with 2 1/2 cups water and Braggs for 15 minutes. Set aside. Water sauté onion, corn and cauliflower until soft and tender. Remove from heat and add oil. Coat pie plate with some olive oil. Press half of the millet into pie plate. Layer the vegetables, then the seitan and top with remaining millet mixture. Carefully press together. Let cool and solidify enough to hold its shape when sliced.

Millet Quinoa Pilaf

1/2	cup millet
1/2	cup quinoa
1/2	tsp. herbamare
2	ears corn, decobbed
1/2	red pepper, minced
1/2	tsp. dried basil
6	spears asparagus, minced
1/2	tsp. dried sage
1/4	cup fresh parsley, chopped
1	tbsp. extra virgin olive oil

Soak millet and quinoa separately. Drain both and combine together in a pot. Add 1 3/4 cups water and herbamare. Bring to a boil and cook for about 15 minutes until all water is absorbed. Mix in remaining ingredients. Remove from heat. Let sit ten minutes before serving.

Millet Croquettes with Onion Sauce*

1	cup millet
1	carrot, shredded
1	small onion, minced
2	stalks broccoli, minced
1	tsp. herbamare
1	tbsp. fresh ginger juice
1	tbsp. extra virgin olive oil
2	tbsp. fresh parsley, minced
2	large Bermuda onions, sliced
2	tbsp. kuzu dissolved in 2 cups water
	Braggs
	parsley garnish

Pressure cook millet with 2 1/2 cups water and one tsp. herbamare for 20 minutes. Steam the carrot, minced onion and broccoli until tender and add to the millet. Add ginger juice, olive oil and parsley with Braggs to taste. Mix well, roll into croquettes and set aside. Pressure cook sliced onions with Braggs for 15 minutes. Combine kuzu mixture with onions to create a thick sauce. Serve over croquettes. Garnish with more parsley. Use this mixture to stuff red peppers for variation. Bake or steam peppers until soft and serve with onion sauce.

Simple Dinner Rice

1	cup medium grain brown rice
2	cups water
1	bay leaf
$1/4$	tsp. thyme
1	tsp. extra virgin olive oil
1	tsp. Braggs

Put all ingredients in a pot. Bring to boil. Cover and simmer about 40 minutes until all water is absorbed and rice is soft.

Millet Squash Loaf *

1	cup millet
1	large onion, chopped
1	small butternut squash
1	bay leaf
1	tsp. Braggs
$1/2$	tsp. dried thyme

Peel, seed and chop squash into small pieces. Layer onion, squash and millet in a pressure cooker. Add two cups water and remaining ingredients. Cook 20 minutes. Remove bay leaf. Mix well and enjoy. This is a sweet dish that can be pressed into a loaf pan. It will harden as it cools. Cut it into slices and serve. Interchange different hard squashes for variation. Add more Braggs if desired.

Millet Mashed Potatoes *

1	cup millet
3	cups water
1	head cauliflower, chopped
1	onion, chopped
$1/2$	tsp. dried basil
1	tbsp. white miso
1	tbsp. extra virgin olive oil
$1/2$	cup baby peas (optional)

Pressure cook first five ingredients for 20 minutes. Place in food processor with S blade and blend until creamy. Add oil and miso. For a richer taste, omit one cup water when cooking. Add one cup plain soy milk when blending. For a variation, mix in some baby peas.

Millet Sauerkraut Casserole *

1	cup millet
1	cup sauerkraut, chopped
1	red pepper, diced
2	leeks
$1/2$	lb. tofu, cubed
1	large parsnip, peeled and minced
	dash cayenne
2	tbsp. olive oil
	Braggs

Pressure cook millet and parsnip with three cups of water for 15 minutes. Wash leeks thoroughly and chop. Water sauté leeks, red pepper and tofu with some Braggs until vegetables are tender. Mix all ingredients together and press into a 9"x13" casserole dish. Use commercial kraut in this recipe.

Shepherd's Pie

	millet mashed potatoes
8	oz. pkg. tempeh
2	large carrots, sliced
1	cup green peas
	bechamel sauce
	olive oil and Braggs

Make one recipe portion of the millet mashed potatoes. Cut into small cubes and bake tempeh until well browned. Coat with Braggs and olive oil. Set aside. Steam peas and carrots until tender. Coat a 10-inch pie plate with olive oil. Layer half the millet mixture, tempeh, carrots and peas and smooth over the top with remaining "mashed potatoes". Let sit until millet hardens and serve with bechamel sauce.

Quinoa with Miso Gravy *

1	cup quinoa
2	tbsp. extra virgin olive oil
1	small onion, diced
2	cloves garlic, minced
2	tbsp. white miso
2	tbsp. mirin (optional)
1/2	tsp. rosemary
1/4	cup fresh parsley, minced
2	tbsp. kuzu
	Braggs

Soak quinoa and discard water. Cook with one 3/4 cups water and some Braggs until all water is absorbed. Set aside. Pressure cook onion, garlic, miso, mirin and rosemary for ten minutes. Mix kuzu with one cup water until dissolved. Mix into hot onion mixture with parsley to create a delicious sauce. Add more water as needed. Serve over quinoa.

Stuffed Grapeleaves

1	cup long grain brown rice
1	parsnip, shredded
1	tsp. fresh mint, minced
1	tbsp. fresh dill, minced
1	large bermuda onion, chopped
	juice of one lemon
1/4	cup extra virgin olive oil
1	bottle grapevine leaves
	Braggs to taste

Cook rice with two cups water, parsnip, onion and some Braggs until all water is absorbed, about 40 minutes. Mix in herbs and set aside. Remove leaves from jar and quickly blanche to remove brine. Separate carefully and add some filling to each leaf. Roll tightly and place in heavy skillet side by side until all the filling is used. Sprinkle with lemon juice and 1 cup water. Cover skillet and simmer about 45 minutes. Drizzle olive oil over the stuffed leaves. Let sit about 20 minutes before serving. Add more Braggs as needed. Grapevine leaves can be purchased in specialty stores. Read the labels and chose the ones without additives. Substitute steamed cabbage leaves for grapeleaves.

Rice and Tofu Jardiniere

1	cup white basmati rice
1	small onion, minced
1	small zucchini, juliénned
1	ear corn, decobbed
1/2	tsp. dried oregano
1	tbsp. fresh cilantro, minced
2	tbsp. extra virgin olive oil
4	oz. tofu, cubed
	herbamare

Cook rice in two cups water with some herbamare. This rice cooks in about 15 minutes. Mix remaining ingredients into hot rice and let sit for ten minutes before serving.

Roasted Rice and Kale

1	cup long grain brown rice
1	bunch young kale
1	cup mung bean sprouts
3	scallions, minced
1/2	tsp. dried oregano
	Braggs and cayenne to taste
2	tbsp. extra virgin olive oil

Roast rice in a heavy pan until golden brown. Bring two cups of water to a boil with some Braggs. Pour over roasted rice and continue to cook until water is absorbed. This process makes the rice kernels burst open producing a very light taste. Remove stems from kale and chop into small pieces. Blanche until crisp but tender. Mix all ingredients together with the hot rice. Adjust seasonings and serve.

Quinoa Salad

1	cup quinoa
1	large carrot, shredded
2	stalks celery, minced
1	yellow pepper, minced
	sweet miso sauce

Cook quinoa with 13/4 cups water for 20 minutes. Mix in carrot, celery and yellow pepper. Add miso sauce to taste and chill before serving. Remember to soak quinoa and discard water.

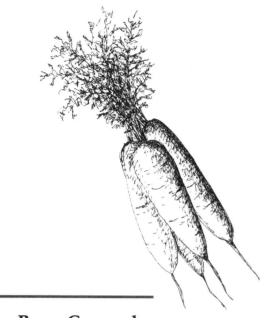

Rye Berry Casserole

1	cup sprouted rye berries
1	large bermuda onion, sliced
1/2	small red cabbage, chopped
1	parsnip, peeled and shredded
1/2	tsp. caraway seeds
1	tbsp. extra virgin olive oil
	Braggs to taste
1/4	cup fresh parsley, minced

Water sauté onion, cabbage and parsnip with some Braggs until tender. Steam rye berries until they are tender, about 15 minutes. Combine all ingredients, mix well and adjust seasoning.

Sweet and Spicy Rice Salad

2	cups cooked short-grain brown rice
1	large carrot
2	stalks celery, minced
1/2	cup plain soy milk
1	small jicama
1/4	tsp. each coriander, tumeric and curry
1	tbsp. maple syrup (optional)
	mung bean sprouts
	Braggs to taste

Peel and shred jicama and carrot. Mix carrot, celery and jicama into piping hot rice. Add remaining ingredients, mix well and adjust seasonings. Serve over bed of sprouts. Omit jicama if unavailable.

Sweet Rice Porridge *

1	cup sweet rice
1/2	cup millet
1/2	cup sprouted wheat berries
	Braggs to taste

Wash rice and millet. Soak in pressure cooker with 2 1/2 cups water. When soaking time is over, add sprouted wheat berries and pressure cook for 30 minutes. Add Braggs or any sauce of your choice.

Wheat Berry Casserole

1	cup sprouted wheat berries
1	bay leaf
1	small onion, sliced
1	large carrot, sliced
1/2	rutabaga, peeled and cubed
1/2	tsp. dried marjoram
1	tbsp. extra virgin olive oil
1	tbsp. toasted sesame seeds (optional)
	Braggs

Cook berries with 1 1/2 cups water and bay leaf in a covered pot until desired softness is achieved. Water sauté vegetables until tender. Add oil, seeds and marjoram. Mix all together and adjust seasonings before serving. Remember to remove bay leaf.

Whole Oat Stew

1/2	cup oat groats
3	cups water
1	small rutabaga
1	small onion, chopped
1	carrot,
2	tbsp. fresh parsley, minced
1	tbsp. Braggs

This recipe is created in a crock pot. Peel and chop rutabaga, carrot and onion into small pieces. Place the oats in the crock pot. Add water, rutabaga, onion, carrot and Braggs. Cook at high setting for about eight hours or until tender. You will have a delicious oat stew ready to eat for your evening meal. Garnish with parsley.

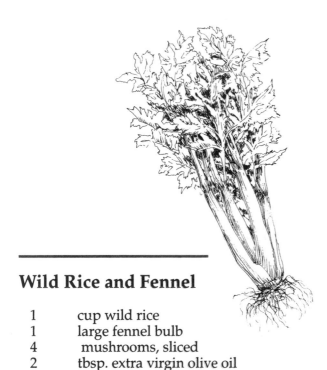

Wild Rice and Fennel

1	cup wild rice
1	large fennel bulb
4	mushrooms, sliced
2	tbsp. extra virgin olive oil
1	tsp. dried orange rind
1	tbsp. Braggs
	dash cayenne
1/2	cup scallions, minced
2	tbsp. fresh parsley garnish

Cook wild rice in three cups water for 45 minutes with Braggs. Clean and remove any inedible parts of fennel and shred into small pieces. Combine all ingredients except oil with hot rice and continue to cook for another five minutes. Remove from heat and add oil. Adjust seasonings and garnish with parsley.

Wild Rice L'Orange

2	cups long grain brown rice
1/2	cup wild rice
1	large onion, diced
1	cup somen noodles, crumbled
1	tbsp. orange peel, grated
1/2	tsp. thyme
1/2	tsp. herbamare
2	tbsp. extra virgin olive oil

Sauté somen noodles in olive oil until lightly browned. Set aside. Bring four cups water to a boil. Combine all ingredients in one pot and cook about 45 minutes until rice is tender and water is absorbed. Toss well and serve.

Wild Rice, Broccoli and Baked Tofu

1	cup wild rice
2	cups small broccoli florets
1/2	lb. baked tofu, sliced
1	tbsp. kuzu
1	cup plain soy milk
1	tsp. garlic, minced
1	tbsp. extra virgin olive oil
1	tbsp. fresh basil, minced

Cook rice in 2 1/2 cups water about 45 minutes until tender. Water sauté garlic, small broccoli florets and tofu slices several minutes until broccoli is crisp. Mix kuzu in soy milk until dissolved. Heat in saucepan stirring constantly until thickened. Combine rice, broccoli mixture and kuzu sauce together. Mix well and serve with fresh basil.

Millet Salad

1/2	cup millet
1/2	lb. artichoke pasta
1	cup broccoli florets
1/2	cup green peas
1	small red pepper, minced
1	small carrot, shredded
1/4	cup parsley, minced
2	tbsp. basil, minced
4	scallions, minced
1/4	cup extra virgin olive oil
1/2	tsp. dried oregano
	juice of one lemon
	cayenne to taste
	Braggs to taste

Cook millet in one cup water for 20 minutes. Set aside. Cook pasta according to directions on box. Just before pasta is done, throw in broccoli and peas to blanche for a minute. Drain pasta and vegetables. Rinse with cold water. Combine all ingredients and toss well. Let sit a while before serving for flavors to blend.

PASTA

Udon Noodle Salad

1	lb. udon noodles
1	red pepper, sliced
1	large carrot, matchsticked
1/2	cup snow peas, stemmed and slivered
6	mushrooms, sliced
6	scallions, sliced
2	tbsp. toasted sesame or olive oil
1/2	cup mirin (optional)
1/4	cup Braggs
	juice of 2 lemons
1/4	cup water
2	scallions, minced as garnish
1	sheet nori, slivered

Cook udon noodles. They should still have a bite to them. Rinse well to remove starch. Combine all the vegetables and quickly blanche together in a pot of boiling water. Drain. Mix with noodles. Combine oil, mirin, Braggs, lemon juice and water to create a dressing. Mix into noodles. Garnish with nori and scallions. This dish tastes better after it sits for a while.

Somen Salad

1/2	lb. somen noodles
1	yellow squash, juliénned
1	carrot, shredded
2	tbsp. lemon juice
1	tbsp. umeboshi paste
2	tbsp. extra virgin olive oil
3	scallions minced, green part only

Prepare the dressing in a suribachi with the last four ingredients. Set aside. Bring a pot of water to a boil and add somen. This pasta cooks in minutes so watch the pot or they will be mushy. Add the squash and carrots the last few seconds the pasta is boiling to blanch them. Rinse in cold water and drain. Mix the dressing into the noodles as soon as they are done so they don't stick together. Chill and serve. There are different types of somen so experiment.

Creamy Macaroni Salad

1	lb. artichoke pasta elbows
1	lb. tofu
1/2	cup water
1	bunch watercress
6	red radishes, minced
1/4	cup instant wakame
1	pickle, minced
2	tsp. umeboshi paste
2	tbsp. fresh parsley
2	tbsp. lemon juice
1	tbsp. extra virgin olive oil

Cook pasta and drain. Coat with olive oil. Set aside. Clean and chop watercress. Blanche in boiling water for seconds and drain. Rehydrate wakame and drain. Blend tofu, umeboshi paste, lemon juice and parsley with 1/2 cup water until smooth. Mix in watercress, radishes, wakame and pickle. Combine with pasta tossing until well combined. Adjust seasonings and chill.

Hot Savory Soba

1/2	lb. lotus root soba noodles
1/4	head cabbage, shredded
3	scallions, minced
1	carrot, julienned
2	tbsp. rice syrup
2	cloves garlic, minced
2	tbsp. tamari
2	tsp. ginger juice
1	tbsp. dark sesame oil
1/4	cup hiziki
1/2	tsp. cayenne
	scallion garnish

Rehydrate hiziki for about 20 minutes. Drain, rinse and set aside. Sauté garlic in sesame oil. Add cabbage and carrot and stir fry until crisp. Add rice syrup, tamari, ginger juice and cayenne. Set aside. Cook soba, rinse well and drain. Do not overcook. Mix together soba, hiziki and vegetable sauce. Garnish with scallions.

Vegetable Lasagna

1	lb. lasagna noodles
1	lb. tofu
1	tbsp. umeboshi paste
1	tbsp. white miso
12	oz. pkg. soya kaas jalapeño cheese
1	lb. mushrooms, sliced
1	large onion, thinly sliced
2	yellow squash, thinly sliced
10	oz. package soysage (optional)
	mock spaghetti sauce
2	tbsp. extra virgin olive oil
	parsley garnish

Boil noodles according to package directions. Drain. Coat with a little olive oil and set aside. Prepare spaghetti sauce from recipe in cooked section. Mash tofu with miso and paste. Slice soy cheese. Sauté onions, mushrooms and squash in olive oil with some herbamare until soft. Using a 15"X11" baking dish, layer sauce, noodles, tofu, soy cheese, vegetables, sauce, noodles, tofu, soy cheese, vegetables, sauce, etc. If you use too much sauce, lasagna will be too loose. If you use too little, it will be dry. Be careful. Bake in oven at 400° for about 20 minutes until bubbly and lightly browned. Let cool for a while before serving so it can settle. Garnish with parsley. Soysage is an imitation sausage made from soybeans. For variation, add it to the lasagna if it is available in your area.

Cold Soba with Umeboshi Dressing

8	oz. wild yam soba noodles
1	tsp. umeboshi paste
2	tbsp. lemon juice
1/4	cup water
1	tbsp. toasted sesame or olive oil
1	tsp. wasabi powder
1	tsp. Braggs
3	scallions, minced

There are many different kinds of soba noodles with different percentages of buckwheat and other ingredients varying cooking time and taste. Use any kind you like. Buckwheat noodles cook very quickly and must be rinsed well to remove the starch that will cause stickiness. Combine remaining ingredients to create a dressing. Toss with the noodles and serve warm or cold.

Buckwheat Noodles and Scallions

1/2	lb. lotus root or wild yam soba noodles
1	bunch scallions minced, green part only
	extra virgin olive oil to taste
	tamari to taste

Boil your noodles. Be careful not to overcook. Add scallions the last few seconds of cooking and quickly drain. Add oil and tamari to taste. This combination is simple but incredibly delicious.

Noodle Loaf

1/4	lb. rice udon noodles
2	cups cooked pinto beans
1	medium onion, minced
1	carrot, shredded
1	stalk celery, minced
1	tsp. dried oregano
1	tbsp. extra virgin olive oil
	Braggs to taste

Cook udon noodles that have been broken into pieces. Drain and set aside. Make sure beans are very well cooked. They should be soft and creamy. Sauté onion, carrot and celery with olive oil and Braggs until soft. Mix together all ingredients, adjust seasonings and press into a loaf pan. Chill. It will solidify. Slice and serve on a bed of sprouts. There are different kinds of udon to try with this recipe.

Green and Red Noodle Dish

1/2	lb. artichoke noodles
1	cup broccoli florets
1	pkg. red radishes, sliced
2	tsp. umeboshi paste
2	tsp. kuzu dissolved in 1/4 cup water
4	oz. tempeh, cubed
	olive oil and cayenne
2	tbsp. parsley garnish

Blanch broccoli until crisp. Set aside. Cook radishes with umeboshi paste and 1/2 cup water until tender. Add kuzu mixture to thicken. Set aside. Broil tempeh until crisp and brown on all sides. Boil and drain noodles. Combine all ingredients and adjust seasonings. Garnish.

Noodle Stew

1/2	lb. udon noodles
1	3 inch piece kombu, slivered
1	onion, sliced
1	cup napa cabbage, chopped
4	mushrooms, sliced
1/2	cup snow peas, stems removed
1	carrot, matchsticked
1	tsp ginger, minced
	tamari to taste
2	scallions, minced
1/2	cup fresh watercress minced

Boil noodles, drain and rinse. Set aside. Boil kombu in three cups water for ten minutes. Add onion. Cook two minutes. Add carrots. Cook one minute. Add cabbage. Cook one minute. Add mushrooms and ginger. Cook two minutes. Add remaining ingredients including noodles. Cook two minutes more. Adjust seasonings and serve. Use soba as a substitute for udon noodles.

Mung Bean Vermicelli Noodles

2	2-oz. packages mung bean threads
1	carrot, matchsticked
1/2	cup snow peas, stems removed
1	bunch watercress, chopped
2	scallions, minced
2	tbsp. toasted sesame oil
	Braggs

These noodles are light and transparent. They are made of mung beans and take only a few minutes to cook. Serve them in soups, sautés and salads. Cook them in a pot of boiling water for five minutes. Rinse under cold water, drain and coat with sesame oil. Blanch watercress a few seconds and drain. Blanch carrots and snow peas until crisp. Combine noodles with all vegetables and Braggs to taste. Sometimes these noodles stick together. Cut them up a little after you cook them to help separate.

Pasta and Escarole Stew

10	oz. package vita-spelt pasta
1	large head escarole
4	cloves garlic, minced
2	tbsp. extra virgin olive oil
1/4	cup fresh parsley, minced
1	tsp. fresh oregano
	Braggs

Wash escarole well to remove dirt and drain. Chop into small pieces and simmer on low heat for about five minutes until soft and tender. Add garlic and oil. Cook the spelt pasta and drain. Mix together pasta and escarole. Add parsley, oregano and Braggs to taste. For a variation, add some sprouted, steamed chickpeas.

Buckwheat Noodle Orientale

1/2	lb. soba noodles
1	large carrot, juliénned
1	large onion, sliced
1	tsp. ginger, minced
2	tsp. kuzu dissolved in 1/2 cup water
1	tbsp. toasted sesame oil
2	tbsp. fresh parsley garnish
	tamari

In heavy skillet, stir fry onions and carrots in sesame oil until nicely browned. Add ginger and tamari to taste. Set aside. Boil noodles, rinse and drain well. Combine noodles with onion mixture. To create a delicious sauce, add the kuzu dissolved in water. Stir a few minutes until clear in color. Top with minced parsley and serve.

Fettucini Alfredo

1/2	lb. fettucini noodles
	tofu alfredo sauce
1/4	cup fresh parley, minced

Prepare your pasta. Top with gently warmed alfredo sauce and garnish with parsley. The sauce recipe is in the following chapter. Find an Italian specialty store in your area and treat yourself to some high quality imported pasta. There are many varieties of shapes.

Noodle Sushi Nori

8	oz. package udon noodles
1	pkg. pickled ginger
1	bunch watercress
1	cucumber
1	carrot
3	scallions
1	package toasted nori sheets
	umeboshi paste

Boil udon noodles until done and drain very well. Let sit in a colander and set aside. Blanche watercress in boiling water a few seconds and chop. Set aside. Peel, seed and slice cucumber in long strips. Peel and shred carrot. Remove white part of scallion and slice green part in long thin strips. Place sheet of nori on sushi mat. Layer noodles followed by some pickled ginger, watercress, cucumber, carrot and scallion. Put some umeboshi paste on the closing end of the nori. Roll tight and slice. Pickled ginger is found in the health food store in the macrobiotic section. It is made by Eden foods.

Pasta Primavera

10	oz. package vita-spelt spaghetti
2	cloves garlic, minced
1	small red onion, sliced
6	mushrooms, sliced
1	tbsp. each fresh basil, parsley, oregano
1	zucchini, juliénned
2	red peppers, sliced
1	cup small broccoli florets
3	tbsp. extra virgin olive oil
	Braggs and cayenne

Water sauté garlic and onion with some Braggs until wilted. Add mushrooms. Cook one minute. Add red peppers, broccoli and zucchini. Cook several more minutes. Remove from heat. Add minced herbs and olive oil. Cover. Set aside. Boil pasta, drain and combine with vegetables. Toss well adding Braggs and cayenne to taste. Use any choice of pasta for this dish.

Pasta Bean Salad

2	cups cooked artichoke rigatoni
2	cups cooked chickpeas
1/2	red pepper, minced
1	medium red onion, minced
2	tbsp. extra virgin olive oil
2	tbsp. umeboshi vinegar
2	tbsp. fresh parsley, minced
2	tbsp. fresh dill, minced
1	jalapeño pepper, minced (optional)
	Braggs to taste

Combine all ingredients and mix well. Adjust seasonings. The umeboshi vinegar is salty, so be careful. Use quinoa pasta as a substitute or any other pasta. Quinoa pasta will fall apart easily if it is overcooked.

Linguini with Tofu Meatballs

1/2	lb. linguini pasta
6	tofu meatballs
	mock spaghetti sauce
2	tbsp. parsley, minced

The recipes for tofu meatballs and spaghetti sauce are in other chapters of the cooked section. Boil the pasta and drain. Top with meatballs and sauce. Garnish with minced parsley.

Fusilli Pasta with Tofu

1/2	lb. fusilli
1	small bunch young kale
1/2	lb. tofu
2	tbsp. sweet white miso
1/4	tsp. nutmeg
1/2	tsp. umeboshi paste
2	tbsp. fresh basil, minced
	dash cayenne

Clean and remove all stems from kale. Chop into small pieces and blanch until tender. Set aside. Mash tofu together with remaining ingredients. Cook the pasta and combine with kale and tofu mixture tossing well. Adjust seasonings and serve. Heat the tofu mixture gently before mixing with the pasta if you plan on serving this dish hot. Substitute watercress for kale.

SEITAN

Herbed Seitan Strips

1	lb. seitan, cut into strips
1	cup corn meal
1	tbsp. poultry seasoning
1/2	tsp. herbamare
1/8	tsp. cayenne
	extra virgin olive oil

Combine cornmeal, poultry seasoning, herbamare and cayenne in a bowl. Dredge seitan strips and sauté on both sides until crisp and brown. Seitan is sold in many shapes. Cut it any way you find convenient for preparation. I am told by a friend who makes seitan commercially that four ounces of seitan contains one gram of carbohydrate, 13 grams of protein, one gram of fat.

Seitan with Peppers and Onions

1	lb. seitan, sliced
2	red peppers, sliced
2	yellow peppers, sliced
1	large onion, sliced
1/4	tsp. marjoram
3	tbsp. extra virgin olive oil
1/4	cup fresh parsley, minced
	tamari to taste and cayenne

Water sauté onions with a dash of tamari until wilted. Add peppers and cook covered for about five minutes. Add remaining ingredients and cook another five minutes. Adjust seasonings and top with more minced parsley.

Seitan in Wine Sauce

1	lb. seitan, sliced
4	shallots, minced
4	mushrooms, sliced
1	tsp. white miso
1	tsp. kuzu dissolved in 1/2 cup water
1/4	cup marsala wine (optional)
1/2	tsp. oregano
2	tbsp. extra virgin olive oil
	arrowroot
2	tbsp. fresh parsley, minced

Dredge seitan in arrowroot and sauté in olive oil until crisp, turning occasionally. Add shallots, mushrooms, miso, wine and oregano. Cook several minutes more. Add kuzu mixture to create a sauce. Adjust seasonings. Top with minced parsley. The addition of marsala wine makes this a gourmet treat. Add more water if sauce gets too thick. For variation, do not sauté seitan. Cook all ingredients together and add the olive oil at the end.

Seitan in Mustard Sauce

1	lb. seitan, sliced
2	tbsp. whole grain mustard
1	tsp. white miso
1	tsp. kuzu dissolved in 1/2 cup water
1/4	cup sherry
2	tbsp. extra virgin olive oil
2	tbsp. scallions garnish
	arrowroot

Dredge seitan in arrowroot and sauté in olive oil until crisp. Add remaining ingredients except kuzu and cook together for about ten minutes. Add kuzu to create a delicious sauce. Adjust seasonings and serve with the minced scallion garnish. For variation, leave out directions in first sentence and cook all ingredients together adding olive oil at the end.

Seitan Stroganoff *

1	lb. seitan, cut into chunks
1	large onion, sliced
6	mushrooms, sliced
2	cloves garlic, minced
1/4	cup couscous
1/2	lb. noodles
2	tbsp. extra virgin olive oil
	dash of cayenne and nutmeg
1	tbsp. white miso
1	tbsp. umeboshi paste
1/4	cup fresh parsley, minced

Pressure cook onion, mushrooms, garlic, couscous, one cup water, miso and umeboshi paste for ten minutes. Process in blender with enough water to make a creamy sauce. Combine seitan with sauce and simmer for five minutes. Add oil, cayenne, nutmeg, minced parsley and adjust seasonings. Boil noodles until tender but firm. Ladle seitan stroganoff over noodles and serve.

Seitan Sloppy Joe

2	cups seitan
1	red pepper
1	onion
1	stalk celery
1	clove garlic
1/2	tsp. dried oregano
1/2	tsp. dried basil
1	cup mock spaghetti sauce
2	tbsp. extra virgin olive oil
	tamari

Finely mince the seitan, red pepper, onion, celery and garlic. Water sauté with herbs and a dash of tamari until soft. Add spaghetti sauce and olive oil and mix well. Serve over vegetables or any way you like. Substitute other sauces of your choice in this recipe.

Gingered Seitan Stew

1	lb. seitan
2	large carrots
2	large onions
8	oz. Brussel sprouts
1	bay leaf
1	3 inch strip kombu
1	cup string beans, chopped
1	tsp ginger, minced
	herbamare to taste
1	tsp. kuzu dissolved in 1/2 cup water

Cut seitan, carrots and onions into chunks. Clean Brussels sprouts and cut in half. Cut kombu into strips. Layer kombu, bay leaf, onions, string beans, Brussel sprouts and carrots in a pot. Add 1/2 cup water with some herbamare. Cover and simmer for about 15 minutes or until vegetables are soft. Remove bay leaf. Add remaining ingredients. Cover and let sit five minutes. Toss gently before serving. Substitute white cabbage for Brussels sprouts.

Sweet and Sour Seitan *

1	lb. seitan, sliced
1	carrot, sliced
2	stalks celery, chopped
1	onion, sliced
1	parsnip, shredded
1	cup vegetable stock
4	scallions, minced
1	tbsp. umeboshi paste
1	tbsp. kuzu dissolved in 1/4 cup water
1/2	cup rice syrup
1	tsp. fresh ginger juice
	Braggs to taste

Put first six ingredients into a pressure cooker and cook 15 minutes. Open pot and add remaining ingredients. Let simmer a few minutes more to thicken the sauce. Adjust seasonings and serve.

CONTENTS
SAUCES, DRESSINGS, DIPS, SPREADS AND PICKLES

Sauces, Dressings, Dips, Spreads, and Pickles

I've compiled an interesting array of sauces and dressings that can be used on any dish of simply prepared foods, either raw or cooked. Serving them separately allows people to use as little or as much as they desire and any leftovers can easily be stored for the next day. You can also add your dressing to a recipe ahead of the time you plan to serve the meal for the flavors to mingle. It's up to you. The dips, spreads and pickles in this chapter will add panache, or shall we say that little extra something unusual, to your meals. Pickles are easy to make, fun to eat and aid digestion. Umeboshi products make delicious pickles.

Aside from marinating vegetables to create pickles, umeboshi plums and their by-products also add interesting flavor to cooked vegetables. They are a source of quality salt. Although umeboshi plums originated in China, they have flourished in Japan. Oddly enough, it is really an apricot and not a plum at all. These apricots are harvested while still green and sour. In a process passed down from generation to generation, they are pickled in a salt brine with red shiso leaves to add color and flavor. At some point the apricots are removed from the brine to dry in the sun. Alternating between soaking and drying for a period of time, they are finally left to age in the brine for at least one year. The liquid left after the pickling process is called umeboshi vinegar, also a delicious flavoring agent. Once the process is complete, these "plums" will keep indefinitely without refrigeration.

They are said to have a healing, strengthening, alkalinizing effect on the body. They also have a high concentration of beneficial, non-volatile organic acids that cannot be destroyed by the heat of cooking. These organic acids aid in the absorption of minerals. The use of umeboshi plums dates back thousands of years. They are excellent for treating acidic stomachaches, fatigue, dysentery and alcoholic hangovers. The Orientals believe these plums can help bring the body back to a state of balance if it is too acidic or too alkaline. I have personally experienced their healing nature. Umeboshi can be used a variety of ways in many recipes to enhance flavor. I use the whole plum as well as the plum paste and vinegar. Be careful to purchase products without additives. They can be found in the macrobiotic section of health food stores. These plums are also reputed to have blood-cleansing qualities as well as the ability to assist the liver and kidneys in dissolving and expelling toxins. They have been recognized for centuries by many as an overall digestive, cleansing and healing aid.

Kuzu is also considered a folk medicine in the Japanese culture. It helps to promote and maintain an alkaline condition in the blood and is used as a remedy for intestinal disorders. It is also commonly used by the Orientals for the relief of head colds, fevers and hangovers. Interchange it with arrowroot although the latter does not have the same qualities, medicinal properties, or jelling abilities.

Kuzu has no significant taste, so it can be used for many purposes. It has the ability to add texture and body without a lot of calories to everything from soups to desserts. It is frequently utilized to create creamy sauces often replacing the smooth texture of dairy products, flours and oils. Kuzu, also called kudzu, is sold in the form of little white powdery rocks and is expensive when compared to the cost of arrowroot. This predominantly wild plant is a thickening substance par excellence and is worth the price you pay for it. It is indispensible in the cooked dessert chapter that follows. In order to use kuzu, it must be dissolved in a little cold water before adding to any recipe. You can pulverize the little rocks with a spoon or a mortar and pestle if you want an exact measured amount. Try adding a teaspoon of dissolved kuzu to a steaming cup of tea or hot apple cider for a soothing treat. Kuzu can be purchased in health food stores in the macrobiotic section.

I am sure you will be able to enlarge your menu repetoire with these food complementing recipes. They dress up your meals and keep life at the dinner table interesting.

For those of you who do not have the availability of kuzu, equal amounts of arrowroot can be substituted in any part of this book for good results. In addition, in any recipes calling for the use of a suribachi, use a small blender if you do not have this useful serrated bowl.

For all of the recipes in this section that include tofu, it is best to try and purchase the soft variety to get the smoothest, creamiest results when blending. If you are not able to get the soft tofu, be sure to blend for a much longer time so the tofu is able to completely break down and combine better with the other ingredients.

Many of the sauce and dressing recipes allow for personal creation. A good-tasting combination of ingredients is presented first and then the amount of water added is left up to you. I hope you will enjoy the freedom of having this kind of flexibility. You will want to add a little water at a time to be able to taste the sauce or dressing until it is right for you. Some people enjoy a rich taste and others like a lighter flavor. Once you make the recipes you like a few times, you will know just how much water to add for your particular preference.

SAUCES

Mock Spaghetti Sauce *

6	large carrots
1	beet
3	onions
2	cloves garlic
1	red pepper, chopped
2	tbsp. couscous
2	tbsp. sweet white miso
1	tsp. umeboshi paste
3/4	cup fresh parsley, minced
1/2	tbsp. each dried oregano and basil

Peel and slice carrots, beet, onions and garlic. Put all ingredients in pressure cooker except parsley and add water to one inch above the vegetables. Cook for 20 minutes. Cool and put into a food processor with the S blade. Blend into a sauce adding water to desired consistency. Garnish with parsley and adjust seasonings. If sauce is too thin, add kuzu dissolved in some water to thicken it. This is a great substitute for tomato sauce and I use it to make vegetarian lasagna.

Barbecue Sauce

1/4	cup white miso
1/4	cup barley malt
2	tbsp. tamari

Blend into a thick paste with suribachi. Use it to coat whatever you are barbecuing, broiling or baking. Add water for a thinner sauce.

Chestnut Sauce *

1 1/2	cups dried chestnuts
1	carrot
1	parsnip
1	large onion
	Braggs

Soak chestnuts overnight. Drain and clean off any loose skins. Clean, peel and chop the vegetables. Layer onion, parsnip, carrot and chestnuts in a pressure cooker. Add water to cover about one inch above pot ingredients. Pressure cook 40 minutes. Purée into a sauce, adding water to desired consistency. Add Braggs to taste.

Stroganoff Sauce *

1	large onion, sliced
2	tbsp. white miso
2	tbsp. tahini
1	tbsp. umeboshi paste
1/2	cup couscous
	dash cayenne and nutmeg
2	tbsp. parsley, minced

Pressure cook onion with miso and 1/4 cup water for ten minutes. Add couscous to one cup boiling water and cook for three minutes until water is absorbed. Put all recipe ingredients together in a blender and add enough water to make a thick creamy sauce. Adjust amounts of miso and umeboshi to your own tastes.

Shitake Mushroom Sauce

6	dried shitake mushrooms
1	large clove garlic
1	tbsp. mirin (optional)
2	tbsp. kuzu dissolved in 1 cup water
2	tbsp. extra virgin olive oil
1/4	cup fresh parsley, minced
	tamari

Soak shitakes until soft. The length of time for soaking depends on size and thickness of the mushroom. Discard stems and slice caps. Cook garlic, mushrooms and some tamari together with 1/2 cup water for about 15 minutes in a covered pot. Remove from heat, open pot and add mirin, kuzu, olive oil and more tamari to taste. Adjust consistency with water. Garnish with parsley.

Sauce Bearnaise

1	cup hollandaise sauce variation
1	shallot, minced
1	tsp. fresh tarragon, minced
	cayenne to taste (optional)

Water sauté shallot until wilted. Remove from heat and add tarragon. Add sauce and stir well before serving. The hollandaise sauce recipe is on page 191.

Tahini Miso Sauce

2	tbsp. barley miso
2	tbsp. tahini
1	tbsp. rice syrup
1	tbsp. mirin (optional)
2	tbsp. toasted sesame seeds

Combine all ingredients with a suribachi adding enough water to create a thin sauce. Pour into a small saucepan and heat gently. The tahini and miso will thicken as the sauce heats up. Use water for desired consistency. Don't use a high heat because tahini sometimes curdles. Substitute same amount of tamari for miso to create another taste.

Variation I

2	tbsp. white miso
2	tbsp. tahini
2	tbsp. fresh ginger juice
	juice of 1 lemon and 1 orange
2	scallions, minced

Variation II

1/4	cup tahini
1	tsp. white miso
1	tbsp. tamari

Follow same procedure for preparation of the sauce variations.

Umeboshi Kuzu Sauce

1	tbsp. umeboshi paste
1	tbsp. kuzu
2	scallions, minced

Dissolve kuzu in one cup water. Heat kuzu gently until it thickens. Whisk in the umeboshi paste and scallions. Serve over cooked vegetables. You can adjust consistency with more or less water. Add cooked onion purée for a variation. Turn this into a sweet and sour sauce by adding 1/4 cup each, rice syrup and mirin.

Teriyaki Sauce

1/2	cup tamari mixed with 1/4 cup water
2	cloves garlic, minced
1/3	cup rice syrup
1	tsp. fresh ginger, grated
1/2	cup sake
1	tbsp. toasted sesame oil
1/4	tsp. dried coriander
1	tbsp. kuzu dissolved in 1 cup water (optional)

Combine all except kuzu with a suribachi. Use as a marinade. Cook this sauce with the addition of the kuzu mixture to thicken.

Variation

4	tbsp. barley miso
1/4	cup sake
1	tbsp. sesame oil
1	tsp. ginger, minced
2	cloves garlic, minced
2	tbsp. maple syrup
1/4	tsp. dry mustard
1/2	cup water

Follow same procedure. Substitute sweet white miso for the barley miso for a lighter color.

Basic Onion Sauce *

2	large bermuda onions
	Braggs to taste
1	tbsp. kuzu dissolved in 1 cup water

Peel and slice onions. Place in pressure cooker and coat with some Braggs. Cook without water for 30 minutes. Once the cooker comes to pressure, be sure to turn down heat immediately so that the onions do not burn. When onions are cooked, add kuzu mixture with Braggs to taste. Create your own consistency with more or less water and kuzu. This is a base for many other sauces. You can purée this sauce. In addition, cook other vegetables with the onions. For example, carrots, cauliflower, fennel, sweet squash, celery, parsnips, etc.

Tofu Tartar Sauce

8	oz. tofu
1	large dill pickle, minced
1	tsp. prepared horseradish
	juice of 1 lemon
1	scallion, finely minced
1	tsp. dried dill
1	tbsp. extra virgin olive oil (optional)

Put all ingredients in a food processor except pickle and scallion. Blend until smooth. Mix in pickle and scallion.

Variation

1	cup tofu mayonnaise
1	tbsp. fresh dill
1	tbsp. fresh parsley
1	tbsp. capers (optional)
1	tbsp. onion
2	tbsp. pickle

Mince all ingredients and mix into tofu mayonnaise. Substitute 1/2 tsp. curry for the pickles to completely change the taste.

Tarragon Mustard Sauce

8	oz. tofu
1/2	cup plain soymilk
1	tbsp. whole grain mustard
1	tsp. lemon juice
1	small clove garlic
1 1/2	tsp. curry
1	tbsp. fresh tarragon

Blend all ingredients together until smooth. Heat gently if you want to serve it hot.

Lyonnaise Sauce

1	cup bechemel sauce
1	tbsp. extra virgin olive oil
3/4	cup onions, minced
1	tsp. Braggs
1/4	cup sake

Sauté onions in olive oil with Braggs until soft. Add sake. Cook a few minutes more. Mix in bechemel sauce and serve.

Hollandaise Sauce

1/2	lb. tofu
1	tbsp. olive oil
1	tbsp. kuzu dissolved in 1/2 cup water
1/2	tsp. tahini
1	tbsp. lemon juice
1	tsp. white miso
1/2	tsp. tumeric

Blend all ingredients except tofu. Put the mixture into a small saucepan and carefully heat to allow the kuzu to thicken. Blend with tofu until very creamy and smooth. Add water to thin out the consistency. Add more tumeric for more color.

Variation

1	tsp. white miso
1	tbsp. kuzu
4	tsp. lemon juice
2	tbsp. olive oil
1	cup grated soy cheese
1/8	tsp. tumeric (optional)

Combine kuzu with one cup water. Heat until thick and smooth. Add miso, lemon juice and olive oil. Stir well. Add grated cheese and continue stirring until melted. Don't burn. Add more tumeric for color. Adjust seasonings and serve.

Mexican Hot Sauce

2	tbsp. extra virgin olive oil
1	red onion, minced
1	clove garlic, minced
2	large ripe tomatoes, chopped
2	jalapeno peppers, minced
1/2	tsp. each dried oregano and thyme
1	tbsp. lemon juice
	Braggs
1	tbsp. fresh cilantro, minced

Sauté onion and garlic in oil until wilted. Add remaining ingredients except tomatoes and cook for five minutes. Turn off heat, add tomatoes and cover skillet. Let sit five minutes more. Add Braggs to taste. Serve hot or cold.

Alfredo Sauce

1	lb. tofu
2	tbsp. sweet miso
2	tbsp. extra virgin olive oil
2	cloves garlic, minced
	dash cayenne
	Braggs to taste

Break up tofu and put into food processor with S blade. Add miso, oil, garlic and cayenne. Process with enough water to make a thick creamy sauce adding Braggs to taste. Serve over vegetables, grains or pasta. Heat gently if you want to serve it hot.

Bechemel Sauce

1/2	lb. tofu
1	tbsp. white miso
1	tbsp. tahini
1	tbsp. mirin (optional)
1	tsp. lemon juice
2	tsp. Braggs
	dash cayenne and nutmeg

Blend all ingredients adding water to desired consistency. Heat gently and serve.

Sweet Miso Sauce

4	tbsp. sweet white miso
1	tbsp. fresh ginger juice
2	tbsp. tahini
	juice of one lemon
1	large clove garlic, minced
1	cup water

Blend all ingredients into a sauce and heat gently. Add more water for a thinner sauce. Store in refrigerator and use as needed.

White Sauce *

8	oz. tofu, crumbled
1	large onion, sliced
2	tbsp. extra virgin olive oil
2	cloves garlic, minced
	herbamare to taste
1/2	tsp. dried oregano or basil

Pressure cook onion and garlic for ten minutes in 1/2 cup water. Add remaining ingredients and blend several minutes into a creamy white sauce. Adjust seasonings and serve.

Sesame Sauce

1/2	cup toasted sesame seeds
2	tbsp. sesame oil
2	tbsp. lemon juice
2	tbsp. Braggs
1/2	tsp. dried orange peel

Grind first four ingredients in a suribachi. Gradually add 1/2 cup water to make a sauce. Add orange peel and mix well. Heat gently or serve chilled.

Sweet Onion Sauce

2	tbsp. sweet white miso
2	tbsp. rice syrup
1	tbsp. lemon juice
1	tbsp. olive oil
1/2	bermuda onion, minced

Grind all ingredients in a suribachi adding 1/2 cup water to create the sauce. Heat or serve cold.

Wasabi Sauce

1	tbsp. wasabi powder
1	tbsp. sweet white miso
4	oz. soft tofu, crumbled
2	tbsp. tahini

Grind all ingredients in a surbachi adding water to desired consistency. Wasabi is dried, hot horseradish powder. Serve hot or cold.

Almond Sauce

1	cup almond butter
1	tsp. umeboshi paste
1/4	cup lemon juice
1/4	cup rice syrup

Put all ingredients in food processor with S blade. Blend ingredients together adding desired amount of water to create a creamy sauce. Heat gently. Try to buy the raw almond butter.

Sauce Orientale

1	onion
3	mushrooms
1	clove garlic
1	red pepper
4	scallions
2	tbsp. toasted sesame oil
1	tbsp. kuzu dissolved in 1 cup water
	tamari to taste

Clean and slice vegetables. Stir fry with oil and tamari until tender. Add kuzu mixture and cook until thickened.

Vegetable Gravy *

1	cup celery, chopped
1	small onion, minced
1/2	cup carrots, chopped
1	clove garlic, minced
1	bay leaf and one clove
	dash cayenne
2	tbsp. kuzu dissolved in 2 cups water
	Braggs

Put all ingredients in pressure cooker except kuzu and cook for ten minutes. Remove bay leaf and clove. Blend until smooth. Add kuzu to thicken the sauce and Braggs to taste. Add one tbsp olive oil for flavor.

Light Ginger Sauce

1/4	cup Braggs
1	tbsp. fresh ginger, grated
1	tbsp. kuzu
1	tbsp. maple syrup (optional)

Dissolve kuzu in one cup water. Combine all ingredients and heat gently until thickened.

Tofu Orange Sauce

8	oz. soft tofu, crumbled
2	tsp. white miso
2	tbsp. almond butter
1	tsp fresh orange peel, grated
1/2	tsp. whole grain mustard

Combine all ingredients in food processor with S blade adding water to create desired consistency. Adjust miso amount to your taste and heat gently.

DRESSINGS

Tahini Umeboshi Dressing

1	tsp. umeboshi paste
1	tbsp. tahini
2	tbsp. lemon juice
2	tbsp. red onion, minced
2	tbsp. fresh dill, minced
1/2	cup water

Variation:

1	tsp. umeboshi paste
2	tbsp. lime juice
4	tbsp. tahini
2	scallions, minced
3/4	cup water

In both recipes, blend all ingredients together adding more water for a thinner dressing. These recipes are especially good served with a cooked salad.

Garlic Miso Dressing

4	tbsp. mellow barley miso
2	cloves garlic
2	tsp. prepared horseradish
2	tbsp. lemon juice
1/4	cup mirin

Liquify ingredients adding water to create desired consistency.

Cucumber Dill Dressing

4	oz. tofu
1	large cucumber
2	shallots
1	small clove garlic
2	tbsp. lemon juice
2	tbsp. maple syrup
1	tbsp. tahini
3	tbsp. dried dill
4	oz. plain soymilk
	herbamare to taste

Peel and seed cucumber. Put all ingredients into a blender and liquify. Try substituting one tbsp. cilantro and 1/2 tsp. cumin for the dill. Add some cayenne for some zip.

Italian Dressing

1/2	cup olive oil
1/4	cup lemon juice
1	clove garlic
1	tsp. whole grain mustard
3/4	cup water
1	tsp. maple syrup (optional)
1/2	tsp. herbamare
	dash cayenne
1/4	cup fresh basil, stems removed

Put all ingredients in a blender and liquify until creamy. Use red onion instead of garlic for a twist. Use dill instead of basil for a delightful flavor.

Lemon Garlic Dressing

3   tbsp. lemon juice
2   tbsp. tahini
1   large clove garlic
      Braggs to taste

Mix ingredients together in suribachi. Add water to desired consistency. This is delicious over cooked green beans. Substitute two tbsp. onion for garlic for a variation.

White Miso Dressing

1/4   cup sweet white miso
1   tbsp. toasted sesame seeds
2   tbsp. canola oil
2   tbsp. barley malt syrup
2   scallions, minced
      juice of 1 lemon

Blend all ingredients adding water to desired consistency.

Green Goddess Dressing

12   oz. tofu, crumbled
1   tbsp. extra virgin olive oil
      juice of 1 lemon
1   tsp. whole grain mustard
1/2   cup fresh parsley
4   scallions, chopped, green part only
1   tsp. fresh tarragon
      dash cayenne
      herbamare to taste
1   tbsp. maple syrup (optional)

Variation:

12   oz. tofu, crumbled
1   tbsp. white miso
1   tsp. umeboshi paste
1/4   cup parsley
4   scallions, chopped
1   small clove garlic
      juice of 1 lemon
1   tbsp. tahini
1   tsp. maple syrup (optional)

Blend all ingredients adding water to desired consistency. Adjust seasonings and serve.

Tofu Russian Dressing

8   oz. tofu, crumbled
2   tbsp. extra virgin olive oil
1   dill pickle, minced or 2 tbsp. sweet
      pickle relish
3   tbsp beet, peeled and grated
1   tbsp. umeboshi vinegar or lemon juice
1   clove garlic, minced
1/2   tsp. herbamare
1   tbsp. maple syrup (optional)

Put all ingredients except pickle in a food processor with S blade. Blend ingredients adding water to create a thick creamy dressing. Add pickle or relish after blending. Adjust seasonings and serve. Substitute same amount of ketchup instead of beets for color.

Miso French Dressing

1/4   cup red miso
1/2   cup canola oil
1/4   cup lemon juice
2   tbsp. maple syrup
1/4   cup scallions, chopped
2   tbsp. toasted sesame seeds
1/2   cup water
1/4   tsp. dry mustard
      dash cayenne
2   tbsp. ketchup (optional)

Blend all ingredients adding more water as needed.

Sesame Tamari Dressing

4   tbsp. toasted sesame oil
1   clove garlic, minced
2   tbsp. tamari
1/4   cup orange juice
1   tbsp. maple syrup
1   tsp ginger, peeled and minced
2   tbsp. lemon juice
1/2   tsp. five spice powder
1/4   cup water

Combine all ingredients and blend. This is delicious over a fresh salad.

Creamy Wakame Dressing

4   oz. tofu, crumbled
2   tbsp. tahini
1   tbsp. rice syrup
     dash nutmeg and cayenne
1/4   cup instant wakame, soaked
     Braggs

Put all ingredients in a blender. Liquify, adding water to make a thick creamy dressing. Adjust seasonings to taste.

Tofu Caraway Dressing

4   oz. tofu, crumbled
1   tbsp. tahini
1   tbsp. lemon juice
1   tsp. tamari
1/4   cup red onion, minced
1/2   tsp. caraway seeds

Put all ingredients in a blender and add water to create desired consistency. Substitute same amount of curry for caraway seeds.

DIPS AND SPREADS

Tofu Onion Dip

1   lb. tofu, crumbled
1/3   cup extra virgin olive oil
1   tbsp. maple syrup (optional)
1   tsp. whole grain mustard
1/2   tsp. curry
3   tbsp. lemon juice
1   packet Hain's onion soup mix
1/2   cup water
     dash cayenne
1   tsp. herbamare

Put all ingredients except soup mix in food processor and blend with S blade for several minutes until very creamy. Blend in the dried soup mix quickly and refrigerate. Let sit several hours before serving. It is even better to make it one day ahead. This is a party favorite. Cut back on the amount of soup mix added to create your own taste. You can purchase the soup mix in most health food stores and it has two small packets in each box.

Tofu Sour Cream

1   lb. tofu, crumbled
1   tbsp. umeboshi paste
1   tbsp. lemon juice
1   tbsp. tahini

Blend all to a creamy consistency adding a little water to produce a sour-cream effect.

Tofu Cream Cheese

8   oz. tofu, crumbled
2   tsp. umeboshi paste
1   scallion, minced (optional)
1   tsp. tahini

Put all ingredients in food processor and blend until creamy. Substitute one tbsp. fresh chives for scallion. You can also use a suribachi for this recipe. Use the soft variety tofu.

Tofu Olive Spread

8   oz. tofu, crumbled
1   red pepper, chopped
1   tbsp. tahini
2   scallions, minced
1   tbsp. umeboshi vinegar
1   stalk celery, minced
1/4   cup pitted greek-cured olives, minced

Blend tofu, red pepper, tahini and vinegar in a processor with the S blade until smooth. Mix in scallions, celery and olives to create a thick spread. Chill several hours before serving.

PICKLES

Umeboshi Daikon Pickles

6	inch piece daikon root, julienned
1	tbsp. umeboshi paste

Peel the daikon if the skin is damaged or old. Dilute paste with 1/2 cup water and coat daikon. Let sit several hours or longer. Wash off daikon pickles with water to remove excess saltiness if you prefer. Daikon has a very high water content that is released easily with the salty paste. Pickles aid digestion, create a stimulating flavor for the palate and add character to a meal.

Cucumber Pickles

2	large cucumbers
1	tbsp. flint corn miso or white miso
2	tbsp. water

Peel cucumbers if not organic and slice in half lengthwise. Remove seeds with a spoon and slice into small thin pieces. Coat with miso diluted with water. Let sit for two hours. If you have a pickle press, use it. Rinse slices with water if too salty.

Vidalia Onion Pickles

	Vidalia onions
1/4	cup tamari
1/4	cup umeboshi paste
1 1/2	cups water (approx.)

Thinly slice onions and fill a quart jar snugly. Blend tamari, paste and enough water together to fill the jar. Cover and let sit in the refrigerator for a day. Eat onions out of jar as you need them. Rinse to remove salt if you prefer. Each day they will become more marinated and take on a slightly different taste. Vidalia onions are a particularly sweet variety and make great pickles.

Refrigerator Pickles

1	large carrot
1	white turnip
1/2	cup small broccoli florets
1/2	cup small cauliflower florets
5	scallions cut into 1" pieces
1/4	cup tamari
1/4	cup lemon juice
1/4	cup mirin

Peel and julienne carrot and turnip. Make sure broccoli and cauliflower are very clean. This is an estimate of the amount of vegetables needed to fill a covered quart jar. Pack the jar snugly and combine last three ingredients with enough water to fill jar. Pour out this liquid and bring to a boil. Immediately turn off heat and pour again over the vegetables. Cover with a sushi mat or kitchen towel and let sit about six hours. Cover jar with lid and store in refrigerator. Let sit for a day and then dig in.

Sweet and Sour Pickles

1	cup daikon
2	cups carrots
1	cup parsnip
1/4	cup lemon juice
1/4	cup umeboshi venegar
1/4	cup mirin

Peel and julienne daikon, carrot and parsnip. Pack vegetables into a quart jar. Add remaining ingredients and fill the jar to the top with water. Cover with sushi mat or towel and let sit about eight hours. Cover jar with lid and refrigerate. Wait until the next day to eat.

CONTENTS
DIGESTIBLE DESSERTS

Digestible Desserts

I compare the choice of ingredients in the following dessert recipes to an artist's palate. With different combinations of tastes, colors, textures and methods, one can create an edible work of art. Each design is unique. A culinary sweet delight is made for consumption by both body and mind. Fruits, vegetables, beans, grains and seaweed have given me an infinite combination of healthy pleasurable dessert choices. These recipes are separate meals that can be enjoyed without destroying your health.

In this chapter you will find great-tasting alternatives to the traditional habits of American sweet snacks prepared with calorie-laden combinations of refined sugar and flour, excess saturated fats, chocolate, chemically preserved fruits and cooked nuts. It is hard to break away from old habits, especially if you have children who have gotten used to the ready-to-eat desserts that are often loaded with additives, preservatives and stabilizers. One could write a thesis on the list of ingredients in a commercial frozen cake or pie at the supermarket.

For my food preparations, use a 10-inch springform pan, a 10-inch pie plate, an 8-inch square pan, cookie sheets, muffin tins, 9-inch round cake pans and various casserole baking dishes. I suggest using glass or stainless steel cookware. In addition, I would like to say a few words about three important pieces of equipment used throughout the entire book: a juicer, blender and food processor. I own and enjoy different juicers. When you make fresh juice everyday, it is important to invest in a machine that is durable and also suits your personal needs. Each juicer has its own different advantages. Every family should have one because it provides us with the living electro-magnetic energy of food enzymes lost in the world of cooked foods.

For those of you who do not have a food processor, a strong blender can be used in many of the recipes that call for thorough mixing. I recommend the quality of Oster products. They have different-size blenders, including a large commercial size. I have several Cuisinart food processors and can say from experience they stand behind their product guarantees, replacing and repairing quickly and easily if necessary. I have had the same Cuisinart for 15 years.

It is easy to prepare healthful desserts while satisfying the sweet-tooth habit, and also eliminate many empty calories. I have substituted many ingredients in traditional recipes in favor of presenting you with nutritious and digestible choices. A well rounded selection of recipe ideas for pies, cakes, cookies, puddings, simple cooked fruits, aspics, tortes, breads, pancakes, muffins, icings and candies have all been created for your enjoyment.

For those of you who love sweet bread, sprouted unleavened essene bread is superior in quality and choice. Many people are not familiar with it. Essene bread has no flour, oil, sweetener, salt, additives, preservatives, dairy or eggs. It is yeast free and non-constipating. Grains are sprouted, blended and baked at a low temperature to produce an incredibly sweet moist bread. This bread is often found in the fresh or frozen section of health food stores. There is a company called Sprout Delights located in Florida that will ship it to you fresh and it is listed in the source section.

Please note. It is best to bake tofu desserts in a *"bain marie"*, which is another larger baking pan with about one inch of water. Place the dessert baking dish in this larger pan to prevent the tofu from burning or cracking. Check the water level if you are baking for more than 30 minutes. In addition, use the soft variety of tofu whenever possible, for it is more easily combined with the other ingredients.

I hope you find the time to try these recipes. When I prepare desserts for friends they appreciate the taste sensation and also the fact that they are wholesome. Just remember, one of the ways to keep healthy your loved one's heart is through the stomach. Give the gift of life in all your food preparations.

Note: For those allergic to whole wheat flour you may substitute spelt flour in any recipe calling for wheat products.

DIGESTIBLE DESSERTS

Coconut Custard Pie

1 1/2	lbs. soft tofu
1/2	cup plain soymilk
1/2	cup maple syrup
1 1/2	cups fresh flaked coconut
1	tbsp. vanilla extract
1	tsp. Braggs
1/4	cup coconut for topping

Blend tofu, soymilk and syrup in food processor with S blade until smooth. Add extract and Braggs. Blend again. Add coconut and blend again. Use the pie crust of your choice or none at all. (You can just coat a ten inch pie plate with canola oil and pour in filling). Bake at 350° for about 35 minutes until set. Test for firmness with a knife. It should come out of the pie clean. Top with remaining coconut and bake another five minutes until coconut is lightly browned. Serve chilled. Add more syrup for a sweeter pie. Substitute dried coconut if fresh is unavailable.

Parsnip Squash Pie *

1	butternut squash
1	lb. parsnips
4	tbsp. agar flakes mixed with 1/3 cup water
2	tbsp. kuzu, finely ground into powder
1	tbsp. vanilla extract
1	tsp. cinnamon
1	tsp. fresh ginger juice
1/2	cup barley malt
1	tsp. Braggs

Peel and seed squash and chop into small pieces. Peel and chop parsnips. Remove all inedible parts of both vegetables. Mix together the vegetables and pressure cook for 15 minutes with 1/4 cup water and Braggs. Open pot and while still piping hot, add remaining recipe ingredients and mix well. Pour into a 10-inch pie plate with crust of your choice. Graham cracker crusts are nice. Chill to set before serving.

Pumpkin Pie

2 1/2	cups cooked pumpkin, pureéd
8	oz. soft tofu, crumbled
1/2	cup maple syrup
1	tsp. pumpkin pie spice
1	tsp. fresh ginger juice
1/4	tsp. each nutmeg and cinnamon
1	tsp. Braggs

Crust

2	cups rice cakes, crumbled
1/2	tsp. pumpkin pie spice
2	tbsp. barley malt

First make your crust. Using S blade, put rice cakes into processor and combine with spice and malt. Grease 10-inch pie plate with some canola oil. Press in the rice cake crust the best you can. Process filling until smooth and creamy. Pour into rice-cake crust and bake at 350° about 50 minutes until filling is set. A knife should come out of the pie clean when set. Add more maple syrup for a sweeter pie. Substitute the same amount of pureé of other hard squashes or chestnuts for pumpkin purée as a variation.

Pear Torte

6	cups ripe pears, chopped
5	tbsp. agar flakes
2	cups apple juice
1	tsp. cinnamon
2	tsp. fresh ginger juice
1	tsp. Braggs
2	tbsp. kuzu dissolved in 1/4 cup water
1	basic nut crust

Press nut crust into a 10-inch springform pan. Set aside. Dissolve agar in apple juice by heating until clear. Add two cups of the pears to the agar mixture. Cook a few minutes. Add all other ingredients except remaining pears and stir until thickened. Cool slightly and purée in a food processor. Put remaining pears in the springform pan. Pour prepared mixture over the pears and chill until firm.

Carob Cream Pie

1	cup pignoli nuts, soaked and drained
2	tsp. agar flakes
1/2	cup maple syrup
1/2	cup fresh coconut, grated
1/4	cup kuzu dissolved in 1/2 cup water
1/4	cup carob
1	tsp. Braggs
2	tsp. vanilla extract
1	cup walnuts for crust

Oil a 10-inch pie plate and coat with one cup walnut meal. Set aside. Blend pignolis in two cups water to make a creamy liquid. Set aside. Dissolve agar in 1/2 cup simmering water until clear. Combine all ingredients in a blender. Move to a pot and gently heat, stirring constantly until very thick. Pour filling into pie plate and chill until set. For a twist, add one tbsp. yannoh or one packet of Café Roma from the health food store to achieve a mocha flavor. Substitute any crust.

Fresh Apricot Pie

3	cups apricots
1/2	cup maple syrup
1	tbsp. lemon juice
1	tsp. agar flakes
2	tsp. lemon rind, grated
2	tbsp. kuzu dissolved in 1/2 cup water
1	basic nut crust

Bring large pot of water to a boil. Drop in apricots for a few seconds until skins split. Peel off skins, remove pits and slice enough for three cups. Set aside. Combine remaining ingredients in a saucepan and simmer until thickened. Mix in apricots. Turn off heat and let sit about 15 minutes. Prepare crust. Spoon into the 10-inch pie plate and chill.

Almond Fruit Pie

Filling

1 1/2	lbs. soft tofu
1/2	cup maple syrup
1/2	cup plain soy milk
1	tbsp. vanilla extract
1/4	tsp. almond extract

Crust

1 1/2	cups almonds
1/2	tsp. Braggs

Topping

1	cup dried apricots
3/4	cup apple juice
2	tbsp. maple syrup (optional)
1/2	tsp. cinnamon

Soak apricots overnight in apple juice in your refrigerator. Blend with syrup and cinnamon in processor with S blade. Set aside. Process almonds and Braggs to a fine meal with S blade. Press into the bottom of a 10-inch pie plate. Next, process the pie filling ingredients until smooth. Pour into nut crust and bake at 350° until set, about 35 to 45 minutes. Use a bain marie if possible. Try not to over bake tofu because it gets dried out. Let the pie cool completely and then spread apricots over the top. Chill before serving.

Pecan Pie

2 1/2	cups pecans
1	cup barley malt
1/4	cup maple syrup
1/4	cup apple juice
1	tsp. vanilla extract
2	tbsp. arrowroot
1	tsp. Braggs
1	tsp. cinnamon
1	tbsp. agar flakes

Oil a 10-inch pie plate. Set aside. Blend one cup of the pecans with the rest of the ingredients to a buttery consistency. Place remaining nuts into the pie plate. Pour in the blended mixture. Bake at 350° for 35 minutes. Do not over bake. Remove and cool before serving. It will harden as it cools. Use any crust that you prefer.

Strawberry Mousse

2	pints strawberries, stemmed
2	cups apple juice
4	tbsp. agar flakes
1/4	cup kuzu dissolved in 1/2 cup water
1	tbsp. lemon juice
1/4	cup maple syrup
	dash cinnamon
1	tsp. vanilla extract

Clean and remove stems from berries. Cut in half and refrigerate. Bring juice to a boil with agar flakes. Simmer until flakes are dissolved and clear. Add kuzu mixture and stir until thickened. Add remaining ingredients except berries. Chill until firm and whip. Add berries and whip again. Put into parfait cups and chill. If you add the berries to the hot liquid, their color and texture will change, so it is better to chill and whip twice.

Chocolate Pudding

1/2	cup unsweetened cocoa or carob
1/4	cup maple syrup
1	tbsp. tahini
1	tsp. vanilla extract
1/2	tsp. Braggs acids
1	cup soymilk
1	tbsp. agar flakes dissolved in 1/2 cup water
2	tbsp. kuzu dissolved in 1/2 cup water

Combine cocoa or carob, syrup, tahini, Braggs and soymilk in a blender. Set aside. Heat agar mixture until clear. Combine with the above ingredients and bring to a boil. Turn down heat; add kuzu mixture and simmer until pudding thickens. Pour into cups and chill.

Lemon Pudding

2	cups apple juice
2	tbsp. agar flakes
2	tbsp. kuzu dissolved in 1/4 cup water
	juice of 2 lemons
1/2	tsp. lemon rind
1/2	tsp. Braggs
1/4	cup maple syrup (optional)
1	tsp. vanilla extract

Dissolve agar flakes in apple juice by heating gently. Add kuzu to thicken stirring constantly. Add remaining ingredients and mix well. If pudding is too tart, add maple syrup and then chill until firm. Whip the pudding after chilling if you want to change the texture. Substitute lime juice for lemon juice for variation.

Strawberry Apple Custard

1 1/2	cups apple juice
2	large apples
3	tbsp. agar flakes
1	tsp. kuzu dissolved in 2 tbsp. water
2	tbsp. tahini
1	tsp. vanilla extract
1	tsp. Braggs
1 1/2	cups ripe strawberries, stemmed and sliced

Dissolve agar flakes in apple juice by heating until liquid is clear. Peel, core, and chop apples. Add to apple juice and cook until soft. Mix in kuzu and stir a minute until thick. Remove from heat and put into food processor with S blade. Whip all ingredients together except berries until well combined. Chill and whip again. Mix strawberry slices into apple custard. Spoon into serving cups and chill.

Basmati Rice Pudding

1	cup white basmati rice
2	cups plain soymilk
2	tsp. vanilla extract
$1/2$	tsp. cinnamon
$1/2$	tsp. Braggs
1	cup rice syrup
2	tbsp. each, kuzu and arrowroot

Bring two cups water to a boil and add rice. Cook about 15 minutes until all water is absorbed. Dissolve kuzu and arrowroot in $1/2$ cup water. Combine all ingredients together and cook for about ten minutes until well blended and thickened. Serve hot or cold.

Indian Pudding

$3/4$	cup yellow corn grits
1	lb. soft tofu
3	cups soy milk
$1/2$	cup maple syrup
1	tsp. Braggs
$1/2$	tsp. pumpkin pie spice or cinnamon
1	tbsp. vanilla extract
$1/2$	tsp. fresh ginger juice

Bring soy milk to a low simmer. Add grits stirring constantly until well combined. Cook about five minutes and continue to stir. Put into a food processor with the S blade and blend with tofu until smooth. Add remaining ingredients and blend all thoroughly. Add maple syrup to taste. Bake in oiled six cup casserole dish for about 35 minutes at 350°.

Cantaloupe Pudding

1	large ripe cantaloupe
	kuzu as needed

The melon must be ripe and sweet. Peel, seed and chop into pieces. Cook fruit with a small amount of water until tender. Purée. Measure the amount of purée adding one tbsp. of kuzu for each cup of purée. You must first dilute the kuzu in a little water before adding to the purée. Reheat on a low flame carefully until kuzu thickens the cantaloupe. Pour into dessert cups and chill.

Dried Chestnut Pudding *

1	lb. dried chestnuts
	dash cinnamon
	dash Braggs
	soymilk

Soak chestnuts overnight. Drain and wash off any skins. Put into a pressure cooker and cover with water about one inch above chestnuts. Cook for 45 minutes and then drain. Save the liquid to drink or flavor other dishes. Put chestnuts into food processor with the S blade and slowly add soy milk using as little as possible to create a thick chestnut pudding. Mix in Braggs and cinnamon to taste. Chill before serving. Add some sweet hard squash (peeled chunks) to the pressure cooker for a variation.

Amasake Custard

2	cups commercial amasake
4	tsp. kuzu dissolved in $1/4$ cup soymilk
$1/2$	tsp. dried orange rind
	dash Braggs
1	tsp. vanilla extract
	dash cinnamon

The tastiest brand of commercial amasake is produced by a company call Grainaissance. I use their product when I don't have time to make my own. Bring amasake to a low simmer. Add the kuzu mixture to the simmering amasake stirring constantly until thickened. Mix in remaining ingredients, pour into dessert cups and chill. You can add lemon rind or almond extract for varied taste instead of orange rind. This amasake is found in the refrigerated section of the health food store.

Pineapple Coconut Pudding

2	cups pineapple juice
1	cup coconut, grated
1/2	cup tahini
1	tbsp. lemon rind
1	tbsp. agar flakes
1	tbsp. kuzu dissolved in 1/2 cup water
1	cup fresh pineapple, minced (optional)

Heat agar flakes in one cup pineapple juice until dissolved. Add kuzu mixture stirring constantly until thick and clear. Remove from heat and blend all remaining ingredients. Pour into dessert cups and chill. Add one cup fresh minced pineapple for more consistency.

Squash Pudding

1	large butternut squash
1/2	cup maple syrup
3	tbsp. kuzu dissolved in 1/2 cup water
1	tbsp. vanilla extract
1	tsp. pumpkin pie spice
1	tsp. Braggs

Peel, seed and chop the squash. Bake or steam until soft. Mash enough for three cups. Blend piping hot squash, syrup and kuzu mixture. Let sit five minutes. Mix in Braggs, extract,and spice. Spoon into parfait cups and chill.

Quinoa Pudding

3/4	cup quinoa
2	tbsp. canola oil
1/3	cup maple syrup
2	cups soy milk
2	tsp. vanilla extract
1	tsp. Braggs
1	tsp. dried orange rind
1/2	tsp. nutmeg
2	tsp. kuzu dissolved in 1/2 cup water

Be sure to soak quinoa and discard water. Put quinoa into a blender with soy milk and liquify. Combine all ingredients except vanilla and kuzu. Cook about ten minutes on a low heat. Mix in kuzu and vanilla and simmer until thickened. Stir well and pour into a glass serving bowl. It tastes especially good warm.

Cranberry Pudding

2	cups cranberries
1	cup raisins
2	cups apple juice
1	tbsp. vanilla extract
	dash Braggs
1/2	tsp. dried orange rind
	crushed walnuts (optional)

Clean and remove stems from cranberries. Put all ingredients in a pot and bring to a boil. Mash the berries with a potato masher. Ladle mixture into dessert cups and chill. Top with crushed walnuts. For a lighter pudding, heat one cup water with one tablespoon agar flakes until dissolved. Add to pudding, mix well and chill.

Carob Orange Mousse

1	lb. soft tofu
1/3	cups carob powder
	grated rind from 1 orange
1/2	cup maple syrup
1	tsp. vanilla extract
	soy milk

Steam tofu for five minutes and break into small pieces. Place all ingredients except soy milk in food processor with S blade. Blend until smooth. Gradually add only enough soymilk to create mousse consistency. Pour into parfait cups and chill.

Carrot Pudding

2	lb. carrots
1/2	cup soymilk
1/2	cup maple syrup
1/2	tsp. cinnamon
1/4	tsp. cloves
1	tsp. dried orange rind
	canola oil

Peel, remove all inedible parts and shred the carrots. Steam until soft and tender. Take one cup cooked carrots and blend with soymilk. Mix all ingredients together. Grease baking dish with canola oil. Pour carrot mixture into pan and bake at 375° for about 25 minutes or until lightly browned.

Strawberry Kanten

2	cups apple juice
2	tsp. agar flakes
1	tbsp. kuzu dissolved in 2 tbsp. water
1	tsp. Braggs
2	pints strawberries
1	tsp. vanilla extract

Clean strawberries, remove stems and cut in half. Set aside. Place agar flakes and juice in a pot and simmer five minutes until dissolved. Remove from heat and add kuzu mixture, Braggs and extract. Let it cool down 15 minutes and add berries. Refrigerate until set. Use any choice of fruit for this dish. This is comparable to a fruit jello.

Baked Apples

4	large Rome apples
1/2	cup currants
1/2	cup walnuts
	juice of 2 oranges
	cinnamon

Remove the core and pits from the centers of the apples. Chop walnuts and combine with currants to stuff the centers of the apples. Squeeze the juice of two oranges over the top of the apples placed in an 8"x8" baking dish. Sprinkle with cinnamon and bake at 350° for about 30 minutes or until soft. Cool and serve. Use any apple variety. Substitute raisins for currants.

Poached Pears

4	pears
1	cup apple juice
2	tbsp. raisins
1	tbsp. kuzu dissolved in 1/4 cup water
1	tsp. fresh ginger juice
1/2	tsp. Braggs

Slice ripe pears in half. Scoop out core and seeds. Place pears in a pan, cut side down. Add apple juice mixed with raisins and Braggs. Poach until soft. Add kuzu and ginger juice. Stir gently until thickened. Serve hot or cold.

Steamed Stuffed Apples

4	large Rome apples
1	cup mixed dried fruit, soaked and chopped
1	tsp. kuzu dissolved in 1/4 cup water apple juice

Wash and remove core from the center of the apples, providing a large space to stuff. Make a horizontal cut with a knife all around the center skin of each apple to prevent splitting. Put apples in a small pan and add one inch of apple juice. Stuff each apple with mixed fruit and dust with cinnamon. Bring to a boil, cover and turn down heat to a simmer until apples are soft. Add kuzu to pan juices and thicken into a sauce. Serve warm or cold. Substitute other apple varieties for variation.

Cooked Fruit Compote

1/2	cup each dried pears and apricots
1 1/2	cups apple juice
2	ripe peaches, sliced
1/4	cup currants
1	tsp. lemon rind
2	tbsp. kuzu dissolved in 1/2 cup water
1	tsp. Braggs
1/2	tsp. cinnamon

Soak dried fruit in apple juice for about six hours. Bring to a boil. Add sliced peaches, rind, cinnamon, Braggs and mix well. Add kuzu mixture and stir until thickened. Cool and serve.

Grilled Fresh Peaches

4	peaches, halved and pitted
2	tsp. mirin
1/4	cup pecans, chopped
2	tsp. tahini
1	tsp. white miso

Arrange fruit cut side up on baking sheet. Mix together mirin, nuts, tahini and miso. Spoon into fruit. Broil five minutes until lightly browned. Cover and leave in oven another ten minutes with heat turned off. Cool and serve.

Orange Nut Squares

2   cups orange juice
2   tbsp. agar flakes
1   cup almonds, finely chopped
1/4   cup maple syrup
1/4   cup kuzu dissolved in 1/4 cup water

Dissolve agar flakes in one cup orange juice by heating gently. Add kuzu mixture stirring until thick and clear. Mix in remaining ingredients and pour into 8"x8" glass dish rinsed with cold water. Chill until firm. Slice into squares and serve.

Orange Cranberry Aspic

2   cups cranberries
2   navel oranges, peeled
1/2   cup orange juice
1/2   cup maple syrup
2   tbsp. agar flakes dissolved in 1/2 cup
        water
1   tsp. dried orange rind

Grind cranberries in processor with S blade until coarsely chopped. Set aside. Process oranges with orange juice, rind and syrup. Heat agar to dissolve flakes in the water. Add cranberries and orange mixture to the agar. Pour into a mold and chill until firm.

Coconut Delight

4   cups fresh grated coconut
2   cups boiling water
2   tsp. maple syrup
2   tbsp. kuzu dissolved in 2 tbsp. water
1/2   tsp. Braggs
1   tbsp. agar flakes

Pour boiling water over coconut and agar flakes and let sit 30 minutes. Strain through cheesecloth or sprouting bag to remove liquid. Combine this liquid(coconut milk), syrup, kuzu and Braggs. Heat gently, stirring constantly until thickened. Do not boil. Add more syrup for a sweeter taste. Pour into 8"x8" glass pan and chill.

Banana Bake

3   cups ripe bananas, sliced
1/2   cup pineapple juice
1/2   cup peacan meal
2   tsp. maple syrup
1/4   tsp. each nutmeg and cinnamon
1/4   cup pecans garnish

Soak bananas in pineapple juice about 30 minutes. Mix drained bananas with the peacan meal, maple syrup and spices and fill an 8"x8" glass baking dish . Bake covered at 425° for 15 minutes. Remove cover and top with finely chopped pecans. Cool and serve.

Fruit Crunch

2   lbs. apples
2   lbs. pears
1   cup pecans, finely ground
1/2   cup hulled sesame seeds
1   cup almonds, chopped
1/2   cup raisins, soaked
1   tsp. cinnamon
2   tsp. Braggs
3/4   cup rice syrup

Peel, core and slice apples and pears. Bake fruit covered for 1/2 hour at 375° or until soft. Heat the syrup to soften. Mix remaining ingredients with rice syrup and coat the mixture well. Top cooked fruit with crunchy mixture and return to oven (uncovered) until top is lightly browned, about five minutes.

Cracker Jacks Popcorn

3   cups popped corn
1/4   barley malt
1/4   brown rice syrup
        dash Braggs

Heat malt and syrup together with Braggs. Pour over popped corn and mix by hand as best you can. It will stick to your fingers and you'll eat half before you're done. Oil your hands before handling popcorn if you want to prevent stickiness. Put popcorn on oiled cookie sheet and bake at 300° for five minutes or until lightly crisp. Don't burn.

Brownies

1	cup whole wheat bread flour
1/2	cup unbleached white flour
1	tsp. baking powder
1	tbsp. arrowroot
1/2	cup carob or cocoa powder
2/3	cup maple syrup
1/2	cup canola oil
1/2	cup soymilk
1	tsp. vanilla extract
	Pinch of sea salt

Combine dry ingredients. Combine wet ingredients. Mix together. Spread into oiled 8x8 pan. Bake in oven at 375° for about 25 minutes . Don't over bake. Test brownies with a knife. It should come out clean.

Banana Cream Torte

4	large ripe bananas, sliced
1	cup walnuts, finely ground
1	tsp. vanilla extract
1 1/2	cups thick almond milk
1/4	cup maple syrup
2	tbsp. agar flakes dissolved in 1/2 cup water
2	tbsp. kuzu dissolved in 1/4 cup water
1/2	tsp. Braggs

Heat agar mixture until dissolved. Add almond milk, maple syrup, Braggs and kuzu mixture. Stir constantly until mixture is thickened. Remove from heat and add two sliced bananas with vanilla. Set aside. Sprinkle one cup walnut meal in a springform pan. Layer remaining bananas on top. Pour in hot banana mixture. Garnish top with more walnuts. Chill about two hours until set.

Carrot Coconut Macaroons

1	cup carrots, grated
1	cup coconut, grated
1/4	cup maple syrup
1/4	cup arrowroot
1/4	tsp. almond extract

Blend all ingredients in food processor with S blade. Spoon onto oiled cookie sheet. I use the smallest ice cream server to make little round macaroons. Bake at 350° for 20 to 30 minutes until golden brown.

Nutty Banana Cookies

1	cup walnuts
1	cup pecans
1	cup coconut, grated
3-5	ripe bananas, sliced
1/4	cup pitted dates (optional)
	cinnamon

Place nuts and coconut in a food processor with the S blade and grind to a coarse meal. Process enough bananas into nuts until mixture forms a cookie dough. Add cinnamon for flavor. For a sweeter cookie, add 1/4 cup pitted dates to the nuts before adding banana. Measure cookies by tablespoons and spoon onto lightly oiled sheet. Bake at 375° for about 15 minutes.

Sprouted Rye Bread

2	lbs. rye berries

Soak berries overnight and drain the next day. Rinse them twice a day while sprouting for two days. On the last day of sprouting, do not rinse that evening so the berries are dry. You need to grind the berries into a sticky dough using a food processor with a S blade or a grinder of some kind. Wet hands with cold water and form dough into small flat loaves. Place on an oiled cookie sheet and bake at 250° for about two hours. It may take longer depending on the size of the loaves. They should be firm when done. Cool and refrigerate. Also use wheat berries to make this bread. This is a version of essene bread.

Boston Brown Bread

3/4	cup whole wheat flour
1	cup rye flour
1	cup cornmeal
2	tsp. baking soda
1	tsp. Braggs
1	cup soymilk
3/4	cup water
1/2	cup barley malt syrup

Combine flours and baking soda. Combine milk, syrup, water and Braggs in a blender. Mix all ingredients together. Pour batter into four cup oiled glass casserole dish with an oiled cover. Put this dish in a big pot with about two inches of water on the bottom. Cover and simmer for approximately two hours adding more water if necessary. Test for doneness with a knife. Cool and remove from bowl. Slice and serve.

Corn Bread

2	cups corn meal
1	cup whole wheat flour
1	ear corn, decobbed
1	tbsp. baking powder
1/4	cup corn oil
1 1/2	cups plain soymilk
1	tsp. Braggs
2	tbsp. maple syrup (optional)

Combine corn meal, flour and baking powder. Combine oil, milk and Braggs. Mix all ingredients together with corn kernels. Pour into and 8"x8" oiled glass or stainless steel baking dish. Bake at 375° for 25 minutes or until done. Do not overbake. Test with a knife. Cool before cutting into squares.

Tofu Cheesecake

2	lbs. soft tofu, mashed
1/4	cup tahini
1/2	cup maple syrup
1/2	cup apple juice
1	tsp. vanilla extract
2	tbsp. arrowroot
1	tsp. fresh lemon rind, grated
1	tbsp. lemon juice
1	cup Graham cracker crumbs

Put all ingredients except cracker crumbs in a food processor and blend for five minutes. Cover the bottom of springform pan with cracker crumbs. Carefully pour the tofu batter over the crumbs. Bake at 325° for approximately 45 minutes or until set. Don't over bake or it will be dry. Use a bain marie. If your oven runs hot, baking time could be cut back as much as ten minutes. Watch carefully. Cool completely and chill. This cake tastes better the next day. Buy quality Graham crackers in the health food store.

Homemade Amasake

1 1/2	cups short grain brown rice
1/2	cup sweet brown rice
2	cups white koji

Pressure cook rice in four cups water for one hour. Pour into crock or glass bowl. Mix in two cups koji and two more cups water. Cover and let sit in an oven that has been preheated to 200° and quickly turned off. It takes about eight to ten hours for the rice to ferment and become very sweet. The last step is to put the rice mixture into a pot and heat gently to stop fermentation. Cool and chill. This amasake can be used to make various desserts like puddings, cakes and cookies. It can be stored in the refrigerator for about a week.

Other variations include using one cup short grain brown rice mixed with one cup pearled barley, or one cup millet, or one cup sweet brown rice. You can also use two cups sweet brown rice only. The finished product should be very thick. You can blend it into a delicious flavored drink by adding more water and some choice of extract.

"Homemade" Amasake Pudding

2   cups homemade amasake
1   tbsp. agar
1   tbsp. kuzu dissolved in 1/4 cup water
1/2   tsp. lemon extract

Dissolve agar in 1/2 cup water by heating until clear. Add kuzu mixture and stir until thickened. Add remaining ingredients. Mix well, pour into dessert cups and chill. For a more refined dessert, blend and chill. Use other extracts for variation. Be careful not to use too much because extracts are very strong. Homemade amasake and commercial amasake can be quite different so interchanging may be done, but the final product will taste different.

Amasake Macaroons

2   cups homemade amasake
1   cup puffed brown rice cereal
2   cups coconut, grated
1   tbsp. vanilla extract
1   tsp. cinnamon
1/4   cup maple syrup
1   tbsp. kuzu

Grind kuzu into a fine powder with a suribachi. Mix all ingredients together to get a tight cookie dough. Add more cereal if necessary. Bake at 425° on oiled cookie sheets for 20 to 30 minutes until golden brown. These cookies are soft in texture.

Amasake Cake

2   cups thick homemade amasake
2   cups puffed brown rice cereal
1/2   cup wheat germ
1   tbsp. vanilla extract
1/4   tsp. almond extract
1   tsp. cinnamon
1   tbsp. agar flakes

Mix agar into amasake and then mix all ingre-dients together. Pour into an oiled quart casse-role dish and bake at 400° for 30 minutes or until done. Cool and serve. This is a soft, moist cake. Give it a try. It's different.

Amasake French Toast

       bread slices
       homemade amasake
       cinnamon

Liquify the amasake in a blender with some cinnamon so that it is smooth. Take your bread and soak it in the amasake for a few minutes. Bake or broil on oiled cookie sheet until golden brown. Serve with maple syrup. Commercial amasake works well here.

Aduki Bean Amasake Cookies

1   cup cooked aduki beans
1   cup rolled oats
1 1/2 cups homemade amasake
1   tsp. cinnamon
1   tbsp. vanilla extract
1/4   cup maple syrup

Make sure the beans are well cooked and drained. Mash them and combine with re-maining ingredients. Let sit about 15 minutes for the oats to absorb liquid. Add more oats for a drier cookie. Bake at 350° on oiled cookie sheet for about 30 minutes or until golden brown. These cookies are soft in texture. Add more syrup for a sweeter cookie.

Pancakes

2	cups whole wheat flour
1	tbsp. baking powder
1	tbsp. kuzu, finely ground to a powder
1	tbsp. Braggs
2	cups plain soymilk
	canola oil

Combine dry ingredients. Combine wet ingredients. Mix together. For a thicker batter, add less milk. Spoon pancakes onto a hot non-stick skillet that has been coated with some canola oil. When bubbles start to appear and pancake is holding together, flip over and finish cooking. What you serve it with is up to you. To make waffles, add three tbsp. canola oil to the batter and pour into greased waffle iron.

Sweet Potato Pudding

3	cups cooked sweet potato
1 $1/2$	cups soymilk
3	tbsp. agar flakes
8	oz. soft tofu, cut into chunks
$1/4$	cup kuzu dissolved in $1/2$ cup water
1	tsp. vanilla extract
1	tbsp. fresh orange rind, grated
$1/4$	cup maple syrup
1	tbsp. pumpkin pie spice
$1/4$	tsp. nutmeg

Process with S blade the potatoes, milk, tofu chunks, agar and kuzu until creamy. Add remaining ingredients and blend well. Add more syrup for a sweeter pie. Pour into an oiled 1 $1/2$ quart casserole dish and bake (covered) at 350° for about 30 minutes or until set. Chill before serving.

Sesame Candy

1	cup sesame seeds
$1/2$	cup barley malt
$1/2$	cup tahini
1	tsp. vanilla extract
$1/4$	cup currants
1	tsp. Braggs

Heat barley malt in a heavy saucepan or cast iron. On low heat, add the tahini and stir with a wooden spoon until combined. Quickly add remaining ingredients and mix well. Remove from heat and spoon into an 8"x8" oiled glass dish. Pat down the candy. Let it sit for about one hour and then cut into pieces. Use hulled or unhulled sesame seeds. For variation, lightly toast the seeds before adding to the recipe.

Oatmeal Cookies

$1/2$	cup rolled oats
$1/2$	cup whole-wheat flour
1	tsp. baking powder
$1/2$	tsp. cinnamon
$1/4$	cup canola oil
$1/4$	cup maple syrup
2	tsp. vanilla extract
$1/2$	tsp. Braggs

Variation:

2	cups rolled oats
1	cup whole wheat pastry flour
$1/2$	tsp. cinnamon
$1/4$	cup corn oil
$3/4$	cup barley malt
2	tsp. vanilla extract
$1/2$	cup water
1	tsp. Braggs

Combine dry ingredients. Combine wet ingredients. Mix together and let sit 15 minutes. Drop by teaspoons onto oiled cookie sheet. Bake at 350° for about 15 minutes until golden. Do no overbake.

Almond Cookies

1 1/2	cups leftover almond pulp
1/2	cup raw tahini
1/2	cup maple syrup
2	tbsp. arrowroot
2	cups sprouted wheat berries
1	tsp. Braggs
1	tsp. vanilla extract

Here is an opportunity to use the leftover pulp from making almond milk. Put tahini, almond pulp and sprouted wheat berries in a food processor with the S blade and grind into a cookie dough. Add remaining ingredients and quickly blend. Add more arrowroot to hold cookie together if necessary. Drop cookies onto an oiled sheet and bake at 350° for about 15 minutes or until golden brown. Try them in a dehydrator. Add 1/4 cup carob powder for a twist.

Variation

4	cups almonds, blanched
1/2	cup apple juice
1	tbsp. dried orange peel
1	tsp. cinnamon
2	tsp. vanilla extract
1	cup rice syrup

Grind almonds in a food processor with S blade. Add remaining ingredients and quickly process to combine. Drop by teaspoons onto an oiled cookie sheet. Bake at 350° for ten minutes or until lightly browned. Don't over bake.

Ginger Snaps

1	cups whole wheat pastry flour
1	cup unbleached white flour
1	tsp. each: ginger, cinnamon
1/2	tsp. each: baking soda, coriander
1/2	cup canola oil
1/2	cup maple syrup
1	tsp. each: vinegar, molasses

Combine flours and ginger. Combine remaining ingredients. Mix all ingredients together. Drop by teaspoons onto oiled cookie sheets. Bake at 375° for approximately ten minutes or until lightly browned. Don't's over bake. Press cookies flat after baking.

Carob Chip Cookies

2 1/4	cups whole wheat pastry flour
2	tsp. baking powder
1/2	tsp. baking soda
1/2	tsp. Braggs
1/2	cup canola oil
1	cup maple syrup
3/4	cup carob chips

Combine flour, baking powder and soda. Combine syrup, oil and Braggs. Mix together. Add chips. Drop by teaspoons onto oiled cookie sheet. Bake at 375° for about ten to twelve minutes or until lightly browned. Cool before removing from sheets.

Three Grain Dinner Muffins

1/2	cup millet
1/2	cup quinoa
1/2	cup cornmeal
2	tbsp. white miso
2	tbsp. olive oil
1/2	cup onions, finely minced
2	tbsp. arrowroot

Cook millet and cornmeal in three cups of water for 20 minutes. Soak quinoa and discard water. Blend with remaining ingredients. Combine all, mix well and bake at 350° for 40 minutes in oiled muffin tins. Muffins should be lightly browned. This is not a traditional muffin. It is soft and moist.

Whole Wheat Muffins

2	cups whole wheat flour
1	tsp. baking powder
1	tsp. baking soda
1/2	tsp. salt
1/2	cup canola oil
1/2	cup maple syrup
1/2	tsp. orange extract
1	cup water

Combine dry ingredients. Combine wet ingredients. Mix them together. Pour into oiled muffin tins. Bake at 375° for 20 to 25 minutes. Extracts and spices will vary the taste of the muffins.

Carrot Bran Muffins

1	cup bran
1	cup whole wheat flour
1	tbsp. arrowroot
1	tsp. baking powder
1	tsp. baking soda
1/3	cup maple syrup
1	cup water
1	tsp. Braggs
1/4	cup canola oil
2/3	cup carrots, grated
1	tsp. pumpkin pie spice
1/2	tsp. dried orange peel

Combine dry ingredients. Combine wet ingredients. Mix them together. Spoon batter into oiled muffin tins. Bake at 375° for about 25 to 30 minutes or until done.

Corn Muffins

1	cup corn meal
1	cup whole wheat pastry flour
1 1/2	tsp. baking powder
1/2	tsp. baking soda
	dash Braggs
1/4	cup canola oil
1/4	cup maple syrup
3/4	cup soymilk

Combine wet ingredients. Combine dry ingredients. Mix together. Ladle into oiled muffin tins. Bake at 350° for about 20 to 25 minutes. Don't over bake or muffins will be dry. For a sweeter muffin, add another 1/4 cup maple syrup and reduce soymilk to 1/2 cup. Substitute water for soymilk if you prefer.

Maple Tahini Glaze

1/2	cup maple syrup
1/4	cup tahini
1	tsp. Braggs

Heat syrup and tahini in a saucepan to combine. Add other flavorings like fruit rind or spice or seeds. Stir in the Braggs. Mix well and chill.

Basic Cake Recipe

2	cups whole wheat flour
2	cups unbleached white flour
1/2	tsp. sea salt
2	tbsp. baking powder
1/2	cup canola oil
1	cup maple syrup
2	cups water
2	tsp. vanilla extract
1	tbsp. dried orange peel

Combine wet ingredients. Combine dry ingredients. Mix together. Bake at 350° in two oiled 9-inch cake pans. It takes about 30 to 35 minutes. A knife should come out clean when inserted into cake. Don't overbake if you want a moist cake. Cool the cake completely and prepare your glaze or eat it plain. Because this recipe uses regular whole wheat flour, the cake has a lot of body. If you want a lighter cake, use two cups whole wheat pastry flour instead. Add different extract flavors or spices as well as interchange lemon and orange rinds, fresh or dried for variation. Add one cup grated or shredded vegetables like carrots or zucchini for another variation.

Tofu Whipped Cream

1	lb. soft tofu
1/4	cup maple syrup
2	tbsp. tahini
1	tsp. dried orange rind
1/4	cup water
2	tsp. vanilla extract
1/2	tsp. Braggs

Steam tofu for five minutes. Place all ingredients in a blender and whip until smooth and creamy. Chill before serving. The longer you whip it, the smoother it gets.

Tofu "Cream Cheese" Icing

1	lb. soft tofu
1/4	cup tahini
1/4	cup maple syrup
1/4	cup apple juice
1	tsp. vanilla extract
	dash Braggs
3/4	cup coconut, grated

Steam tofu for five minutes. Blend for several minutes until very smooth and chill. This is good on carrot cake. Add carob powder for a variation.

Cinnamon Apple Glaze

2	cups apple juice
2	tsp. cinnamon
1	tbsp. fresh ginger juice
2	tbsp. kuzu

Dissolve two heaping tbsp. kuzu in the apple juice. Combine all and heat in a saucepan. Simmer until mixture gets thick and clear. Chill and use as a glaze over cakes and other desserts. Top the glaze with crushed nuts or coconut for a variation.

Dried Fruit Glaze

2	cups dried fruit
2	tbsp. tahini
1	tsp. Braggs

Boil pitted fruit of your choice in two cups water for 15 minutes. Drain and save liquid. Put fruit into a blender. Add tahini and Braggs and just enough of the cooking water to create a thick glaze. Be creative and add grated coconut, or poppy seeds, or different spices like cinnamon.

Carob Icing

3	tbsp. carob powder
3	tbsp. tahini
1	tsp. vanilla extract
1/4	cup rice syrup
1	tsp. Braggs

Heat all ingredients in a saucepan adding just enough water to make a thick icing. Mix well and chill.

Aromatic Party Tea

6	herbal tea bags
1	tsp. cardamon seeds
1	tsp. whole cloves
2	inch piece of fresh ginger
2	sticks cinnamon
2	quarts water

Use the tea you prefer. Slice the ginger into thin rounds. Bring all the ingredients to a boil. Simmer 15 minutes. Remove tea bags and ginger. Strain tea before serving. Add more water if too strong. Drink hot or cold.

Hot Apple Toddy

1 1/2	cups apple cider
	dash of cinnamon
1	tsp. Kuzu dissolved in 1/2 cup apple cider

Combine all and heat gently. Serve immediately. Substitute Apple juice for cider.

GLOSSARY

aduki beans: a small, dark red bean imported from Japan, but also grown in the U.S.; it is reputed by the Orientals to be healing to the kidneys

agar flakes: a colorless mineral rich source of gelatin derived from a sea vegetable and used to make aspics; it comes in flakes, bars and powder form.

amasake: a food made from rice and sometimes other grains that is combined with an inoculated grain to create a thick sweet fermented liquid; it is eaten alone or used as a sweetener for other dessert recipes.

arame: a thin wiry black sea vegetable rich in iron and calcium.

arrowroot powder: a starch processed from the root of an native American plant used as a thickening agent similar to corn starch.

arugula a small spicy-flavored, green leafy vegetable that is sold in bunches; it is popular in the Mediterranean.

barley malt: a thick, dark-brown sweet syrup made from sprouted barley; often used for preparing desserts.

couscous: a traditional North African grain made from semi-refined wheat; it can be used for a main course as well as a dessert.

Braggs amino acids: a lighter alternative to soy sauce and seasalt; it is made with soybeans and water only

buckwheat: this nutrient-rich hearty grain is well known in Russia, Poland and Japan; roasted buckwheat, called kasha, is also available in unroasted form.

bulghur: a food prepared from whole wheat that is cracked, steamed, and dried; it is popular in the Middle Eastern countries.

bok choy: Chinese green leafy vegetable with thick juicy stalks

canola oil: a refined oil lowest in saturated fat and the most easily digested.

carob: a natural substitute for chocolate or cocoa powder without the harmful effects of caffeine, theobromine, and calcium oxylate.

curry: a term for a combination of certain spices well known in India.

chickpeas: a nutty-flavored bean (also called garbanzo) used in India, Africa and America that is rich in nutrients.

daikon: a long large Japanese white radish known for helping dissolve animal fat deposits in the body.

dried herbs: they add variety to all meals and their concentrated flavors need time to be released in any preparation.

dulse: a reddish-purple seaweed especially rich in iron, vitamin A, and phosphorus.

garlic clove: one small almond-shaped segment of a whole bulb of garlic.

ginger: a pungent golden-colored root used in a variety of ways; it increases circulation and aids in the breakdown of fats in the body.

gomasio: a Japanese condiment of lightly toasted sesame seeds finely ground with a little sea-salt.

herbamare: delicious combination of dried herbs with added sea salt sold in health food stores.

hummus: a Middle Eastern food usually made from puréed chickpeas, tahini, garlic and lemon juice.

jalapeno pepper: a very small hot banana-shaped pepper that is green (or red when ripe).

jicama: a somewhat round vegetable that looks like a very large potato with brown skin and a sweet, white, juicy, crunchy center; it is popular in Mexico.

kanten: a type of jello dessert made from agar and fruit juice.

koji: innoculated grain (usually rice) used in making foods like miso, amazake and tamari

kombu: a broad, thick green seaweed that grows in deep waters and is rich in minerals; especially good for cooking soup stocks and beans.

kuzu: also called kudzu, a white pebbly, powdery starch from the root of the wild kuzu plant used to thicken much like cornstarch or arrowroot.

legumes: the edible seeds or pulses of pod bearing plants; they include foods like lentils, peanuts, peas, beans, alfalfa, clover and fenugreek.

lentils: used in Middle Eastern and Indian cooking, they are quick-cooking beans that are especially good for creamy soups and patés.

millet: small, yellow alkaline grain that grows throughout the world; it is a staple in China, Japan and India.

mirin: a sweet Japanese wine made from rice.

miso: a fermented grain and/or bean paste of many varieties both sweet and salty; it is protein rich, beneficial to the circulatory as well as digestive organs and is used to flavor everything from soups to desserts.

mung beans: a small green bean common to the Near East and India; it is usually sprouted and eaten as a fresh vegetable.

napa cabbage: Chinese-style long-leaf cabbage often used in stir-fry dishes.

nori: large thin pressed sheets of dried nori seaweed that are black, rich in vitamins A, B_1, B_2, C, D and calcium; often used in making sushi rolls.

nouvelle cuisine: a French term describing a new attitude that is freeing chefs from the confines of traditional, classical cooking techniques and presentation.

olive oil: produced from the fruit of the olive tree predominantly in the Mediterranean. It is considered cold-pressed if you purchase the "extra virgin" first pressing of the olive.

pignoli nuts: also called pine nuts, a small white, soft nut that is harvested from large pine cones; it is predominatly found in the Mediterranean and used in the making of pesto sauces.

psyllium seed husks: used as a thickening agent, they are the coverings of the seed called Plantago ovata, an excellent source of dietary fiber; they can be more finely ground into a powder that is often used to congeal foods

radicchio: a small leaf lettuce that comes in many varieties; it is popular in the Mediterranean.

rice syrup: a sweet thick syrup made from brown rice and sometimes barley; it is often used in sauces and desserts.

sake: a dry Japanese wine made from fermented rice.

seitan: a wheat gluten, also called wheatmeat, that is cooked in a seasoned broth; high in protein, it was developed long ago in the Orient and used as a meat substitute.

shitake mushrooms: dried or fresh, they are well known in the Orient for their effectiveness in neutralizing excessive salt and fat consumption.

shoyu: naturally brewed soy sauce, with the addition of wheat, is aged traditionally for two or three years; no chemicals or coloring are added.

soba: long, thin noodles made from buckwheat that can also be combined with other flours and vegetables like lotus root or yam.

somen: very, very thin Japanese noodles made of different grades of refined wheat.

soymilk: a drink made from soybeans, an excellent substitute for cow's milk.

soy sauce: a generic term for all dark, salty, fermented seasonings made from soybeans, water and salt.

stevia: a herb best used in the form of an extract; it is a substitute for processed sweeteners.

suribachi and **suricogi:** a special serrated glazed clay bowl and pestle used for grinding, puréeing, and combining foods.

tahini: a smooth paste made from finely ground sesame seeds popular in Middle Eastern recipes.

tamari: a naturally brewed soy sauce that is usually wheat-free.

tempeh: a cultured food made from split soybeans, water and a special inoculating bacteria that is allowed to ferment forming a solid cake of precooked beans.

toasted sesame oil: made from whole sesame seeds that are toasted and then pressed; this oil contains the natural preservatives of vitamin E and lecithin.

tofu: a bean curd made from soybeans and nigari, a coagulant taken from sea salt water; it originated in Asia and is a meat substitute.

tororo kombu: a type of finely shredded kombu seaweed.

udon: a long, thick Japanese noodle made from different grades of wheat and also rice.

umeboshi paste or **plums:** a preserved fruit made with salt and shiso leaves that stimulates the appetite and aids in maintaining an alkaline blood quality; it takes one to two years to produce and is also sold in paste form.

umeboshi vinegar(ume-su): a flavorful liquid that is a byproduct left after the pickling process of the umeboshi plum; it can be used to replace commercial vinegars.

wakame: a delicate green, leafy sea vegetable rich in minerals like iron and magnesium.

wasabi: a dried horseradish powder popular in Japan; it is traditionally used with raw fish (sashimi or sushi) to kill of any harmful bacteria.

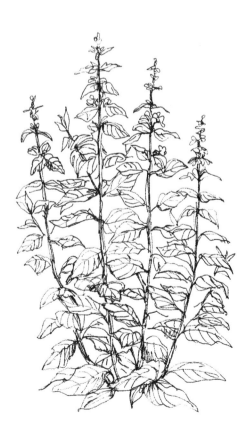

FOOD PREPARATION TERMS

adjust: to taste just before serving and add more seasoning if needed.

al dente: to cook pasta so that it is tender but firm

bain marie: a French term for a hot water bath used in the baking and steaming process.

bake: to cook in an oven with dry heat.

barbecue: to grill foods with a spicy sauce.

beat: to whip foods briskly.

blanch: to dip in boiling water for seconds to help remove produce skins or to cook quickly.

blend: to combine two or more ingredients together in a recipe.

boil: to heat a liquid until it bubbles.

chill: to put food in a refrigerator to become cold.

chop: to cut into small pieces.

coat: to cover a food with a wet or dry ingredient.

cool: to allow a hot food to come to room temperature.

core: to remove the center stem and seeds of produce.

cream: to beat together until smooth.

crumble: to break into little pieces with the fingers.

cube: to cut foods into small, square ,somewhat uniform pieces.

decob: to remove corn kernels from the cob by scraping with a knife.

dice: to cut into very, very small square pieces or cubes.

dissolve: to cause a solid food to be broken down into a solution.

drain: to draw off all liquid or strain.

drizzle: to pour a liquid over food in a very light stream.

drop: to use a spoon to place cookie dough onto a cooking sheet.

fold: to mix gently and quickly.

freeze: to chill until very hard.

garnish: to add a decorative food to a dish when serving.

glaze: to coat food with a glossy topping.

grate: to shred food into tiny particles with the smallest hole of a grater.

grill: to broil with the heat source underneath the food.

grind: to break up food into very fine particles or even a paste.

husk: to remove the outer covering of foods like corn or shuck.

julienne: to cut foods into long or short matchstick shaped pieces.

marinate: to steep in a salty liquid with added herbs and/or spices for several hours.

mash: to press into a pulp.

matchstick: to julienne

mince: to cut into extremely small pieces.

mix: to stir recipe ingredients together to combine.

mold: to place food in a contained shape long enough for it to hold that shape.

peel: to cut off the skins of produce.

pit: to remove the pits of produce.

plumb: to soak dried foods until soft with liquid.

prick: to make holes with the tines of a fork.

pureè: to produce a paste with a blender, food mill or processor.

rehydrate: to restore dried foods to a moist consistency with water.

roast: to cook in the oven without a cover.

saute: to cook in a pan over direct heat with small amounts of oil or water.

score: to make cuts with a knife over a food surface.

season: to use salts and other food additions like herbs and spices.

seed: to remove seeds from produce.

shred: to press food through the larger side of a grater to create thin strips.

simmer: to heat foods or liquids below the boiling point

skewer to push small chunks of food onto wooden or metal sticks.

slice: to cut foods with a knife into somewhat thin pieces

sliver: to cut into very, very thin pieces by length and width or snip.

soak: to allow foods to sit in water.

steam to cook in a pot with a cover over another pot with boiling liquid.

steep: to allow foods to stand in any hot liquid.

stew: to cook foods that are covered by a simmering liquid

stir fry: to toss foods quickly as they fry.

stock: the strained broth of boiled foods.

stuff: to fill a food mixture into the cavity of another food.

thicken: to concentrate a liquid by adding a starch or flour.

thin: to dilute a mixture by adding more liquid.

toast: to make a food lightly browned by heating.

toss: to combine by turning foods many times over in a bowl.

whip: to beat a food over and over with a whisk or blender until it is stiff.

MEASURES AND CONVERSIONS

VOLUME

Metric	Standard	Imperial
5 ml	1 tsp.	
15 ml	1 tbsp.	1/2 fl.oz.
30 ml	2 tbsp.	1 fl. oz.
60 ml	1/4 cup	2 fl. oz.
120 ml	1/2 cup	4 fl. oz.

or

1/4 lb.

180 ml	3/4 cup	6 fl. oz.
240 ml	1 cup	8 fl. oz.

or

1/2 lb.

480 ml	2 cups	16 fl. oz.

or

1 lb. =

1 liter	4 1/4 cups	34 fl. oz.
2 liters	8 1/2 cups	68 fl. oz.

APPROXIMATE CONVERSIONS

5 gm	1 tsp.	
15 gm	1 tbsp.	1/2 oz.
29 gm		1 oz.
58 gm		2 oz.
113 gm	1/4 lb.	4 oz.
227 gm	1/2 lb.	8 oz.
454 gm	1 lb.	16 oz.
908 gm	2 lb.	32 oz.
1000 gm	2.2 lb.	35 oz.
1 kilogram	2.2 lb.	35 oz.

LENGTHS

5 mm	1/4 inch
10 mm(1cm)	1/2 inch
2 cm	3/4 inch
2.5 cm	1 inch
5 cm	2 inch

Oven Temperature

F°	C°
250	120
300	150
325	160
350	180
375	190
400	200
450	230

To convert Fahrenheit to Celcius (Centigrade):
$$(F° - 32) \times 5/9 = C°$$

To convert Celcius to Fahrenheit:
$$(C° \times 9/5) + 32 = F°$$

U.S. WEIGHTS AND MEASURES

dash or pinch	less than 1/8 tsp.
3 tsp.	1 tbsp.
2 tbsp.	1/8 cup or 1.fluid oz
4 tbsp.	1/4 cup
5 1/3 tbsp	1/3 cup
8 tbsp.	1/2 cup or 4 fluid oz.
10 2/3 tbsp.	2/3 cup
12 tbsp	3/4 cup
16 tbsp.	1 cup or 8 fluid oz.
2 cups	1 pint
2 pints	1 quart
4 quarts	1 gallon

SOURCES

Seed Sources

CROSS SEED COMPANY
HC 69 Box 2
Bunker Hill, KS 67626
(913) 483-6163

DIAMOND K ENTERPRISES
RR 1 Box 30
St. Charles, MN 55972
(507) 932-4308

JAFFE BROTHERS
P.O. Box 636
Valley Center, CA 92082
(619) 749-1133

LIVING FARMS
Box 50
Tracy, MN 56175
(507) 629-4431

WALNUT ACRES
Penns Creek, PA 17862
(717) 837-0601

Dehydrator Sources

BEE BEYER'S FOOD
DRYERS
1154 Roberta Lane
Los Angeles, CA
(213) 472-8961

EXCALIBUR
6083 Power Inn Rd.
Sacramento, CA 95824

Produce, Sprouts, Wheatgrass Sources

CHICAGO'S INDOOR
GARDEN
Lauri Roberts
(312) 989-0774

COMMUNITY WORKS
San Diego, CA
(619) 282-1851

DEMATTEIS, JOE
Route 4, Box 1158
Little Torch Key, FL
(305) 872-9057

DIRT CHEAP ORGANICS
Corte Madera, CA
(415) 924-0369

GLORIOUS GRASS
San Francisco, CA
(415) 826-1914

GOURMET PRODUCE
Rochester, NY
(716) 461-3558

GOURMET SPROUTING
Leucadia, CA
(619) 753-4281

GREENSWARD
Santa Cruz, CA
(408) 728-4136

LIVING LIQUIDS
Oakland, CA
(415) 536-8019

SUNSHINE SPROUTS
6915 Imperial Drive
West Palm Beach, FL 33463
(407) 688-6579

MORNING STAR
San Anselmo, CA
(415) 454-6563

OUR PLACE EATERY
830 Washington Ave.
Miami, FL
(305) 674-1322

PERFECT FOODS
3748 Oceanic Ave.
Brooklyn, NY 11224
(718) 946-0004

TOTALLY ORGANIC FARMS
2404 F St., Suite 101
San Diego, CA 92102
(619) 231-9506

WHOLE FOODS STORE
117 Prince St.
New York, NY 10012
(212) 673-5388

Herb Sources

FRONTIER HERB CO.
Box 69
Norway, IA
(800) 669-3275

SAN FRANCISCO HERB CO.
250 14th St.
San Francisco, CA 94103

Seaweed Sources

GOLD MINE
San Diego, CA 92102
(619) 234-9711
(800) 475-FOOD

MAINE SEAWEED CO.
Box 57
Steuben, ME 04680
(207) 546-2875

MENDOCINO SEA
VEGETABLE CO.
Box 372
Navarro, CA 95463
(707) 895-3741

Enzyme Supplements

21ST CENTURY ENZYMES
1-(800) 593-2665 or
contact Viktor Kulvinskas
P.O. 331
Royal, Arkansas 71968

More Food Sources

ALBERT'S ORGANICS
Los Angeles, CA 90058
(213) 234-4595

BANDWAGON BROKERAGE
INC. PRODUCE
Los Angeles, CA 90021
(213) 622-5601

COLVADO DATE CO.
P.O. Box 908
51-352 Hwy 86
Coachella, CA 92236
(619) 398-3441

ERNESTON ORGANIC
PRODUCE
West Palm Beach, FL
(407) 832-2446

GLASSER FARMS FRUITS
Miami, FL
(305) 238-7747

HARDSCRABBLE
ENTERPRISES
Rte. 6, Box 42
Cherry Grove, WV 26804
(304) 567-2727

KAHUILLA GARDENS
(Organic Dates)
P.O. Box 2328
Borrego Springs, CA 92004
(619) 540-5693

MOUNTAIN ARK
TRADING CO.
Fayetteville, AR 72701
(501) 442-7191
(800) 643-8909

PARADISE BANANAS
(Organic Dried)
Pahoa, HI
(808) 965-8522

SPROUT DELIGHTS, INC.
Essene Bread
Miami, FL 33168
(305) 687-5880

Equipment Sources

CUISINART PROCESSORS
Greenwich, CT 06830
(203) 975-4600

OSTER BLENDERS
Professional Products
Rt. 9 Box 541
McMinnville, TN 37110
(800) 356-7837

QUALITY HEALTH
(Champion Juicers)
922A Black Diamond Way
Lodi, CA 95240
(800) 826-4148
(800) 521-5455

BIBLIOGRAPHY AND SUGGESTED READING LIST

Spiritual Nutrition and the Rainbow Diet, Dr. Cousens, Cassandra Press, 1986, CA

Enzyme Nutrition, Dr. Howell, Avery Publications, 1985, NJ

Diet and Salad, Dr. Walker, Norwalk Press, 1971, AZ

Food Enzymes, Dr. Santillo, Holm Press, 1987, AZ

Raw Vegetable Juices, Dr. Walker, Norwalk Press, 1936, AZ

Juice Fasting, Dr. Airola, Health Plus Publishers, 1971, AZ

Hippocrates Diet and Health Program, Wigmore, Avery Publications, 1983, NJ

Survival Into the 21st Century, Kulvinskas, 21st Century Publications, 1975, IA

The Wheatgrass Book, Wigmore, Avery Publications, 1985, NJ

Hippocrates Health Program, Clement, Hippocrates Publication, 1989, FL

Love Your Body, Kulvinskas, 21st Century Publications, 1972, IA

Recipes For a Longer Life, Wigmore, Avery Publications, 1978, NJ

Inner Cleansing, Wade, Parker Publishing, 1983, NY

The Juicing Book, Blauer, Avery Publications, 1989, NJ

Salt Free Health Sauerkraut Cookbook, Bragg, 1979, CA

Complex Carbohydrate Handbook, Ross, Morrow Inc., 1981, NY

Diet for the Atomic Age, Shannon, Avery Publications, 1987, NJ

Food Combining for Health, Grant and Joice, Healing Arts Press, 1989, VT

Raw Cultured Vegetables, Richards, Rejuvenating Publishing, 1987, CA

Preserve It Naturally, Reston Publishing, 1983, VA

How to Dry Foods, DeLong, H.P. Books, 1979, AZ

The Book of Kudzu (Kuzu), Shurtleff and Aoyagi, Avery Publications, 1986, NJ

The Encyclopedia of Nutrition, Natow and Heslin, Pocket Books Publications, 1986, NY

Nutrition Almanac, Kirschmann, McGraw Hill Publications, 1979, NY

Food Additives and Your Health, Hunter, Keats Publishing, 1972, CN

Encyclopedia of Fruits, Vegetables, Nuts, and Seeds for Healthful Living, Kadans, Parker Publications, 1973, NY

Poisons in Your Body, Null, Arco Publishing, 1977, NY

Growing and Using Healing Herbs, Gaea and Weiss, Rodale Press, 1985, PA

Fresh Produce A to Z, Sunset Books Lane Publishing, 1987, CA

Everything You Always Wanted to Know About Nutrition, Reuben, Avon Books, 1978, NY

Complete Handbook of Nutrition, Null, Dell Books, 1972

Cooking With Sea Vegetables, Rhoads, Autumn Press, 1978, MA

INDEX

ORDER FORM

To Order: **Dining in the Raw   Cooking with the Buff**

PLEASE SEND ME _____ COPIES AT US$ 29.95 PER COPY

FOR A TOTAL OF _____

PLUS shipping and handling of
$ 3.00 per book for USA
$ 5.00 per book for Mexico and Canada   _____
$ 10.00 per book for all other location

TOTAL _____

MAKE CHECKS PAYABLE TO: **RITA ROMANO**.

Sorry, no credit cards accepted.

SHIP BOOKS TO:

NAME

ADDRESS

CITY,   STATE,   ZIP CODE

PHONE

MAIL ORDER FORM AND CHECK TO:

RITA ROMANO
P.O. BOX 5893
KEY WEST, FLORIDA 33045
Telephone and FAX
1-500-449-4490